Feminist Fiction

Feminist Fiction

FEMINIST USES OF GENERIC FICTION

Anne Cranny-Francis

Polity Press

Copyright © Anne Cranny-Francis 1990

First published 1990 by Polity Press
in association with Basil Blackwell

Editorial office:
Polity Press, 65 Bridge Street
Cambridge CB2 1UR, UK

Marketing and production:
Basil Blackwell Ltd
108 Cowley Road, Oxford OX4 1JF, UK

ISBN 0 7456 0527 3
ISBN 0 7456 0528 1 (pbk)

British Library Cataloguing in Publication Data
A CIP catalogue record for this book is available from the British Library.

Typeset in 10 on 12 pt Palatino by
Wearside Tradespools, Fulwell, Sunderland
Printed in Great Britain by TJ Press, Padstow, Cornwall.

Contents

For Jack Lindsay: critic, writer, socialist

Acknowledgements

The author and publishers wish to thank the following who have kindly given permission for the use of copyright material. Every effort has been made to trace all copyright holders, but if any has been inadvertently overlooked the publishers will be pleased to make the necessary arrangement at the first opportunity.

A. M. Heath and Company Ltd and Lescher & Lescher Ltd on behalf of the author, and Atheneum Publishers, an imprint of Macmillan Publishing Company, for 'And Then the Prince Knelt Down and Tried to Put the Glass Slipper on Cinderella's Foot' from *If I Were in Charge of the World and Other Stories* by Judith Viorst. Copyright © 1981 by Judith Viorst; Virginia Kidd on behalf of the Estate of Alice B. Sheldon, for extracts from *Warm Worlds and Otherwise* by James Tiptree, Jr. Copyright © 1975 by James Tiptree, Jr.; and *Out of the Everywhere and Other Extraordinary Visions* by James Tiptree, Jr. Copyright © 1981 by James Tiptree, Jr.; Anthony Sheil Associates Ltd for extracts from *The Edge of Time* by Marge Piercy, Women's Press. Copyright © 1979 by Marge Piercy.

I should like to thank the staff of the English Department, University of Wollongong for their encouragement and practical support during the writing of this book. In particular I thank the following colleagues for their discussion of many of the issues raised by this study: Marele Day (writer, Sydney), Patricia Gillard (Canberra College of Advanced Education), Dorothy Jones (University of Wollongong), Stephen Knight (University of Melbourne), Gunther Kress (University of Technology, Sydney), Cate Poynton (South Australia College of Advanced Education), Tony Thwaites (University of Queensland), and Terry Threadgold (University of Sydney).

Many thanks to my parents for their continuing support and encouragement, and special thanks to Jim Martin for reading the manuscript and just for being there ... And thanks also to U2 whose music got me through the worst/best part, the writing.

1
Introduction

One of the most innovative and interesting areas of contemporary literary production is feminist genre fiction – the feminist appropriation of the generic 'popular' literary forms, including science fiction, fantasy, utopian fiction, detective fiction and romance. This is genre fiction written from a self-consciously feminist perspective, consciously encoding an ideology which is in direct opposition to the dominant gender ideology of Western society, patriarchal ideology. Not all women writers are feminist writers. Many writers work conscientiously within the dominant ideologies of gender, race and class; after all, that is the best way to make a living (Lovell, 1987 (A))[*] – and it does not preclude the expression of oppositional views within their texts, even if one suspects that these views are effectively subsumed by the conservatism which colours the text as a whole. The fiction in which I am interested here, however, does not admit this compromise. Its writers work against, not with, conservative ideological discourses and what I am concerned with is the effect of this oppositional stance on their texts – not just on the events and characters represented in their texts, but also on the conventions and structure of the genres in which they operate. Not only do their texts tell slightly different kinds of stories, the texts function differently. Sometimes they do not seem to function at all – as traditional generic texts; sometimes they exhibit a complexity supposedly inconsistent with popular fictional forms. This feminist discourse, it seems, has structural, as well as semantic consequences for the texts in which it is encoded.

Sexist discourse defines, describes and delimits how men and

---

[*] In bibliographic references, letters in brackets refer to sections A–F of the References and Bibliography.

women must act in order to be considered masculine and feminine, how to be 'real' men and 'real' women in a patriarchal or male-dominated society (Kress, 1985 (A)). It similarly orders the interactions between the sexes, what constitutes normal or acceptable sexual behaviour and, equally oppressively, what constitutes normal social behaviour for both sexes, in both private and public areas of activity. Masculinist discourse is the discourse derived from sexism which is specifically male directed; that is, it defines, describes and delimits what it is to be masculine in a patriarchal society, the masculine subject. The feminine subject of patriarchy is also defined by a specifically female directed discourse which, but for its difficulty of pronunciation, might be called femininist discourse. These gendered discourses define primarily the power available to their own subjects under patriarchy; predictably female power is limited to the private, interpersonal spheres of nurturing and homemaking or to areas where these skills might be seen to apply, such as education. As part of the formation of subjectivity of women and men from a very early age sexist discourse (including its gendered component discourses) determines not only what they do, but how they think – about themselves as well as others. This discourse is 'naturalized' as the obvious mode of representation and self-representation of women and men. The most important role and task of feminist discourse is to challenge this naturalization, this obviousness, this common sense. And to challenge it, feminist discourse has to make it visible. In feminist fiction, including feminist genre fiction, feminist discourse operates to make visible within the text the practices by which conservative discourses such as sexism are seamlessly and invisibly stitched into the textual fabric, both into its structure and into its story, the weave and the print.

But why genre fiction? The answer lies with the synonym by which these texts are described – popular. People enjoy genre fiction; it sells by the truckload. As a conscious feminist propagandist it makes sense to use a fictional format which already has a huge market. The Women's Press manifesto printed at the front of each of the books in their SF series implicitly acknowledges this aim. Part of their statement reads as follows: 'We hope that the series will encourage more women both to read and to write science fiction, and give the traditional science fiction readership a new and stimulating perspective.' The same might be said for feminist writers in each of the genre forms. Their aim is to give the traditional readership, whether of fantasy, utopian fiction, detective fiction, romance, a new and stimulating perspective. The important recognition in this statement is that there is an existing readership worth tapping. That readership is not only large, but diverse. People of all ages, classes, genders, and races read genre fiction. It is unlikely that quite so many, in quite so diverse a cross-section, read postmodernist texts. As a political practice, then, the feminist use of genre fiction seems very appropriate. It (potentially) enables feminist writers to reach markets which might otherwise be closed, even antagonistic, to them. The feminist discourse which many readers might be totally unfamiliar with is presented within a familiar and much loved format. One result might be that readers are irritated by the disruption of their traditional reading practice since, as I have already noted, the feminist discourse does in varying ways and to varying degrees, transform the operation of the genre text. Another possible result is, as the Women's Press hope, a new and stimulating perspective for the familiar audience on the material and/or their reading practice.

This audience commonly attracts a negative reception from critics who, in accordance with the high/low culture division institutionalized by a now outmoded, but still powerful, modernist aesthetic, regard the mass audience of popular fiction as degraded consumers of formula art. This judgement contains an assumption that modernist writing (and possibly its realist predecessor) is non-formulaic, which is highly questionable. Genre fiction, it might be argued, foregrounds its conventions, rather than stitching them seamlessly into the fabric of the text and so its ideological framework may be, or may appear to be, self-evident; modernist and realist fiction, on the other hand, uses less mannered conventions and so achieves an apparent 'naturalization' which has the effect of obscuring its encoded ideological statements. Both genre fiction and its 'high brow' counterparts (realism, modernism, postmodernism) utilize a variety of textual conventions, some of which are more visible than others, and all of which are part of the discursive practice of the text. It is extremely significant, therefore, that one kind of text and its audience suffer critical disapprobation, while another (that to which the critics belong) is defended as the site of knowledge and truth. This critical – and implicitly political – division of audience extends beyond the recognizable class parameters involved in the high brow/low brow debate to issues of gender. As Terry Lovell notes in her book *Consuming Fiction* (Lovell, 1980 (A)), even critics interested in popular fiction have treated genres read by women with contempt. The well-known studies of nineteenth-century popular fiction by Margaret Dalziel and Louis James[1] differentially value fiction read by women and by men, the latter being assumed to be more important and valuable.

Of course, mainstream nineteenth-century literature and its critics were equally gender-biased, with the female emancipist or feminist activist of the late nineteenth century singled out for especially virulent condemnation. The 'New Woman', as she was known, was characterized as some kind of sexless, undersexed, or oversexed monster. Interestingly she was often characterized alongside the effete or effeminate dandy of *fin de siècle* decadence as a probable cause of the demise of bourgeois society. The two were linked by their inability to bear children, the dandy by sexual preference, the New Woman by her unfemininity. The latter is almost a parody of ideological biologism (that is, the explanation of ideologically con- structed social roles in biological terms: women are not strong enough to do 'male' jobs or are biologically less intelligent than men) and yet appeared in the pages of *Punch* magazine as late as 1894.[2] In fact both dandy and New Woman were disruptive of the patriarchal gender ideology characteristic of nineteenth-century society; both challenged its normative function, its rigid delimitation of female and male roles, abilities and expectations. In view of the increasingly strong demands for equality by bourgeois women throughout the nineteenth century it is not surprising to discover, as Huyssen (1986 (A)) has done, that the masses, that (other) disruptive, potentially destructive social grouping, which filled with fear the breast of the (male) bourgeoisie, were characterized as female:

> What especially interests me here is the notion which gained ground during the 19th century that mass culture is somehow associated with woman while real, authentic culture remains the prerogative of men . . .
> It is indeed striking to observe how the political, psychological, and aesthetic discourse around the turn of the century consistently and obsessively genders mass culture and the masses as feminine, while high culture, whether traditional or modern, clearly remains the privileged realm of male activities. (p. 47)

Huyssen goes on to describe the alignment of political and psycholo- gical discourses in the bourgeois characterization of the industrial working classes as a dangerous and disruptive mob, which simul- taneously was an image of engulfing female sexuality. Fritz Lang's film, *Metropolis*, operates discursively in terms of this characterization with the Metropolis working class led to a frenzy of destructive violence by the sexually provocative female robot, Maria. Translated into the contemporary aesthetic discourse of modernism, this fear of both women and the potential power of a united working class constituted what Huyssen describes as the 'powerful masculinist mystique' (p. 55) explicit in the work of modernists such as Marinetti, Wyndham Lewis and Jünger. The mass culture, against which modernism antagonistically defined itself, was accordingly characterized as feminine, the main problem with this process, according to Huyssen, being 'the persistent gendering as feminine of that which is devalued' (p. 53). So in the work of both artists and critics of the early and mid-twentieth century a convergence of discourses – aesthetic, political, psychological – maps out the place of the feminine in society and culture, as that which is devalued, inferior, even depraved, disruptive, and potentially violent or revolutionary.

Viewed from this historical perspective, the feminist appropriation of generic forms carries a wonderful irony. Generic fiction, characterized as feminine by a masculinist (political, psychological, artistic) establishment, is now being transformed by feminist ideology. Rather than rejecting the mass culture to which they were relegated (and which, as female, was relegated to them), feminist writers have embraced it, seeing its characteristic popularity as a powerful tool for their own propagandist purposes. They also consolidate the traditional association of women, the feminine, with a major area of cultural production. And it is certainly true that women have published extensively in generic forms. In the nineteenth century women writers, left alone to support large numbers of children without the modern benefit of child welfare, had to publish in formats which brought in as much money as possible, as often as possible. They were also less likely to have their work 'valued' by the artistic establishment if they wrote about the areas they knew best, the home environment. The rigid demarcation of experience into the private/domestic/feminine and public/social/masculine was an ideological hall mark of the nineteenth-century bourgeoisie, the era of the 'angel in the house'. Women's experience was devalued, and it still is. Paul Lauter notes of American writing: 'Some of the most popular texts in United States literature present hunting – a whale or a bear – as paradigms for "human" exploration and coming of age, where menstruation, pregnancy, and birthing somehow do not serve as such prototypes.' (Rabinowitz, 1987 (A), p. 221.) Women writers have, from economic necessity as much as choice, always had a strong presence in generic literature – though not always in the same genres.[3]

Even so, women have had to play by the rules, and the rules were dominated by or produced by the patriarchal ideology which was endemic to society and its cultural products. Feminist writers are now performing a complex aesthetic/ideological manoeuvre; utilizing their relegation as inferior or mass culture producers in order to show the legitimating processes in operation; using generic forms in order to show the ideological processes (of patriarchy) in (textual) operation. They are working with literary forms that have always been women's special providence – from economic necessity and through masculinist characterization (the two not unrelated, of course) – and their contemporary manipulation of these forms is enlightened by the practical advances of the Women's Movement since the 1960s and its accompanying theoretical development. Interestingly attempts have been made to co-opt the 'feminist voice' for postmodernism.[4] Feminist generic fiction may be contemporary with much postmodernist writing and it may use some of the same procedures (primarily, of course, the manipulation of genre conventions and the rejection of the high/low culture classification), even for the same purposes (particularly the revelation of power operations in a patriarchal bourgeois society), but to subsume it into the category of postmodernism(s) is extremely dangerous. The classification of feminism *within* the discourse of postmodernism tends to suppress both the long history of women's oppression under patriarchy and their struggle against that oppression. As Teresa de Lauretis warns in *Technologies of Gender*, much contemporary European philosophy (Derrida, Foucault, Lyotard, Deleuze) is essentially inimical to women because it appropriates women in a similar ahistorical manoeuvre as a category of the oppressed, the subjected, which essentially confirms that categorization by its implicit denial of the *history* of that oppression and subjection and the strategies used by women to fight against it. De Lauretis also notes the failure of poststructuralist philosophy to acknowledge the 'epistemological contribution of feminism to the redefinition of subjectivity and sociality' (de Lauretis, 1987 (A), p. 24); that is, the influence on contemporary philosophy of the feminist theorization of that history of oppression and resistance.

Genre fiction as political practice

As a form of political resistance the use of generic fiction has a long history. Most of the generic forms with which I am concerned here developed or were consolidated during the nineteenth century: fantasy and romance (in the modern sense) became established genres, utopian fiction reached a new height of popularity in the 1880s and 1890s only recently approached in the 1960s and 1970s, and science fiction and detective fiction began their rapid rise to popularity. All were used as vehicles for political debate by political activists in the nineteenth century. The Chartist newspapers published romance and melodrama clearly intended to show the decadence of traditional landowners and to exalt the figure of the working-class hero, the princess inevitably snatched away in the strong arms of a cossack, rather than doomed to a life of ease with an effete member of a decayed aristocracy.[5] These stories were not structurally or textually self-conscious; their propaganda was mostly a matter of plot – though the use of a working-class character in the role of hero does challenge some of the basic assumptions encoded in these narratives. Still the stories were not concerned with why romances and melodramas use certain kinds of plots or characters. No one, for example, was expected to question the concept of the princess as prize, a possession, objectified within the text.

The politicized writers of utopian texts were sometimes more self-conscious, but this was at least partly the result of the time when they were writing. As I noted above, the 1880s and 1890s saw the greatest increase in the production of utopian texts. Between 1516 (More's *Utopia*) and 1895 about 400 utopian texts were written in English; of these 320 were written in the nineteenth century. Furthermore about half that number were written between 1887 and 1896, 1887 being the original publication date of Edward Bellamy's seminal text, *Looking Backward*.[6] Utopian texts are fundamentally political, being organized around the elaboration of a social structure which seems to be totally unlike anything the reader has experienced. During the nineteenth century socialists and feminists both used the utopian text as a means of political debate and propaganda. Few of the feminist texts have survived, but some of the socialist texts are available. Most are fairly literal in their application of socialist ideals to the utopian format, but William Morris's *News from Nowhere* does show an awareness of the formal or structural demands of the text, as well as of the story or plot. There seem to be two major reasons for Morris's self-consciousness. The first was his rejection of *Looking Backward*, which he read as capitalism masquerading as socialism. This reading was a result of his structuralist, rather than literally thematic, analysis of the text (Morris, 1889 (D)). The second was Morris's virulent rejection of the realist aesthetic which characterized mainstream literary production at this time. Morris noted that realist literature was concerned only with the middle classes, the working classes not simply denigrated or rejected, but ignored, silenced (Morris, 1970 (D), pp. 129–30). To echo Terry Lovell on fantasy – 'whose fantasy?' (Lovell, 1987 (A), p. 63) – Morris was asking the question: whose realism? Morris accepted the linear or quest narrative characteristic of the utopian text and used it in an informed (though not necessarily wholly successful[7]) way. So the realist aesthetic came under pressure at the end of the nineteenth century not only from the proto-modernists, but from the denigrated and maligned users of the quest narrative, the producers of mass culture, of popular or generic literary texts.

This kind of questioning is coded into the debate about the role of fiction between one of the 'fathers' of realism, Henry James, and his correspondent, H.G. Wells, Fabian Socialist and one of the popularizers of science fiction. The science fiction genre is generally regarded as having begun with Mary Shelley's *Frankenstein*, a text fundamentally concerned with the ideologies of class and gender.[8] Wells, too, used the genre quite openly to explore ideas and issues, sometimes fundamentally questioning bourgeois ideological practices (his representation of class relations in *The Time Machine* is one example).[9] Science fiction has always been considered a literature of ideas, though sometimes those 'ideas' are woefully banal. In the nineteenth century, when it developed, it was used by writers with strong political convictions to explore the nature of their own society and its ideologies. Some of these writers, notably Wells, were also concerned with how their texts functioned, with their confrontation with realism and the issues, ideological as well as aesthetic, this raised.

Detective fiction also developed as a popular genre in the nineteenth century. The most famous detective of the period was, of course, Arthur Conan Doyle's Sherlock Holmes. Doyle's stories are not without political significance, but I am concerned here with detective fiction used for overtly propagandist ends. Again such stories are to be found in publications intended for a politicized readership, such as Keir Hardie's paper for the newly-formed Independent Labour Party, *Labour Leader*. An outstanding example, which I shall discuss further in the appropriate chapter, is 'By Shadowed Paths' by Albert T. Marles (Yorick the Younger). It is essentially a Socialist *bildungsroman* (or novel of education) telling the story of the hero's early tutorship by a crusty old Chartist, his aspirations to land ownership, his brush with Anarchists (who have him throwing bombs), and his finding of love and political correctness with a sweet young Socialist. So the use of genre forms for political/ideological purposes is not in itself innovative. Socialists used these forms for the same reason that feminists are now using them: because they are popular. People like to read genre fiction and if you are looking for a populist audience, where best to start than with their entertainment, especially when you are also aware of the conservative ideologies otherwise naturalized into those same texts. For contemporary feminists, however, use of generic fiction must be tempered by a complex understanding of the ideological significance of textual practices, the practices and conventions which define and characterize those texts for readers. These practices, these conventions, are not neutral. They carry or encode the ideological function of the text at least as much as does the story. Nineteenth-century socialists often ignored or were unaware of this and their texts consequently carried conflicting ideological messages. William Morris, however, understood this connection and his most openly propagandist work, *News from Nowhere* contains passages which reflect on the practice of the text – clearly an attempt to debate and neutralize the conservatizing effect of realist reading practices.[10] Nevertheless his own text falters in its production of a gender ideology which comprises his (intratextual) discussions of gender roles.[11] Contemporary feminist use of these heavily conventionalized literary forms thus involves writers in a process of constant evaluation of the constitutive practices of their own texts.

Feminist writers, like the socialist writers of the nineteenth century, may find that the use of popular or generic literary forms can operate as a political practice. Generic fiction may be a site for the allegorical description of social injustices displaced in time and/or place from the reader's own society, but still clearly recognizable as a critique of that society. However, this fiction may also be reappropriated by the discourses against which it is written *if* writers are not aware of the ideological significance of generic conventions, as well as of the text's explicit description of a particular (displaced but clearly contemporary) social formation. So, for example, attempts to construct a female hero based on simple substitution fail badly. A female hero who is as blood-thirsty (i.e. brave) and manipulative (i.e. clever) as her male counterpart does nothing to redefine that characterization and the ideology it naturalizes; she may even reinforce it by lending it a new legitimacy. Feminist generic fiction is not simply masculinist generic fiction with female heroes telling stories of oppression; as such it would risk becoming an even more effective apology for patriarchy. Feminist generic fiction, like socialist generic fiction, is a radical revision of conservative genre texts, which critically evaluates the ideological significance of textual conventions and of fiction as a discursive practice. At times this interrogation may transform the feminist text into a virtual parody of the genre; at other times it is sustainable by the text which remains still recognizably SF, fantasy, utopian, detective fiction or romance. Detailed discussion of the conventions of specific genres can be found in the appropriate chapters below, but I begin here an analysis of the one convention common to them all, the use of the quest narrative. (It may be typologically more correct to class generic fiction as a particular type or subset of narrative fiction. The important point for this analysis, however, is that genre fiction is conventionally structured by the linear, quest narrative, with all the implicit ideological consequences that entails.)

Narrative and ideology

The quest narrative is a linear narrative in which temporal sequence is taken to signify material causation. Though other narrative structures do exist, the narrative in which, in Barthes' words, 'the mainspring of the narrative activity is to be traced to that very confusion between consecutiveness and consequence,' (Rabinowitz, 1987 (A), p. 108) is the dominant structure in nineteenth- and twentieth-century Western writing. It may not always be linearly sequential, as the quest narrative usually is, but its essential feature, the equation of temporal sequence with material causation, ranges it genealogically with the quest narrative. When I specify narrative in my text, this is the narrative to which I refer. Peter Brooks writes about this temporal ordering of narrative in *Reading for the Plot*:

> Plot as it interests me is not a matter of typology or of fixed structures, but rather a structuring operation peculiar to those messages that are developed through temporal succession, the instrumental logic of a specific mode of human understanding. Plot, let us say in preliminary definition, is the logic and dynamic of narrative, and narrative itself a form of understanding and explanation. (Brooks, 1984 (A), p. 10)

In other words narrative plotting is one of the major semiotic practices of our society, a way of negotiating meaning from the mass of information which confronts us (Jameson, 1981 (A), p. 26). But this semiosis is not non-ideological or apolitical. It is in the plotting of narrative, the arrangement of events into a meaningful pattern, that the ideological or political framework of a text becomes apparent (Brooks, 1984 (A), p. 323); the (ideological, political) assumptions underlying the patterning procedure are detectable. But this meaningful arrangement involves also temporal patterning; the events of the narrative are meaningful when and if they follow a recognizable temporal logic. And this familiar temporal logic appears to us to be 'natural'. For us the notion of time as a linear process is well established and fundamental to the planning of our lives. Our time is not circular, or transcendent. We do not see each year as an instance of every other year, but as the year following the one before. Brooks speculates on the emergence of narrative in terms of this perception of time:

> The emergence of narrative plot as a dominant mode of ordering and explanation may belong to the large process of secularization, dating from the Renaissance and gathering force during the Enlightenment, which marks a falling-away from those revealed plots – the Chosen People, Redemption, the Second Coming – that appeared to subsume transitory human time to the timeless. (Brooks, 1984 (A), p. 6)

So it is 'natural' for us now to think of time in terms of linear sequence, rather than, for example, in terms of seasonal cycles. If narrative represents events in temporal (linear) sequence as a causal process, then it follows that we will read that causal process, as we read temporal sequence, as 'natural.' That causal process, in turn, inevitably encodes ideological discourses and these discourses too are read as 'natural'. When the discourses involved are dominant in a society, this naturalization is particularly easy; no confrontation with entrenched beliefs occurs, simply reinforcement. Much of the writing in our society operates this way. It is non-oppositional; the discourses it encodes are dominant discourses and so its narrative process is entirely non-problematic. The discourses are 'natural', the causal process is 'natural', the temporal sequence is 'natural' – and the text is very easy to read. The text reproduces the mechanical causality in which we are accustomed to thinking, the arrangement of events in temporal sequence constituting a reasoning process which we regard as 'natural' or obvious or commonsense. Yet when one considers that this process simultaneously encodes ideological discourses, then the problematic nature of narrative is visible perhaps for the first time. Christopher Williams, writing of cinema, commented that 'narrative militates against knowledge' (Masterman, 1983 (A)). The reason for Williams's claim lies with the invisibility of the narrative/narrativizing process. By concealing its own mechanism, Williams claimed, the narrative text also conceals its ideological function. In her book, *Writing beyond the Ending* Rachel Blau DuPlessis corroborates Williams's point by noting that one major strategy of contemporary women writers is the interrogation of conventional narrative, which she designates 'a verson of, or a special expression of, ideology' (DuPlessis, 1985 (A), p. x). Conventional narrative encodes gender discourses which women writers, particularly feminist writers, find disruptive and unusable. These discourses may subvert the oppositional gender discourse also coded into the text, so that feminist writers using narrative must explore and expose its conservative and conservatizing function in order to avoid the appropriation of their work by the dominant discursive formation, the gender ideology of which is patriarchal.

The failure of role reversal strategies in some early feminist genre fiction exemplifies this problem. Mieke Bal comes to the same conclusion in her study of narrative function, *Narratology*: 'Closer analysis will probably reveal that in much traditional literature, women can only function as subject in certain fabulas, in which the object is a characteristic of the subject (happiness, wisdom) and not a concrete object that would necessitate a long journey or physically taxing ordeal.' (Bal, 1985 (A), pp. 83–4.) So the causality which functions in these narratives may not be purely mechanical, not simply a matter of activating particular roles regardless of gender, race, class, etc. It seems that certain preconditions are necessary for the narrative process to operate simply and unproblematically – and those preconditions are ideologically determined.

In *Landscape for a Good Woman* Steedman discusses the interaction of ideology and narrative be reference to Freud's famous analysis of Dora (Steedman, 1986 (A), p. 132). Steedman's point is that the perception of causality must be the same for speaker and hearer for the narrative to operate successfully. In Dora's accounts of the events in which she was involved, her narratives are rejected by Freud because they did not fit the version he intended her to have. Dora's narrative conflicts with the patriarchal version of her that she must learn to accept (to be 'cured', to be 'normal') and Steedman goes on to suggest that Freud, as a member of late nineteenth- and early twentieth-century Western society and ratifier of its gender ideology, cannot accept the coherence and point of Dora's narrative: to him they do not ring true. Dora's narrative does not work because it is ideologically unsound. Because of the naturalization of the patriarchal ideology, its obviousness, its commonsense, Dora's oppositional narrative is then interpreted as unnatural, contrived, hysterical – explanations which feature in Freud's analysis of Dora.

Steedman then continues her discussion of narrative and ideology with an example of oppositional class ideology. She tells the story of the social researcher Henry Mayhew's interview with an eight-year-old watercress seller in London in the winter of 1849–50. Steedman interprets the girl's autobiographical narrative as organized by an economic vision (ideology) appropriate to her class position. The middle-class Mayhew does not understand the coherence or point of her story; its causal relationships are unfamiliar and unacceptable to him. Steedman notes:

> But there is no story for the little watercress girl. The things she spoke to Mayhew about (pieces of fur, the bunches of cress, the scrubbed floor) still startle after 130 years, not because they are strange things in themselves, but because in our conventional reading, they are not held together in a figurative relationship to each other. (Steedman, 1986 (A), p. 138)

So the watercress girl's narrative, too, is unacceptable – irrational, lacking meaningful causality. She, like Dora, is silenced. Her narrative, too, is unsound; it conflicts with, and is marginal to, the dominant class discourse of Mayhew's society, which is middle class. In middle-class terms, in bourgeois discourse, the girl's arrangement of items is meaningless, her narrative lacks causality. It is important, particularly in the context of the present study, to note that Dora and the watercress girl are no longer silent. Feminist critics are leading the way so far as Jameson's injunction concerning marginalized voices is concerned. He wrote:

> ...the affirmation of such nonhegemonic cultural voices remains ineffective if it is limited to the merely 'sociological' perspective of the pluralistic rediscovery of other isolated social groups: only an ultimate rewriting of these utterances in terms of their essentially polemic and subversive strategies restores them to their proper place in the dialogical system of the social classes. (Jameson, 1981, (A), p. 86)

Precisely Steedman's impressive achievement in *Landscape for a Good Woman*. One of the major contributions of feminist critics has been in this area of narrative theory because their rereadings, perhaps more effectively than any others, have revealed the ideological nature of narrative itself; that this 'form of understanding and explanation' is no neutral structure to be applied equally and justly to all, but an ideological mechanism by means of which we are taught to think, to understand and to explain in ways appropriate to the dominant discursive formation. By means of the process of naturalization described earlier, conservative ideological discourses (of gender, class, race) are encoded into our consciousness, our ways of understanding, our common sense. Oppositional, marginalized voices must battle for air-time; must set up pirate stations in order to be heard.

Narrative and desire

Before going on to discuss concepts of genre I want to discuss briefly the use of 'desire' to explain the motivation of narrative. Carolyn Steedman's use of this concept to describe the construction of narrative as a political act is a theoretical conceptualization fundamental to much feminist writing of generic fiction:

> that longing was produced in her distant childhood, what she actually wanted were real things, things that a culture and a social system withheld from her. The story she told was about this wanting, and it remained a resolutely social story. When the world didn't deliver the goods, she held the world to blame. In this way, the story she told was a form of political analysis, that allows a political interpretation to be made of her life. (Steedman, 1986 (A), p. 6)

Steedman writes of desire as a psychosocial, not psychological, construct. This is not the abstract (Lacanian) notion of a lack, metaphorized as a gap or space (another 'neutral' structure!). Rather it is a materialist (re)construction of that lack as it is experienced by the individual subject. Peter Brooks, in *Reading for the Plot*, writes about this desire from a Freudian/Lacanian perspective:

> Narratives both tell of desire – typically present some story of desire – and arouse and make use of desire as dynamic of signification. Desire is in this view like Freud's notion of Eros, a force including sexual desire but larger and more polymorphous, which (he writes in *Beyond the Pleasure Principle*) seeks 'to combine organic substances into ever greater unities.' Desire as Eros, desire in its plastic and totalizing function, appears to me central to our experience of reading narrative. (Brooks, 1984 (A), p. 37)

The first part of Brooks's statement, that narratives present a story of desire, recalls Steedman's analysis of her mother's narratives in *Landscape for a Good Woman*. As she notes, these narratives and the stories they structure are a mode of political analysis often overlooked by orthodox political theorists, by whom they are often dismissed as 'morally' bankrupt (Steedman 1986 (A), p. 23). Feminist writers are now telling stories of desire and feminist critics are reading the desire in these and earlier texts as a political critique of the ideologies (of gender, class, race) of our society. These writing and critical practices have prompted feminists to another crucial question; to echo Terry Lovell once again: whose desire? Is desire itself a neutral conceptual category equally available to feminist and non-feminist writers and theorists? If narrative is envisaged as motivated by desire – as dynamic of signification, as Eros, in its plastic and totalizing function – will it matter if the writer or the reading position produced is female or male? Brooks's own specification of the operation of desire seems to me to contain a metaphorical deconstruction of this category:

> Narratives portray the motors of desire that drive and consume their plots, and they also lay bare the nature of narration as a form of human desire: the need to tell as a *primary human drive* that seeks to *seduce* and to *subjugate* the listener, to implicate him in the *thrust* of a desire that never can quite speak its name – never can quite come to the point – but that insists on speaking *over and over again its movement* towards that name. (Brooks, 1984 (A), p. 61, my italics)

At the very least Brooks's own metaphor of 'human' desire seems to be based on a stereotypically male pattern of sexual response, as the italicized words show very clearly (his reference to the 'love that dare not speak its name' – the nineteenth-century formulation of homosexual love – is also fascinating and deserving of more analysis). Within this stereotypical pattern the place of the female/feminine is to be the seduced, the subjugated. So where and how does female/'human' desire operate? As a pattern of yielding and subjection perhaps? Certainly this is the kind of desire mechanism encoded in much Gothic fiction with its sadistic but irresistible, and essentially tender, hero and passive, acquiescent heroine.[12] Contemporary feminist writers, however, are less than satisfied with this mechanism and yet, if Brooks's description of the masculinism of the desire mechanism operating in traditional narrative is correct, what alternatives do they have? Again feminist writers are forced to confront the inadequacies of contemporary literary theory and practice and to formulate practices capable of expressing their own (marginalized) experience, their desire, and their vision. This may involve the reworking of narrative, its reconstruction on the basis of another pattern of coherence; not the temporal logic of traditional narrative, but contradiction.[13] Feminist writers must engage with, and contradict, traditional narrative patterning in order to (re)construct texts capable of articulating their marginalized, oppositional positioning – both inside, described by, patriarchal ideology (as the idealist construct, Woman) and outside that discourse, experiential witnesses to its contradictions, its mystifications (as women). (de Lauretis, 1987 (A), p. 26)

This is a project very different from Brooks's 'totalizing' function for narrative, or for other psychoanalytic interpretations which locate the Freudian oedipal scenario as the fundamental psychic trajectory of narrative mechanism. As DuPlessis notes, however, 'even the Freudian account somewhat reluctantly presents a recurring tension between the oedipal and preoedipal phases for the female, whereas in most males (as far as the theory tells) the oedipus complex has a linear and cumulative movement' (1985 (A), p. 36). This linear and cumulative movement is sometimes read as the psychoanalytic narrative of 'human' growth and development, a narrative which characteristically encodes a male gender bias and linear causal fallacy. Whether that encoding happens because of the (oedipal) psychic development of those who have long controlled the production of narrative (i.e. men) or whether it is explained in those terms because of the psychoanalytic theorizing of those who have long controlled the production of theory (i.e. men), it seems incontrovertible that the mechanism of narrative, which we might describe as desire, is gender-coded. de Lauretis suggests a viable feminist response:

> Feminist work in film should be not anti-narrative or anti-oedipal but quite the opposite. It should be narrative and oedipal with a vengeance ... working ... to represent the duplicity of the oedipal scenario itself and the specific contradiction of the female subject in it. (de Lauretis, 1987 (A), p. 108)

De Lauretis' strategy is very similar to that used by feminist writers of genre fiction who work simultaneously with and against the characteristic narrative format of popular fiction.

Genre

I am using the term 'genre' as it has been applied to fictional forms, to identify texts which exhibit a specific format or formula or set of conventions. In other disciplines the texts with which I am dealing might be considered to be in the genre of the novel, sub-genre of SF or fantasy or utopian or detective fiction or romance. My use of 'genre' is common in literary critical circles and among publishers (the identification for booksellers provided on the cover), where in both cases it is a means of placing the particular text within the range of writing styles. My use of the term, however, extends beyond this pigeonholing exercise. Study of the feminist use of generic literary forms confirms that genre is a form of social practice as well as a literary or

linguistic category. (Jameson, 1985 (A), pp. 140–1) The conceptualization of the relationship between genre(s) used and social context by
functional linguists is useful in the study of literary (sub)genres.[14]
They describe genres as responses to specific social situations, the
competence of the user being a function of her/his ability to use the
appropriate genre(s) correctly on specific occasions. And that ability
is determined by the subject position of the user, by her/his access to
the powerful discourses of bourgeois, patriarchal society which are
coded into those genres and their use.

Feminist genre fiction makes constant (implicit) reference to several
of these points. Their work reveals genre as a social strategy on a
number of levels. Feminist analysis of generic fiction has shown that
genres encode ideological information. They have a specific social
function to perform as the expression of conservative ideological
discourses, though oppositional voices are often heard – either within
the same texts and in order to be silenced (but still there) or in
self-consciously oppositional works by politicized writers (for example socialists or feminists). Genres work by convention and those
conventions are social constructs; they operate by social assent, not
individual choice (in the same way that the red/orange/green configuration of traffic lights is a social contract, not a matter of
individual interpretation). These conventions are themselves subject
to social pressures and social mediation. As society changes, formerly
accepted conventions become unacceptable or are revised. For example, the last few years have seen the emergence in detective fiction of
a number of professional female detectives, only acceptable since the
higher public profile of professional women in Western society. As
Todorov, in his study of the work of Bakhtin and his circle, explains:
'Genre is a sociohistorical as well as a formal entity. Transformations
in genre must be considered in relation to social changes.' (Todorov,
1984 (A), p. 80.) And these social changes are the result of changes in
the dominant discursive formation, of the renegotiation and recon-
figuration of the discourses describing society at a particular time.
Feminist genre fiction is an intervention in this configuration, an
attempt to subvert the dominance of patriarchal discourse by challenging its control of one semiotic system, writing, and specifically
genre writing.

In *The Political Unconscious* Fredric Jameson explores the useful-
ness of the concept of genre in the attempt to understand social
semiosis: 'The strategic value of generic concepts for Marxism clearly
lies in the mediatory function of the notion of genre, which allows the
coordination of immanent formal analysis of the individual text with

the twin diachronic perspective of the history of forms and the evolution of social life.' (1981 (A), p. 105.) One might amend this statement to read 'Marxism *and feminism*.' Feminist writers and critics are constantly performing this same complex procedure; placing the individual (generic) text within the history of that particular (generic) form, identifying the ideological significance of textual conventions and aligning them with the ideological discourses they encode, placing those discourses in relation to dominant and marginalized voices in society. Jameson adds his own definition of genre: 'Genres are essentially literary *institutions*, or social contracts between a writer and a specific public, whose function is to specify the proper use of a particular social artifact.' (p. 106) The 'proper use' to which Jameson refers is presumably the socially sanctioned use, just as stop/ready/go is the 'proper use' or interpretation of the red/orange/green traffic light system. For feminists to intervene in these social contracts, to de/re/construct them, revealing their ideological significances, means a fundamental intervention in the relationship between reader and text, a disruption of the reader's conventionalized understanding of the contract, the literary institution of the particular genre. To intervene without causing a traffic jam or a major crash is an extremely delicate procedure – and maybe there are times when the crash makes sense (after all, one can be quite sure that readers are quite secure).

Jameson writes also about the changing social use of generic forms:

> what this model implies is that in its emergent, strong form a genre is essentially a socio-symbolic message, or in other terms, that form is immanently and intrinsically an ideology in its own right. When such forms are reappropriated and refashioned in quite different social and cultural contexts, this message persists and must be functionally reckoned into the new form. The history of music provides the most dramatic examples of this process, wherein folk dances are transformed into aristocratic forms like the minuet (as with the pastoral in litera-ture), only then to be reappropriated for new ideological (and nationa-lizing) purposes in romantic music ... The ideology of the form itself, thus sedimented, persists into the later, more complex structure as a generic message which coexists – either as a contradiction or, on the other hand, as a mediatory or harmonizing mechanism – with elements from later stages. (pp. 140–1)

The persistence of ideological messages or discourses within generic forms, coded into their conventions, is one of the characteristics with which feminist writers are most concerned. The gender ideology most often detected in generic fiction is extremely conservative, stereotyping women into the role of virgin or whore, and as the object of a quest or adventure, not the subject. With this ideology sedimented into the text feminist writers are forced to develop innovative strategies for dealing with what appears at first a no-win situation. The answer for many feminist writers, filmmakers, theorists and artists is not a simple rejection of narrative, the genre convention identified as the most obvious source of this conservative gender discourse, though this strategy did dominate film theory/practice for a time. Rather the tactic now seen as most viable is the self-conscious use of narrative, even narratives, intersecting with an equally self-conscious use of other genre conventions, to 'make visible' the socially and politically conservative discourses coded into traditional genre conventions. De Lauretis presents this strategy as a translation of Irigaray's discussion of representation in *The Sex Which Is Not One*:

> To play with mimesis is thus, for a woman, to try to recover the place of exploitation by discourse, without allowing herself to be simply re-duced to it. It means to resubmit herself ... to ideas about herself ... that are elaborated in/by a masculine logic, but so as to make 'visible,' by an effect of playful repetition, what was supposed to remain invisible: the cover-up of a possible operation of the feminine in language. It also means 'to unveil' the fact that if women are such good mimics, it is because they are not simply reabsorbed in this function. *They also remain elsewhere.* (Modleski, 1986 (A), pp. 128–9)

Women are both inside these narratives and outside them; inside the ideology which presents them as 'woman' and outside it. Feminist writers can manipulate these conservative narratives and genre conventions because they both recognize and understand them, can play their game, and yet are not contained by them or subsumed within them. Feminist generic texts are sites of ideological struggle, just as are conservative generic texts – but the feminist texts show the struggle in process. The struggle takes place inside the conventional space of the text (described by traditional use of narrative and convention) *and* outside, on screen and off. The feminist writer continually crosses the boundaries which delimit the operation – formally/aesthetically/ideologically – of the traditional generic text and, in so doing, shows that those boundaries exist.

This complex strategy involves feminist writers in the transformation of generic texts and, as I noted earlier, this can be costly. The readership may find a heavily transformed text unreadable, no longer recognisable as a member of the generic family from which it developed. Todorov noted: 'just as linguistic rules can be violated,

generic rules can be ignored, but not without some consequences.'
(1984 (A), p. 84) The consequences may be positive in some cases, the
eradication of particularly offensive conventions (such as the dumb
blonde, the stupid black, the Neanderthal working-class man); in
other cases, the consequences may be a loss of readership so severe as
to call into question the whole concept of the feminist appropriation
of popular fiction. If the appropriation is such that the fiction is no
longer popular, where then? At this point the centrality of the notion
of audience to this whole area of study must be extremely apparent,
and I shall deal with this shortly. Firstly, though, I must address a
couple more points about genre and genre criticism.

No text is the unequivocal construct of a single genre.[15] Even if
writing about literary (sub)genres it is difficult to find a text which
does not exhibit some characteristics of other genres, for example
romance conventions in detective fiction, SF or utopian fiction;
detective fiction conventions in any of the above. Jameson argues that
what we call the 'novel' is not a coherent, organic whole, but a
symbolic process or act harmonizing heterogeneous generic conventions, including narratives, each with their own ideological significance. He describes the novel as layered or marbled by *generic
discontinuities* (1981 (A), p. 144). The traditional generic text can be
theorized in these terms: it customarily presents a resolution of the
contradictions engendered by the simultaneous presence of heterogeneous generic conventions, each with their own reference to
specific ideological discourses. When the discourses motivated are in
harmony, this is not very difficult. However, a text may be found to
encode conflicting discourses; oppositional or marginalized voices
may be heard. In the latter case the text often presents a resolution of
the conflict in which the oppositional voice is shown to be invalid or
incorrect or unnatural: many Mills & Boon romances, for example,
voice a feminist discourse which is subsequently devalued by being
associated with a particularly unpleasant character or with the
temporary misjudgement of the main female character. Nevertheless,
it is interesting that the oppositional or marginal voice must be heard
in order to be silenced. The feminist strategy with genre fiction is not
unlike that of the Mills & Boon texts, except that the other side wins;
the oppositional or marginal voice is shown to have value and
significance. Of course, this conflict, this ideological struggle does not
always happen so literally; it is rarely built so thematically into the
story. In the feminist text the struggle often occurs at the site of the
convention. For example, the professional female detective of recent
feminist fiction is an affront to many traditional readers for whom

detecting is 'man's work.' The convention itself thus becomes the site of ideological contention. The multigeneric nature of many texts is merely a complicating factor, as writers, readers and critics are implicated in a more complex negotiating process – a process in which generic discontinuities mobilize ideological contestation in which the tenuousness of conservative ideological positionings may be recognized and from which new meanings may be constructed.

De Lauretis calls this 'a view from elsewhere,' where 'elsewhere' is defined as 'the spaces in the margins of hegemonic discourses, social spaces carved in the interstices of institutions and in the chinks and the cracks of the power-knowledge apparati.' (1987 (A), p. 25) De Lauretis's model for an oppositional aesthetic also depends on an understanding of traditional textual practice as the mediation or resolution of contradiction, the kinds of contradictions which arise from the presence within the one text of a number of generic strands each with its own ideological significances.

This conceptualization of the operation of genre has usefully replaced the prescriptive work of early genre critics. Contemporary use of this concept is an informed political strategy by critics whose concern is to deconstruct the conventions by which individual genres are recognized, as Peter Rabinowitz explains in *Before Reading*:

> Conventions . . . are one of the grounds on which the politics of art is mapped out; often invisible, they serve as enabling conditions for literature's ideological structures. Thus, study of literary conventions can help illuminate the connections between politics on the one hand and interpretation and evaluation, as the academy currently practices them, on the other. (1987 (A), p. 9)

This study has been invaluable to feminist critics who have traced in all kinds of literary conventions the gender ideology which is so limiting and negative for women. Furthermore it has revealed the institutional mechanism by which oppositional or marginalized voices in literature come to be adjudged 'bad' art. Paradoxically an informed genre criticism can be used to deconstruct the prescriptive critical practices which so often masquerade as apolitical, neutral, objective, purely aesthetic. This informed genre criticism is fully aware of the social construction of the conventions by which it operates and which it must finally deconstruct:

> This final moment of the generic operation, in which the working categories of genre are themselves historically deconstructed and abandoned, suggests a final axiom, according to which *all* generic categories, even the most time-hallowed and traditional, are ultimately

to be understood (or 'estranged') as mere ad hoc, experimental constructs, devised for a specific textual occasion and abandoned like so
much scaffolding when the analysis has done its work. (Jameson, 1981
(A), p. 145)

Feminist critics, along with Marxist critics such as Jameson, have
rejuvenated genre criticism, given it a new complexity and subtlety
through their use of Bakhtinian and other semiotic writings to
produce new conceptualizations of the ideological function of generic
conventions and the multi-generic nature of most literary texts. For
feminist critics this use of genre criticism has also been a way of
addressing one of the most crucial concepts for feminist theory and
practice: the notion of audience.

Audience and textual address

Medvedev/Bakhtin wrote in *The Formal Method in Literary Scholarship*:

An artistic entity of any type, that is, of any genre, is related to reality
according to a double modality; the specifics of this double orientation
determine the type of this entity, that is its genre. The work is oriented,
first, toward its listeners, and recipients, and toward certain conditions
of performance and perception. Second, the work is oriented toward
life, from the inside so to speak, by its thematic content. Every genre, in
its own way, orients itself thematically toward life, toward its occurr-
ences, its problems, etc. (Todorov, 1984 (A), p. 82)

The second point has been covered fairly thoroughly in the discussion of genre criticism and feminist uses of it. However, it is the first
point which has been attracting the most theoretical and practical
attention from feminists in recent years. Thus Craig Owens, writing
about feminism and postmodernism, acknowledged that, although
the notion of the privileging of vision in Western society is not new,
its connection with what he calls 'sexual privilege' certainly is
(Owens, 1985, (A), p. 70), and that connection is most clearly
perceived and theorized in the work of feminist artists and critics.
And in their recent works on literature and film both Terry Lovell and
Teresa de Lauretis have focused on the importance of audience,
reader or viewer. De Lauretis describes an important initiative for
women's film as the 'idea that *a film may address the spectator as female*'
rather than simply ensuring that its portrayal of women is positive.
(1987 (A), p. 135) The question raised by the latter strategy is precisely
– for whom? To which audience is the film directed? Is there such an

entity as a non-gendered audience? Or is audience, too, an implicitly (male) gendered concept?

Lovell contextualizes this position by noting the cultural disposition of literary texts which have addressed a female audience:

> It has been tentatively suggested that it is not so much the sex of the author which secures the exclusion of a text in the process of cultural capitalist accumulation as the address of the text. It is woman-to-woman writing which is excluded. Because those forms have been and continue to be extremely popular they have been drawn upon in the postmodernist high cultural raid upon popular culture, along with forms whose address is not woman-to-woman but whose real as opposed to implied author is often female, such as detective fiction. Clearly there are some circumstances under which women's texts do become cultural capital. (Lovell, 1987 (A), p. 160)

Lovell's wry assessment of the postmodernist appropriation of woman-to-woman texts reinforces her initial point about textual address: woman-to-woman writing is an oppositional mode and unacceptable; it only becomes acceptable when subsumed by an authoritative male (postmodernist) voice. Lovell traces the representation of feminist ideas in literary texts and finds that the ones with 'literary survival value' are in texts by men, such as Gissing and Hardy, whose texts were implicitly addressed to a male audience (p. 107). Much recent feminist research has involved the recovery of texts which have been consistently marginalized and denigrated, very often on the grounds of a lack of 'universality', which is to say, male address. Certainly the history of nineteenth-century writing seems to support Lovell's case. The women writers of that time who are popularly considered 'good' writers (Jane Austen, Elizabeth Gaskell, E.B. Browning, George Eliot) on the whole address a male reader. Perhaps the major exceptions are the Brontës – and they have only relatively recently been rescued from their marginalization by Leavis et al. Feminist research on nineteenth-century women writers is not only discovering how very many women earned their living or a substantial part of their income by writing (there were thousands[16]), but is also attempting to evaluate why these writers so completely disappeared from literary, let alone popular, memory. To postulate that this was only because of the gender of the author verges on rather a large conspiracy, though gender identity undoubtedly had a great deal to do with the critical reception of the work, and therefore sales, and therefore the future publications of the individual woman writer (consider, for example, the critical reception of *Wuthering*

Heights and its extraordinary gender-bias). Yet this set of reviewing/ sales/publication practices does not explain the marginalization of so many writers, or the success of the few. It is here that the notion of audience address forms a crucial supplement to this historical research.

De Lauretis projects this notion on to contemporary feminist practice:

> Feminist cinema . . . begins from an understanding of spectatorship as gendered . . . and then essays to fashion narrative strategies, points of identification, and places of the look that may address, engage, and construct the spectator as gendered subject; and most recently, as in Lizzie Borden's *Born in Flames*, as a subject constructed across racial as well as sexual differences. (1987 (A), p. 123)

Not all feminist generic fiction can claim to be so self-conscious. Not all feminist generic fiction is so concerned with the gender of its audience. And not all generic fiction engages with issues of race and class. However, a substantial number of feminist popular texts engage with one or other of these issues and, in fact, the very process of writing a feminist text which is not itself subverted by the ideological sedimentation of genre conventions produces an acute awareness of both textual practice and audience reception. In the chapters which follow I shall consider texts by feminist writers written in a variety of genres, not so much as an assessment of the value or correctness of individual texts or writers, but in order to construct a composite image of this innovative and provocative area of literary production. This is not a unified field of endeavour, any more than feminism is a unified field of theory, or feminists a unified group. As de Lauretis notes, the feminist subject is 'constructed across racial as well as sexual differences' (1987 (A), p. 123). This description must be supplemented by the category of class (and in many societies religion is another important difference between women and between feminists). But it is only lately that this lack of unity, these differences, have been recognized as enabling and enriching, rather than divisive. Traditionally women have no presence in literature other than as 'Woman,' an idealist construct composed from the negatives of masculinity. As 'Woman', women are represented as basically good or bad (according to whether they help or hinder masculinist practices); female characters have no complexity, no subtlety, no 'real' presence. In feminist genre fiction writers are attempting to break down that simplistic characterization, and, in so doing, to challenge patriarchal discourses. They are not just breaking through boundaries, but showing boundaries which readers were not meant to perceive. These include boundaries between women, as well as between women and men. In textual terms this means an increasingly complex engagement with narrative, with genre conventions, and with the discourses they mobilize.

Subject position, reading position

The most useful concept in dealing with the audience constructed by a literary text is reading position. This is the position assumed by a reader from which the text seems to be coherent and intelligible. It is essentially a set of instructions about how to read the text, constructed by the text by means of the conventions which simultaneously encode discursive positionings (Kress 1985 (A), p. 37). Of course, the reading position produced in generic texts by sedimented ideological discourses will often conflict with the reading position produced by feminist ideology; hence the discomfort readers may experience with these texts. Yet, as I noted earlier, these contradictions are also the site of struggle, of negotiation, and of the production of new meanings (pp. 83–4). Feminist writers are at the forefront of this struggle to make new meanings. Here too is the rational for the appropriation by feminist writers of generic forms. With no other literary forms are the boundaries so discernible and the ensuing struggle so palpable. And given the popularity of these generic forms, the struggle can even be fun. More importantly the resultant production of new meanings is an essential part not only of literary experimentation, but also of social change. Feminist genre fiction is not the result of an 'instance of postmodernist thought' but is an important phase in the development of a feminist consciousness and of the complex feminist subject.

Subject position is the discursive equivalent of reading position; it describes the position of the individual subject in relation to a particular discourse or set of discourses, rather than a particular text.[17] The feminist subject is the subject position constructed by feminist discourse, an oppositional gender discourse predicated on the experiential recognition of contradictions and injustices generated by the dominant gender discourse of patriarchy. A feminist text is one in which the reading position constructed by the text – the position from which the text is coherent and meaningful – corresponds with this subject position. That is, the text operates to reveal the contradictions and injustices within the dominant gender discourse and to make visible the strategies by which that discourse is naturalized, including genre conventions and narrative.

Each of the following chapters traces the construction of this feminist reading position by feminist writers of genre fiction. The study begins with science fiction, which was the first genre form to become part of the recent strategic intervention by feminists in textual practice. As a literature of estrangement (that is, a literature concerned primarily with the alienation experienced by individual subjects, realized textually by a setting displaced in time and/or space), science fiction was used initially to show how different women's and men's experience of their world were, and to demonstrate the practice of sexist discourse. Subsequently feminist SF writers began to engage with the problems of textual convention, to investigate how these conventions and their sedimented discursive practices intervene in the formulation of a feminist reading position. The chapter begins by tracing the historical development of the genre as a literature which explored the impact of technological change on society, its earliest manifestation being Mary Shelley's *Frankenstein*. Changes in the overt political concerns of the genre are charted, as are the uses to which it has been put as political propaganda. The generic conventions of SF are then considered in some detail and the use to which they have been put by feminist writers is analysed. The work of a number of feminist SF writers is considered, beginning with a short story by James Tiptree Jr. (Alice Sheldon) entitled 'The Women Men Don't See' which might serve as an exemplar for feminist science fiction.

In the next chapter feminist use of the fantasy genre is considered, with particular reference to three modes of the fantastic – secondary world fantasy, fairy-tale and horror. In each case feminist use of the conventions of the genre is analysed starting with the estranged form, the secondary world fantasy. Again the genre is used to explore the different experience of women and men of the contemporary social formation and to reveal the practice of patriarchal discourse. The fairy-tale mode achieves a similar deconstructive practice, but this is based quite explicitly on the evocation and revaluation of traditional fairy-tale narratives. Feminist horror is not common, but exists, and its practice is also very much a referential one, familiar horror stories and characters reworked to show not only patriarchy in social practice, but also encoding of patriarchal discourse in textual practice. Again a number of writers are considered, from best sellers such as Marion Zimmer Bradley to political activists as Suzy McKee Charnas, and to highbrow writers (who may also be political activists) such as Angela Carter.

Feminist utopian fiction is considered next and, as with science fiction, the chapter begins with an analysis of the history of this genre which so conspicuously deals with the discursive formation of the society in which it was produced. The use of utopian fiction as political propaganda is discussed, with particular reference to the proliferation of utopian writing during the politically turbulent closing decades of the nineteenth century. The modifications effected by late nineteenth-century writers to the conventions established by Thomas More in his seminal work, *Utopia*, serve as a gloss on the transformations of these same conventions by recent feminist writers. Writers such as William Morris used the utopia in the late nineteenth-century to interrogate not only specific discursive practices of his society, but also the role of fiction in those discursive practices. Feminist utopias, including Charlotte Perkins Gilman's early twentieth-century novel, *Herland*, as well as more recent texts such as Marge Piercy's *Woman on the Edge of Time* and Joanna Russ's *The Female Man*, engage with either or both of these textual strategies and they, too, modify the conventions of the genre in accordance with their own discursive practice, which is the construction of a feminist reading position.

Feminist detective fiction is one of the most recent ventures into genre fiction by feminist writers. The female detective, either 'hard-' or 'soft-boiled', leads the way in the appropriation by feminists of a genre which deals primarily with the process of discovery, of finding out, of demystification. The next chapter deals with detective fiction, its development since Poe's detective, Dupin, extended Gothic eccentricity into the realm of the rational, and its conventions including the detective, the criminal, the off-sider/helper, and the crime. All of these conventions are challenged in various innovative ways by contemporary female and feminist writers of the genre, from Sara Paretsky with her super-cool professional detective, V.I. Warshawski, to Valerie Miner and her amateur sleuth, Nan Weaver. Reworkings of the genre raise a number of issues: how far can the conventions be modified before the text ceases to be recognizable as a detective novel? how can feminist writers best exploit the 'detective' framework of the genre as part of the construction of a feminist reading position?

A historical study of the development of romantic fiction, the final genre form considered in this study, raises several issues which are pertinent to attempts to construct a feminist reading position in these texts. Romantic fiction seems to be predicated on the elaboration of a relationship between a powerful, active male character and a weak, submissive female character. The inequality between the characters, based essentially on gender difference, often constructs the sexual tension developed by the narrative as a rape fantasy. And the rape fantasy signals another level of signification altogether; that romantic fiction may be a displaced representation and negotiation of class relationships. Feminist romantic fiction seems to be a contradiction in terms, a parody in practice. Feminist uses of this genre are accordingly complex and subtle. This is the genre most recently approached by feminist writers, with equivocal results.

Feminist genre fiction is an exciting initiative for writers attempting to construct a feminist reading position within their texts. Furthermore it is a significant contribution to feminist political practice, a highly self-conscious intervention in the signifying practices of contemporary Western society. It is a new way of making meanings, of renegotiating the complex of discourses which constitute the dominant ideological framework of contemporary society – and, in particular, of renegotiating the gender discourses which define what and how it is to be a woman or man in contemporary Western society.

2

Feminist Science Fiction

'The Women Men Don't See': feminist science fiction

I see her first while the Mexicana 727 is barreling down to Cozumel
Island. I come out of the can and lurch into her seat, saying 'Sorry,' at a
double female blur. The near blur nods quietly. The younger one in the
window seat goes on looking out. I continue down the aisle, registering
nothing. Zero. I never would have looked at them or thought of them
again. (Tiptree, 1975 (B), p. 131)

The hero/protagonist/narrator of James Tiptree Jr.'s short story 'The
Women Men Don't See' recalls his first sighting of the Parsons,
mother and daugher, two women who prefer to leave for an unknown planet to live with physically repulsive aliens than to stay
where they are comfortable and safe, on Earth. As he notes, they were
to him a 'blur', 'nothing', 'Zero'. Tiptree's story was praised by editor,
Robert Silverberg as a 'profoundly feminist story told in entirely
masculine manner' (p. xvi). Knowing that Silverberg's 'ineluctably
masculine' (p. xii)[1] writer Tiptree was actually the scientist and writer
Alice Sheldon alerts contemporary readers to what is perhaps a more
profoundly feminist story than even Silverberg suspected.

The 'entirely masculine manner' to which Silverberg responded is a
construct of masculinist discourses which Tiptree uses to compose
her narrator, Fenton. Fenton is the tough guy of space opera,
adventure story, detective fiction, or Western. At least Fenton talks
that way and thinks in those terms: 'My paranoia stirs. I grab it by the
collar . . .' (p. 148). Fenton's dialogue sounds right in the mouth of
Humphrey Bogart as Sam Spade. Fenton progresses from not seeing
the Parsons to objectifying them in stereotypically masculine, sexist
terms:

As we clamber into the Bonanza, I see the girl has what could be an attractive body if there was any spark at all. There isn't . . . (p. 132)

The women are now in shorts, neat but definitely not sexy . . . (p. 137)

. . . my eyes take in the fact that Mrs. Parsons is now quite rosy around the knees, with her hair loose and a sunburn on her nose. A trim, in fact a very neat shading-forty . . . (p. 139)

Miss Parsons is even rosier and more windblown . . . A good girl, Miss Parsons, in her nothing way . . . (p. 140)

The woman doesn't mean one thing to me, but the obtrusive recessiveness of her, the defiance of her little rump eight inches from my fly – for two pesos I'd have those shorts down and introduce myself. If I were twenty years younger. If I wasn't so bushed . . . (pp. 142–3)

As the quotes show, Fenton's awareness of them *as women* leads directly to an expression of sexual desire which is explicitly a rape fantasy. Yet this rape fantasy is apparently a normal part of the masculine manner Silverberg identifies. Fenton is surprised by and annoyed by the Parsons' failure to fulfil stereotypical female roles: they do not panic when the plane crashes; they do not complain when forced to live rough while waiting for rescue; and they do not respond physically to him. The 'spark' which Fenton decided was missing from Miss Parson's body is surely the flirtatious response to male gaze which Fenton consistently fails to find with the Parsons. When Fenton is unable to resolve this dilemma (for him) of the Parsons' behaviour, he deflects his anxiety into another masculinist fantasy, the legendary sexual proficiency of non-white males. His own inability to seduce or rape Mrs Parsons finds relief in erotic fantasies of Miss Parsons and the Mayan pilot, Captain Estéban:

Captain Estéban's mahogany arms clasping Miss Althea Parsons' pearly body. Captain Estéban's archaic nostrils snuffling in Miss Parsons' tender neck. Captain Estéban's copper buttocks pumping into Althea's creamy upturned bottom . . . (p. 150)

Fenton relates this as the vicarious desire of Mrs Parsons, but it is his own formulation and he uses it to excuse his 'failure': 'I feel fairly silly and more than a little irritated. *Now* I find out . . .' (p. 150). Mrs Parsons does not respond to him, he decides, because *she* is preoccupied with erotic fantasies about her daughter and Captain Estéban. Tiptree assigns to Fenton the racist, white male fantasy that white women are slavishly attracted to non-white men, a scenario which objectifies both non-white men and white women; both are reduced to their sexual function. As Tiptree's use of it in this story implies, this fantasy is a projection of white male fears about their own sexuality mingled with guilt about white colonialist abuse of non-white women. And it is a fantasy which appears frequently in all kinds of literary texts, from *Othello* to contemporary pulp. It is one of the defining discourses which Tiptree represents in the character and actions of Fenton. Fenton also personifies the he-man adventurism of that same discourse. When the aliens approach, Fenton's first response is to attack them with a revolver, but he only manages to shoot Mrs Parsons. Undaunted by his incompetence at the original meeting Fenton next plans to steal the alien's boat: 'Schemes of capturing it swirl in my mind. I'll need Estéban' (p. 160). Like so many of the adventurers of quest, romance, fantasy and detective fiction, Fenton's answer to the unknown, the alien, is violence; his response to a superior technology is to steal it. Fenton characterizes a violent, colonialist, white, male discourse which is fundamentally sexist – and Tiptree introduces him in these terms via his description of the Mayans at the beginning of the story. It is a mixture of racism and sexism:

> Our captain's classic Maya profile attracts my gaze: forehead sloping back from his predatory nose, lips and jaw stepping back below it. If his slant eyes had been any more crossed, he couldn't have made his license. That's a handsome combination, believe it or not. On the little Maya chicks in their minishifts with iridescent gloop on those cockeyes, it's also highly erotic. (p. 133)

Tiptree simulates an 'entirely masculine manner' in the story by constructing a narrative voice from a number of sexist discourses which are so effectively naturalized that even the editor, Silverberg, did not suspect that the narrative voice was a part of, not simply the authoritative medium for, the 'feminist story'. Perhaps this credulousness on Silverberg's part was also a function of the dominance of the SF genre by male writers, many of whom openly espoused the ideological discourses mouthed by Fenton.

The feminist discourse of 'The Women Men Don't See' is expressed primarily in the behaviour and characterization of the Parsons. Fenton is surprised when Mrs Parsons declares that women's lib is 'doomed':

> 'Women have no rights, Don, except what men allow us. Men are more aggressive and powerful, and they run the world. When the next real crisis upsets them, our so-called rights will vanish like – like that

smoke. We'll be back where we always were: property. And whatever has gone wrong will be blamed on our freedom, like the fall of Rome was. You'll see. (p. 153)

When Fenton offers the platitudinous comfort that the world would stop without women's labour, Mrs Parsons' reply is a testament to the political realities of the situation:

'That's fantasy ... Women don't work that way. We're a – a toothless world ... What women do is survive. We live by ones and twos in the chinks of your world-machine.' (p. 154)

When Mrs Parsons suggests to Fenton that he think of women as 'opposums' ('Did you know there are opposums living all over? Even in New York City' (p. 154)), Fenton is alarmed by her perspective and its implications:

'Men and women aren't different species, Ruth. Women do everything men do.'
'Do they?' Our eyes meet, but she seems to be seeing ghosts between us in the rain. She mutters something that could be 'My Lai' and looks away. 'All the endless wars ...' Her voice is a whisper. 'All the huge authoritarian organizations for doing unreal things. Men live to struggle against each other; we're just part of the battlefields. It'll never change unless you change the whole world ...'
'Men hate wars too, Ruth,' I say as gently as I can.
'I know.' She shrugs and climbs to her feet. 'But that's your problem, isn't it?'
End of communication. Mrs. Parsons isn't even living in the same world with me. (p. 154)

And Fenton thinks to himself: 'Alienation like that can add up to dead pigeons ...' (p. 154). Fenton's musing is the key to the use of SF conventions in this so-far realistic tale. When the aliens arrive, Mrs Parsons attempts to communicate with them and it is then that Fenton recognizes to his horror: 'She's as alien as they, there in the twilight' (p. 158). By this time his pathetic attempts at heroics had resulted in him shooting her in the arm, but even this is highly significant to the feminist discourse developed in the text. In wanting to shoot the aliens Fenton shoots the woman and in one sense achieves his aim: the woman is thereby identified with/as the alien. When he pleads with Mrs Parsons for collaboration, she responds in terms which confirm their (Fenton and hers) difference: '"For Christ's sake, Ruth, they're *aliens*!" "I'm used to it," she said absently' (p. 160). The punchline of the story is that Ruth Parsons pleads with the aliens to take her and her daughter away with them to their own planet, which they do: 'The last I see of Mrs Ruth Parsons and Miss Althea Parsons is two small shadows against that light, like two opposums. The light snaps off, the hum deepens – and they're going, going, gone away.' (p. 162) Tiptree thus reverses the usual sensationalistic bug-eyed monsters steal earth-women for orgies in deep space theme into earth women plead with said monsters to be taken away in to deep space. Fenton is left to muse on this extraordinary event (and usefully to repeat the message for any who have missed it):

> We survive by ones and twos in the chinks of your world-machine . . . I'm used to aliens . . . She'd meant every word. Insane. How could a woman choose to live among unknown monsters, to say good-bye to her home, her world?
>
> As the margharitas take hold, the whole mad scenario melts down to the image of those two small shapes sitting side by side in the receding alien glare.
>
> Two of our opposums are missing. (pp. 163–4)

The feminist discourse of 'The Women Men Don't See' is a function of both the feminist ideology espoused by Ruth Parsons and the contrasting sexism of Fenton. This is not, as Silverberg's 'Introduction' seems to suggest, a story of female alienation narrated by an ordinary, somewhat naïve, male narrator. Tiptree's story achieves both an expression of feminist ideology and a deconstruction of sexism. Not only does Tiptree show the devaluing, negating, silencing, and subsequent invisibility of women in twentieth-century Western society, or at least in its legitimation processes, its exercise of power; she also shows the naturalized operation of the discourse which so relegates women. What, then, is the reading position of this story? Silverberg seems to suggest a reading position which corresponds largely with that of the narrator. He is just an ordinary man who has learned an extraordinary lesson about female alienation; the reader can be assumed to have responded sympathetically to this ordinariness and will learn the lesson with Fenton. My analysis indicates, however, that Tiptree's story is far more complex than this; that the sexist and racist ideologies of her narrator are more apparent than Silverberg implies, that Tiptree's representations of Fenton's mannered language and mindless, stereotypical responses to situations, are the product of a textual self-consciousness and sophistication which negate attempts at simplistic realist readings of the story. The reading position Tiptree negotiates in this story requires the reader to adopt a feminist subjectivity. Only then do all the events of the story make sense – Fenton's preoccupation with the physical appearance of the women, his failure to comprehend women who do not correspond to the gender roles in which he conventionally places them (the women men don't see), his fantasies about Althea Parsons and Captain Estéban, his shooting of Mrs Parsons, and his inability to understand the Parsons' perception of life on Earth. Only then is Fenton's heavily conventionalized dialogue also intelligible, as Tiptree's deconstruction of the discourses which guide, define and delimit masculine (sexist) behaviour.

'The Women Men Don't See' is an example of feminist genre fiction, specifically of feminist science fiction. Tiptree has used the male dominated genre of science fiction to deconstruct male domination. Tiptree demonstrates the behaviour dictated by patriarchal gender ideology in the character and actions of narrator, Fenton. And in writing him, in representing his thought processes, she reveals how ideological discourses in narrative form enter the consciousness of individuals. As writer Marge Piercy noted: 'The myths we imagine we are living (old westerns, true romances) shape our choices.'[2] When those myths, those narratives, encode ideological discourses, sometimes those choices are made for us. At the very least they often contribute to a complex of conservative discourses which the individual must negotiate in order to make meaning of her/his existence, the experiential incidents of which may sometimes clash directly with those discourses and their narratives. The Parsons are in conflict with Fenton's world, to such a degree that they are alienated from it. They are aliens in Fenton's world and must leave, whether that means flagging down a passing starship or developing new meanings for existence in those cracks and interstices of official institutions in which they now exist, cracks and interstices which might thus be strengthened sufficiently to shatter and fragment the institutions: as Ruth Parsons predicts, 'change the whole world' (p. 154). Fenton and his brothers may not notice that two of their sisters are missing, but the point is that most of the time they do not notice the sisters are there at all.

Tiptree's use of the conventions of the science fiction genre in 'The Women Men Don't See' is particularly interesting because she weaves conventional responses into her articulation of an extremely unconventional narrative and encoded discourse. The convention which is most obvious is the alien and, in fact, until the aliens arrive, there has been little to suggest that this story is science fiction, or at least that science fiction will be among the weave of genres which comprise it. As the analysis above shows, Tiptree uses the alienness of the extraterrestials to signifiy the absolute alienness of women in a patriarchal society. The logic of patriarchy equates masculinity with normality, the standard for 'man'; femininity is thereby relegated to some less-than-human status, as the subsequent treatment of women by apologists for this ideology demonstrates. The fatuousness of the 'equal but different' argument of patriarchy is alluded to by Ruth Parsons in her response to Fenton's projection of the consequences for society if women were to withhold their labour. Parsons makes the point that women do not, that is, cannot, operate that way; women are not free to withdraw their labour, because of the kinds of labour for which they are relegated responsibility. So the power they have in theory amounts in practice to nothing; women under patriarchy are powerless. In the same way being equal but different is fine in theory, but in practice it means to be different and most decidedly unequal, again primarily because of the kinds of labour in which women are involved and their virtual exclusion from the public sphere in which power is exercised and decisions made.

In the story Parsons refers repeatedly to this powerlessness. This power differential is fundamental to legitimation processes, to deciding who or what is valid and not valid. Women's powerlessness is a function of and reason for their exclusion from these legitimation processes. The result is the alien/ation of women from their own society. Not only do women feel alienated, not a part of their society, but also men do not see them as equal members of that society. For men, too, women are alien/ated. In the most extreme case women are reduced simply to their biological function; it is the ultimate determinant of their existence. The women men don't see might be read as all women; men only see a sexist feminine construct which has little to do with the reality of women's lives. The women men especially don't see are the ones who will not or cannot represent themselves in terms of that construct. Those women are absolutely alien; they cannot be comprehended, cannot be perceived, except as something fundamentally other, different, alien. The interaction between Fenton and the aliens in the story then becomes a kind of ghastly allegory of the interaction of the patriarchal male with the alien/ated female: appropriate its labour (technology) and/or shoot it. Tiptree consolidates this connection in the story by having Fenton aim at the aliens and shoot Mrs Parsons. The concept of the alien is therefore used very effectively by Tiptree to represent the 'otherness' of women in contemporary society. Simultaneously her representation of sexist discourse via the Fenton character shows the ideological mechanisms by which that 'otherness' is confirmed, reinforced and naturalized.

Another science fiction convention Tiptree uses is estrangement, the use of a different or alien environment or character to show the reader the everyday in a different light, from another perspective. In this story the other or different perspective comes not from another world or an alien character but from the alienated Ruth Parsons. Parsons gives the reader the non-patriarchal view, both in what she says to Fenton and in her interactions with him. To Fenton her view, her perspective, is dangerous, alienated, doomed, liable to result in 'dead pigeons.' This dual perspective on the world we know is a convention familiar to readers of science fiction and Tiptree assumes that familiarity in setting up the interaction between Parsons and Fenton. It is as if, the story having been designated science fiction (by the publisher, or by association with this writer), readers constantly expect something strange or alien to happen, and the longer they wait, the more crucial that demand becomes. When Fenton shoots Parsons by mistake, and the identity of woman as alien is consolidated, suddenly the whole story falls into place: readers expectations are fulfilled, the contract is ratified. Thus the presentation of the story as science fiction, and the expectations that creates in readers, is fundamental to the impact of 'The Women Men Don't See.'

Science and technology do not play a major role in the story, though Tiptree does use high technology in the conventional way, by associating it with the aliens. As I noted above, Fenton's response to the alien technology is a desire to appropriate it. In this Tiptree evokes many of the adventurers of SF, as well as all those B-movies of the 1950s in which the threat of high-tech alien invaders was a thinly disguised allegory of the West in the Cold War (*The Thing* (1951), *It Came from Outer Space* (1953), *War of the Worlds* (1953) *The Quatermass Experiment* (1955), *Earth vs the Flying Saucers* (1956), *It Conquered the World* (1956)). By that stage in the story Fenton's characterization is established as a component of the discursive formation of sexism which Tiptree mobilizes in the text. Through Fenton's attitude to the Mayans Tiptree also relates this formation to an acquisitive, colonialist discourse which generates the frontiersman type behaviour Fenton displays in relation to the aliens, when he tries to shoot them and later when he wants to capture them and their technology. Tiptree again utilizes a standard SF convention while at the same time deconstructing it, relating it to the ideological discourse it encodes but usually represents as entrepreneurship, courage or enterprise.

Related to several of these conventions is Tiptree's use of the tough-talking male narrator, the Han Solo type of adventurer whose hallmarks include the treatment of women as sex objects and aliens as enemies. Yet, as I have suggested above, Tiptree almost overwrites his dialogue; Fenton is almost too much of a stereotype, his constant comments on the women's bodies a parody of objectification, especially in light of his own consistent failure to act on any of these statements. In fact Fenton's sequence of failures – his inability to interest either of the women, his jealousy of Captain Estéban, his careless injury to his leg in the swamp and subsequent reliance on Ruth Parsons, his shooting of Parsons instead of the aliens, his failure to capture either the aliens or their technology – is perhaps Tiptree's most successful deconstruction of that tough-guy characterization. The discrepancy between Fenton's dialogue and his actions is not simply an indication of failure by the individual; it is rather an example of self-representation in terms of a stereotype. As women are incited by patriarchy to don the mask of femininity, so men are meant to take on that of masculinity. Fenton's tough talk is his attempt to comply, but his actions show just how fanciful this role can be. The tough guy is not so tough in person but what he does do is live out the racism and sexism fundamental to the discourses which make up this characterization. This, Tiptree implies, is the danger of these roles: men who adopt them risk not seeing a great deal of what happens around them.

Tiptree also conventionally employs the quest narrative in her story, but then subverts it. Conventionally the hero of this narrative should be Fenton, but he achieves little by its resolution. He does not get the 'girl', and he does not understand why she and her daughter have gone off with the aliens. The consciousness raising which occurs in the story does not effect Fenton; he never adopts or understands or even sees the feminist subject position. Tiptree parallels Fenton's quest with that of Ruth Parsons. Parsons is the female hero of a narrative motivated by feminist ideology. Parsons's quest does not begin in the events of the story; they are just another part of the same struggle – to live in a society in which she has no place, where she and those like her are alien, other, different. And there is a resolution here for Ruth and Althea Parsons; they leave with the aliens. What this resolution signifies is an acceptance by the female characters of their difference and their decision to live as aliens. Their removal is not so much a physical one as a political one. In rejecting entirely the sexist ideology of their own society they are, of necessity, forging totally new identities which will not be legitimated by the patriarchal order. The Parsons are no longer content to be opossums; they will be monsters instead. Monsters have power, unlike opossums, and so have to be seen.

The resolution of 'The Women Men Don't See' is only non-problematic when the story is read from a feminist reading position. Only then do both the Fenton plot and the Parsons plot make sense, only then is their interaction intelligible, and only then do the endings of both plots make sense in themselves and in relation to each other. I agree with the editor, Silverberg, then, that this is 'a profoundly feminist story' and this is at least partly the reason for giving it such prominence in this study. However, I am a little less sure of his judgement that it is 'told in entirely masculine manner', particularly given Silverberg's outspoken support of patriarchal masculinity in this same preface. Rather it seems that Tiptree has used the conventional/ized response to this 'masculine manner' in her story and so effectively subverted that manner, which speaks but does not see. And this is my other reason for beginning with this story: the effectiveness of Tiptree's subversion of SF conventions. She succeeds in writing a feminist story that even those who most support the 'masculine' will read, even if they fail to understand that she includes them as part of the problem. The more persistent their masculinist reading, the more disturbing is the resolution of the Parsons plot. Tiptree achieves this degree of political sensitivity by attending closely to the expectations, needs and demands of her audience, by inscribing them into the dynamics of her narrative. In 'The Women Men Don't See' Tiptree demonstrates the 'aesthetic of reception' that Teresa de Lauretis describes as the focus of contemporary feminist cinema (1987 (A), p. 141). 'The Women Men Don't See' is an outstanding example of science fiction as political fiction, of the subversive use of genre fiction to produce an unconventional discursive position, the feminist subject.

History of the genre

Science fiction developed as a genre during the nineteenth century, a time of enormous social turmoil in Western society. The Industrial Revolution changed the lives of countless people as work practices familiar for generations disappeared apparently overnight. The growth of the cities was a consequence of changed work conditions on the land and huge slums were formed, from where the new class of machine-tenders was drawn for the factories. Crisis after crisis shook this society to its foundations. Socialist and other radical political movements accompanied the consolidation of this new industrial working class and demands for social justice accompanied the spread of the democratic process. Middle-class and working-class women joined the call for social justice with a demand for equality for women, before the law and in the ballot box. Darwin's theory of evolution shook the white middle-class male belief in their unique position as the pinnacle of God's creative achievement, though they were soon able to assimilate this theory to their ideological practice as Social Darwinism. Geological research and the accumulation of the fossil record challenged the familiar, literal interpretations of Genesis, prompting religious and spiritual trauma. Research into the nature of individual consciousness challenged the notion of the undifferentiated self, and Freud's research in the later decades of the century corroborated the need for a more complex model of the operation of consciousness. All the certainties of life were being questioned: class positions and class loyalty, the roles of women and men in society, the nature of God, the nature of the self. Writers responded in a variety of ways to these challenges, which they attempted variously to explore and/or resolve.

Science fiction was one of the literary responses to this age of crisis. The conventions we now classify as science fiction first appeared in texts which showed also the conventions of Gothic fantasy, most notably in Mary Shelley's *Frankenstein*, now generally accepted as the first science fiction novel. *Frankenstein* in one of the first novels in which science or technology occupies a pivotal role, and Shelley's concern is not science *per se* but science in relation to society. Victor Frankenstein's fault is not simply the pursuit of forbidden knowledge, but his failure to consider the consequences of his research, the dilemma faced by scientists in many areas of research today (for example nuclear technology, genetic manipulation, *in vitro* fertilization). This technology/society conflict is the site at which Shelley simultaneously mobilizes an exploration of other discourses, principally that of gender. In making his creature Frankenstein not only usurps the place of God, he also usurps the role of woman. Frankenstein's creature therefore signifies the result of the masculinist attempt to appropriate and exploit this biological capability of women, which in a patriarchal society is their defining, and limiting, characteristic. The patriarchal order appropriates and exploits maternity, and therefore women, by subsuming it/them into its male-dominated gender discourse of sexism. Maternity is thereby placed not in relation to women, but men. It is the opposite of paternity, and paternity is where the power is (within this discourse). In *Consuming Fiction* Terry Lovell notes this same negation and relates it to the exclusion of women from cultural history: 'Like the biblical account of father begetting sons, which omits the mediating body of the mother, so this cultural begetting omits her mind' (1987 (A), p. 5). Frankenstein literally negates the body of the mother; sexist discourse ideologically negates women, whom it identifies solely as the body of the mother. In either case the result is a disaster, a monster which is not so much an individual subjectivity as an embodied fragment of the consciousness of the creator. Frankenstein's monstrous creation signifies the chaos of a technology out of touch with its society. It also signifies the distortion of gender relations produced by sexist discourse, and particularly the distortion of women subsumed within that discourse as the 'feminine.' In writing about the ideological disposition of women Shelley continued a thematic preoccupation of the Gothic, particularly Gothic literature written by women. The simultaneous articulation of both concerns suggests that the debate about the social consequences of technological change is somehow fundamentally connected with the debate about gender roles and the power differential which defines masculinity and femininity under patriarchy.

These two issues, however, did not continue to receive the same amount of attention, perhaps because the next prominent writer, or group of writers, using the genre was male. While gender issues may have been a concern for men, they were not so obviously problematic as for women who had to contend with the limiting consequences of patriarchal discourse in their own professional and personal lives. H.G. Wells and Jules Verne were the next major writers of science fiction and in their work women rarely appear except as the 'love interest' for one of the male characters; women occupy the role of object, prize. Wells and Verne were, nevertheless, very different writers and their work gave rise to two distinct strands of science fiction. Verne was interested, even fascinated, by new technology. His works, such as *20,000 Leagues Under the Sea* and *From the Earth to the Moon*, have simple, even simplistic, adventure plots which Verne builds around the technological masterpiece at the centre of the narrative. Of course, gender issues are not thereby avoided; in fact, Verne's evasion of them, and of female characters almost entirely, is extremely revealing in itself, signifying the exclusion of women from the technology which was the source of power and wealth in contemporary society. And Wells, though a supporter of women's rights in his political work as a Fabian Socialist, did not address these issues in his science fiction. He did, however, use science fiction to speculate about the nature of his own society, particularly its class ideology. In works such as *The Time Machine*, *The First Men in the*

Moon, *The Invisible Man* and *The Island of Dr. Moreau* Wells debates the nature of bourgeois society, its class structure and the dehumanization of the working classes, its colonialism, its abuse of technological achievement. The contrast between Verne and Wells is apparent in Verne's own judgement of Wells:

> I make use of physics. He invents. I go to the moon in a cannon-ball, discharged from a cannon. Here there is no invention. He goes to Mars in an airship, which he constructs of a material which does away with the law of gravitation. *Ça c'est tres joli* . . . but show me this metal. Let him produce it. (Parrinder, 1980 (B), p. 7)

Wells's fault, so far as Verne is concerned, is that he is unscientific, unlike Verne himself (though I would not like to be in that cannon-ball!). Wells produces unreal, but pseudo-scientific, situations and environments by which to explore his own environment, and in this he follows very much in the tradition of Mary Shelley. Verne's work, on the other hand, establishes a new tradition – a toys for the boys strand of science fiction totally preoccupied, in Frankensteinian manner, with technology and with little interest in the social implications of that technology. Verne's strand of SF dominated the genre throughout the first half of the twentieth century and the significance of this for women hardly needs to be spelled out. Socially and politically conscious science fiction continued to be written, but mostly in the related generic form of the utopian or dystopian novel, a genre which uses many of the conventions of SF, but with some significant differences (see Chapter 4). Until the 1960s science fiction was predominantly a macho genre produced for the Fentons of modern society. The major preoccupations of the genre were scientific extrapolation, given great impetus by the rapid rate of technological change in the twentieth century and particularly by imaginative projections of nuclear technology, and the monsters from outer space scenarios which projected the xenophobic fears of nations existing with the realities of world wars. Very little of this science fiction was self-reflexive or socially or politically investigative.

In the 1960s science fiction changed. This was a time of economic ease in the West, of student radicalism, experimentation with drugs and lifestyles, rejection of bourgeois 'rationalism' and the exploration of the fantastic and bizarre, the freeing of pop culture from the stranglehold of modernist legitimation. Science fiction writers engaged with this negotiation of new meaning and new reality in their work. Philip K. Dick, Stanislaw Lem and Kurt Vonnegut Jr. reanimated the tradition of Shelley and Wells, transforming pulp into philosophy. Again these writers seldom engaged with gender issues as a primary focus for their work, though the growing interest in gender ideology prompted by lifestyle experimentation is apparent in their work, but their writing prepared the way for the more explicitly political work produced in the 1970s.

Throughout the 1960s the Women's Movement had regained strength and a high public profile, as women once again experienced the discrepancy between theory and its practical application: the personal liberation movements of the 1960s usually endorsed stereotypical roles for women as childbearers and caregivers, 'earthmothers,' without challenging the social limitations engendered by that role. Consciousness raising was a buzz word of the rejuvenated feminist movement, recovering from the onslaught of 1950s McCarthyism. Women attempted to throw off the mental shackles of sexist ideology and see themselves and their role in society differently:

> *Only sf and fantasy literature can show us women in entirely new or strange surroundings. It can explore what we might become if and when the present restrictions on our lives vanish, or show us new problems and restrictions that might arise.* It can show us the remarkable woman as normal where past literature shows her as the exception. Will we become more like men, ultimately indistinguishable from them with all their faults and virtues, or will we bring new concerns and values to society, perhaps changing men in the process? How will biological advances, and the greater control they will bring us over our bodies, affect us? What might happen if women in the future are thrown back into a situation in which male dominance might reassert itself? What might actually happen if women were dominant? How might future economic systems affect our societal roles? (Sargent, 1978 (B), p. 48)

Pamela Sargent, in the Introduction to her anthology, *Women of Wonder*, describes how feminist science fiction writers participated in this consciousness raising program. In this explanation Sargent conflates two different but related aspects of the task for feminist science fiction. Because of its estrangement from the everyday world of experiential reality, science fiction (and fantasy) can present women in new roles, liberated from the sexism endemic to their society even in its most emancipated state. In this way science fiction has a role in this task of imagining which is fundamental to change. By this means a rationale can be given for struggle, an endpoint envisaged which is better than the current situation – even if the endpoint is, in a sense, the struggle itself and is transformed in the process of struggle. With an imaginative conceptualization of a better future not only does the fight for change seem worthwhile, but perhaps more importantly the necessity for the change becomes increasingly apparent. The injustices and limitations of the present become increasingly visible and intolerable. In other words this imaginative visualization of a different society is seen as a key element in the perception of the mechanisms of patriarchal ideology, the breakdown of its naturalization. No longer will it be obvious or commonsense or natural that women are better adapted to ironing or food preparation than men, that women are intellectually inferior, that men are more aggressive. Rather the economic and social determinants of these attitudes become visible and with that visibility comes the possibility of change. This is one way in which Sargent envisages science fiction intervening in or contributing to the negotiation by women of new meaning, a new reality, freed of the 'mind-forg'd manacles' of sexism.

The other task for feminist SF is literary. Science fiction is to challenge the conventions of 'past literature' which place women, or female characters, in unremarkable roles. In this work women are not heroes. Science fiction will give the reader female heroes and it will represent social systems in which women are not subordinate, but may even be dominant. Such representations are not just socially unconventional; they are literary heterodoxies. How can a text which operates by the inflection of a number of conventions change those conventions and still be perceived as a text? The literary challenge contained in Sargent's statement is not a simple one and it demands a greater degree of textual awareness than had been exercised in the past by writers of science fiction. It is no surprise that this textual self-awareness should coincide with the self-consciousness of post-modernism, though it is a mistake to regard it simply as an instance of postmodernist thought. Nevertheless the way for a theoretically self-conscious fiction had been prepared by writers whose work spans the boundaries of SF and postmodernism, notably Vonnegut and subsequently Thomas Pynchon, Italo Calvino and Doris Lessing. Feminist SF joined the challenge to modernism – but under a very particular impetus, the feminist challenge to patriarchal ideology and the social structure it engendered. Feminist theory and the experiential knowledge of women went into the making of feminist SF and the result was the remaking of a literary genre, a fundamental investigation of the conventions of that genre, both for their literary or narrative implications and for their embedded ideological significance(s).

Conventions of the genre

Some of the characteristics of science fiction have already been cited, in the discussion of 'The Women Men Don't See.' The first and most obvious is that science fiction is a literature which, in some way, addresses *science* or *technology*. As noted earlier, this is appropriate for a literary form that developed during the period of the first Industrial Revolution. In *Frankenstein* Shelley explores the newly emerging scientific discourse of the Industrial Revolution. In Victor Frankenstein's construction of a creature over which he has no control and for which he feels no empathy, and in that creature's subsequent destructiveness, Shelley represents the disaster which results when scientific or technological achievement and social competence are unequal, when a society has access to power which it does not have the wisdom to use well. Shelley's text establishes the misuse of technology as a characteristic thematic element of science fiction. Shelley also wrote about gender ideology in *Frankenstein*. Victor Frankenstein's non-sexual production of a living creature is more than just a challenge to the role of women under patriarchy; it is a deconstruction of the appropriation of reproduction by the male gender in a patriarchal society. So the deformity of the creature, its quasi-human status, can be read as emblematic of the woman produced by patriarchal gender ideology. This woman is the expression of the 'feminine,' a masculinist construct which has little to do with the experiential world of women. This feminine woman is the 'other,' the defining opposite of the male, which in turn defines the human, humanity, 'mankind.' The 'feminine' woman is, therefore, not quite human, less than human; a deformed and disabled version of women. This use of science fiction to investigate gender relations was a forerunner to that contemporary feminist science fiction which similarly focuses on the nature of patriarchal gender relations. It is interesting to note, however, that it was not until the radical movements of the 1960s and the impact of their theorization on SF writers, female and male, that Shelley's explorations were continued. As I noted earlier, it is also highly significant that both concerns are expressed within the same text, indicating some connection between them. This connection has been the subject of much recent feminist science fiction, particularly that in which the possession of a superior technology has been related to colonialist practices.

Later in the century Wells maintained the social inflection of Shelley's investigation of scientific discourse, writing novels in which futurist technology was primarily an estrangement device allowing Wells to confront the reader with allegorized versions of her/his own reality. So Wells conducted his own challenge to bourgeois ideology, denaturalizing it, showing its class divisiveness, colonialist rapacity, scientific irresponsibility. When Wells wrote about science, he, like Shelley, was concerned with its social consequences. It is quite appropriate that he was taught science by T.H. Huxley. His contemporary, Jules Verne, had no such social interest. Verne was a technologist pure and simple. The Verne quote given earlier outlines his own attitude to the science of science fiction: it should be real science, at least as perceived at the time. In Verne's work gender and class ideologies are non-problematic. Conservative ideologies are naturalized into texts in which technological invention is the focus; Verne's work is an instance of the attitude to science, the unquestioning acceptance of an ideology of 'progress', which Shelley and Wells both challenged so vigorously. Verne's high-tech SF predominated for decades, during those years of the twentieth-century marked by the escalating production of armaments, world wars, and the beginning of the age of nuclear weaponry.

In the 1960s, however, science came under challenge along with all other discursive fields. The objectivity of scientific *knowledge*, its status as some kind of non-ideological mode of inquiry and way of knowing, had been exposed as fallacious from within by theories of relativity and uncertainty espoused by Einstein and Heisenberg, but the popular understanding of science and its everyday application remained in the era of Newton. Social and political theorists and commentators continued to justify the validity of their own interpretations by declaring them 'scientific'. Then scientific knowledge itself came under scrutiny as an ideological construct: the way scientific knowledge is compiled as well as the way it is used was analysed as a function of bourgeois ideology, with its characteristic class, race and gender discourses articulated within scientific experimentation and theory. Stanislaw Lem, in his novel *Solaris*, describes the attempt by Earth scientists to understand the alien life-form which lives on or constitutes the planet Solaris. His main character, Kelvin, is led to the truth about the impossibility of this aim by his reading of work by dissident scientists, rejected by the scientific community as the lunatic fringe. One of these scientists, Grastrom is described as having.

> set out to demonstrate that the most abstract achievements of science, the most advanced theories and victories of mathematics represented

nothing more than a stumbling, one or two-step progression from our rude, prehistoric, anthropomorphic understanding of the universe around us. He pointed out correspondences with the human body – the projections of our senses, the structure of our physical organization, and the physiological limitations of man – in the equations of the theory of relativity, the theorem of magnetic fields and the various unified field theories. (Lem, 1971 (B), p. 178)

Lem's novel constitutes an analysis of the limitations of knowledge, of our ability to perceive and understand. Grastrom's conclusion about the future of Solaristics is that it is doomed to failure, that it is absolutely impossible for human beings, confined by the limitations of their physical selves, limitations which are encoded into their intellectual achievements, to communicate with an entity whose physical/emotional/intellectual configuration is so totally other. Feminist SF writers were also involved in these fundamental epistemological investigations. For many feminists the phallocentricity of most discursive fields was a major impediment to any progress towards equality for women. Women working within any specialized discipline, for example, were apt to be as misunderstood and misrepresented as the sentient ocean of Solaris; women within these disciplines were just as alien, as other, as the Solarian ocean. In other words, feminist writers also recognized in scientific theory the 'projections of our senses, the structure of our physical organization, and the physiological limitations of men' but they further realized that the 'man' of Grastrom's statement was the gendered concept, not the supposedly generalized term. Scientific knowledge, all knowledge, was organized around the sensory projections of men: women were thus excluded from the fundamental ways of knowing the world. The ramifications of this exclusion are vast. On a fundamental epistemological level this means that women can only understand contemporary formulations of the real by adopting a masculine persona, at least so far as that is possible. Women thereby become split subjectivities, their knowledge a masculinist construct which they must use and manipulate as such while simultaneously translating it into terms which have significance for them as women, the excluded, the alien. And if women do not achieve this complex task, they are simply excluded from ways of knowing the real and so are easily exploited, their ignorance characterized as weakness or idiocy or madness (the failure to comprehend the (masculine) real). One of the leading theorists of science fiction, Darko Suvin defines the science of science fiction in this way. For Suvin science is a cognitive function and fiction is a way of making strange the everyday in order to show how it operates: science fiction, then, is the literature of cognitive estrangement. It is a neat formulation which summarizes the major conventions of science fiction. Suvin regards the SF in which the analysis of knowledge is a major focus as the most important and innovative science fiction. It is certainly one of the most useful inflections of the genre for feminist writers.

Feminist writers of science fiction have incorporated the *science/ technology* convention into their works in a variety of ways. Some, like Lem, question the access of women to contemporary ways of knowing. In *Native Tongue*, Suzette Haden Elgin's novel about a future Earth in which women's rights have been negated and patriarchy institutionalized as the official gender ideology, the female linguists upon whom her story focuses discover that their most powerful instrument for liberation is a *language* of their own. The women discover that the language of their planet does not express female experience and so women are negated as human beings; the language encodes male perception and male experience as the universal. They begin to develop their own language, Laadan, which expresses their specifically female experience – and so constitutes a fundamental attack on the male-dominated order:

> REFORMULATION ONE, Goedel's Theorem:
> For any language, there are perceptions which it cannot express because they would result in its indirect self-destruction.
>
> REFORMULATION ONE-PRIME, Goedel's Theorem:
> For any culture, there are languages, which it cannot use because they would result in its indirect self-destruction. (Elgin, 1984 (B), p. 145)

Elgin's novel allegorically represents the phallocentricity of language in our own society, the encoding of male experience and masculinity itself as the universal, the normal, the human. The powerlessness of the female linguists signifies the disempowering effect of the exclusion of women from the mechanisms of power validated in language. There are some problems with this representation; for example, Elgin does not address language structures, just lexical items, and it is arguable that the structure of language, like narrative structure, is a more powerful encoder of conservative ideological discourses than the individual unit of language. Nevertheless, Elgin does address and fictionalize the debate about language and its role in the subjugation of women which has been one of the concerns of the Women's Movement, particularly since the 1970s and the publication of Germaine Greer's *The Female Eunuch* (1971). The relationship between women and language continues to be one of the most important areas of analysis and research for feminists and is fundamental to an understanding of the ideological mechanisms by which women are excluded from knowledge, from ways of knowing the world which in themselves confer power (by which, for example, the individual becomes a member of one of the institutions of knowledge/power in our society).

Ursula LeGuin also evokes this debate about the relationship between women and knowledge in her novel, *The Left Hand of Darkness* (LeGuin, 1981 (B)), set on the planet Gethen (or Winter, as it is known by off-worlders) whose inhabitants have a very unusual sexual morphology. The Gethenians spend most of their time as sexless androgynes, that is, without the primary sexual characteristics of either sex, but with the secondary characteristics, the emotional and intellectual strengths and weaknesses of both. Once a month they experience a *kemmer* period in which they become sexually active, but they are unable to predict which sexual identity, female or male, they will have during this period. Consequently their thinking does not follow the dualist patterns of those societies with two distinct sexes:

> Consider: There is no division of humanity into strong and weak halves, protective/protected, dominant/submissive, owner/chattel, active/passive. In fact the whole tendency to dualism that pervades human thinking may be found to be lessened, or changed, on Winter. (p. 85)

These field notes of Ekumen investigator, Ong Tot Oppong clarify this point. Implicit in the dualisms Oppong cites is the basic dualism, male/female. When the female and male sides of the dualism are assembled from their designated characteristics, the fundamental inequality of the female position is apparent: the weak, protected, submissive, passive chattel. Encoded into our thinking, into our language, is the ideological mechanism by which the unequal position of women is maintained. Later in the novel the Ekumen visitor, Genly Ai, a black male Terran, is questioned about Terran women by the Gethenian, Estraven/Harth:

> 'Do they differ much from your sex in mind behaviour? Are they like a different species?'
>
> 'No. Yes. No, of course not, not really. But the difference is very important. I suppose the most important thing, the heaviest single factor in one's life, is whether one's born male or female. In most societies it determines one's expectations, activities, outlook, ethics, manners – almost everything. Vocabulary. Semiotic usages. Clothing.

Even food. Women . . . women tend to eat less . . . It's extremely hard to separate the innate differences from the learned ones. Even where women participate equally with men in the society, they still after all do all the childbearing, and so most of the child-rearing . . .'

'Equality is not the general rule, then? Are they mentally inferior?'

'I don't know. They don't often seem to turn up mathematicians, or composers of music, or inventors, or abstract thinkers. But it isn't that they're stupid. Physically they're less muscular, but a little more durable than men. Psychologically –'

After he had stared a long time at the glowing stove, he shook his head. 'Harth,' he said, 'I can't tell you what women are like. I never thought about it much in the abstract, you know, and – God! – by now I've practically forgotten. I've been here two years . . . You don't know. In a sense, women are more alien to me than you are. With you I share one sex anyhow . . .' He looked away and laughed, rueful and uneasy . . . (p. 200)

Genley's uneasiness, his description of women as alien, his total inability to differentiate between innate and socialized characteristics, and his 'logical' association of childbearing and child-rearing, constitute a deconstruction by LeGuin of the representation of women, of femininity, in a patriarchal society. It is highly significant that, while Genly recognizes the determining influence of the sex-gender system in the life of the individual, he is still unable to reason out why there are so few female mathematicians, composers, and inventors. This inability displays very clearly the impoverishing, limiting effect of gender ideology on men as well as women; men are blinded by the ideology to the same extent that women are negated – only the consequences for women are far more severe. After all, that blindness is almost entirely self-servicing, from a patriarchal perspective. Genly's blindness is used throughout the book to show the way women are abused and marginalized in a patriarchal society, and that blindness is manifest in his use of language. At the very beginning of the book, for example, Genly is upset at the political intrigue in which Estraven involves him, describing it as 'effeminate' (p. 13), an unusual association which suggests the virulence of the adjective in Genly's consciousness. Later, at Estraven's home Genly describes his distaste at his host's manner in gender-loaded terms: 'I thought that at table Estraven's performance had been womanly, all charm and tact and lack of substance, specious and adroit' (p. 18). Genly's distrust of women is apparent in this statement. Genly ponders on his own distrust:

Was it in fact this soft supple femininity that I disliked and distrusted in him? For it was impossible to think of him as a woman, that dark, ironic, powerful presence near me in the firelit darkness, and yet whenever I thought of him as a man I felt a sense of falseness, of imposture: in him, or in my own attitude towards him? (p. 18)

Again Genly's attitude to women is revealed as a patriarchal construct: women cannot be 'dark, ironic, powerful', just as their behaviour is characteristically 'all charm and tact and lack of substance, specious and adroit'. Repeatedly throughout the text LeGuin shows in Genly's language the encoding of attitudes to women which ensure their exclusion from all positions of power within a patriarchal system. When Genly describes his landlady, for example, his concentration on physical characteristics and the odd mixture of personal qualities is typical of sexist characterizations of women: 'I thought of him as a landlady for he had fat buttocks that wagged when he walked, and a soft fat face, and a prying, spying, ignoble, kindly nature' (pp. 46–7). When Genly considers the absence of war on Gethen, he concludes: 'They lacked, it seemed, the capacity to *mobilize*. They behaved like animals, in that respect; or like women' (p. 47). Genly's parallelling of women and animals is hardly flattering to women, and indicative of a male-centred ideology. And when Genly's sled doesn't work properly on the snow, he describes it as a 'bitch' (p. 185), again a gendered appellation which confirms the low esteem in which its referent is held. The crucial point in the story for Genly Ai is reached when he learns to accept the Gethenians as they are, which means that he learns to accept women as equal viable subjectivities to men. His difficulty in reaching this point, in realizing the import of Tormer's Lay: 'Light is the left hand of darkness/and darkness the right hand of light' (p. 199) – is LeGuin's commentary on the degraded position of women in a patriarchal society, a measure of their exclusion from power and knowledge.

In *Walk to the End of the World*, a savage vision of life after nuclear war, Suzy McKee Charnas also addresses this issue of women and language (Charnas, 1978 (B)). Charnas works from the premise that the same men who started the war survived the war, hidden away in government bunkers. Emerging into the ruined post-holocaust environment they immediately need a scapegoat to explain this devastation for which they cannot and will not accept responsibility: the scapegoats are the women who survived with them, their secretaries and administrative staff. Subsequently words associated with women before the war are invested with new meanings which support the women's new (?) status:

Even at the time, there had been names for fems indicating some understanding of the danger they represented. One Ancient book used in the Boyhouse mentioned fems as 'bra-burners.' Since 'bra' was a word in an old language meaning 'weapon,' clearly 'bra-burner' meant a fem who stole and destroyed the weapons of her masters. (pp. 65–6)

The ironic truth of this description of the bra-burners is available to readers who adopt a feminist reading position, from which the horrific events of the story then read as a ghastly allegory of contemporary Western society. In this obscene society women are ritually burned as witches to open the male ceremony in which boys chant the names of the 'unmen.' After the animals come the 'Dirties,' those gibbering, nearly mindless hordes whose skins had been tinted all the colors of earth so that they were easily distinguishable from true men: "Reds, Blacks, Browns, Kinks; Gooks, Dagos, Greasers, Chinks; Ragheads, Niggas, Kites, Dinks"' (p. 129). These are followed by the 'Freaks' who include '"Lonhairs, Raggles, Bleedingarts; Faggas, Hibbies, Families, Kids; Junkies, Skinheads, Collegeists; Ef-eet Iron-Mentalist,"' the last being a reference to the soft-minded values of the Freaks, iron being notoriously less strong than steel' (p. 129).

Finally, the chant came to the fems, huge-breasted, doused in sweet-stinking waters to mask uglier odors, loud and forever falsely smiling. Their names closed the circle, for being beast-like ('red in tooth and claw,' as some old books said) they had been known by beasts' names: 'Bird, Cat, Chick, Sow; Filly, Tigress, Bitch, Cow . . .'

A counter-chant was being raised now by the Teachers, enumerating the dreadful weapons of the unmen: 'Cancer, raybees, deedeetee; Zinc, lead and mer-cu-ree . . .' (p. 129)

Of course the weapons enumerated by the teachers were the by-products of the military-industrial complex controlled by the one group not mentioned in the lists of unmen, the white middle-class male. The horror of this ceremony lies not in its possibility, but in its reality; in the fact that the groups mentioned are already the scapegoats for the weapons which are destroying life on earth, creating the apocalyptic nightmare vision of the novel. The unmen include all non-whites, the socially critical and non-conformist, families (perhaps Charnas's comment on the anti-family reality of welfare cuts and poverty in the West), and women. The descriptions of women might be drawn from the misogynistic pornography of today, or from the work of writers like Mailer. Charnas's evocation of the animal names given to women is a direct reference to *The Female Eunuch* in which Greer analyses the social power of these descriptions of women, their encoding of misogynistic ideological discourses into everyday language. In *Walk to the End of the World*, then, Charnas constructs a similar critique of language and power to that of LeGuin in *The Left Hand of Darkness*, though her setting and tone are very different. Charnas reinforces her argument about language during the narrative of her female 'fem' character, Alldera:

> There had never been any security, any time, even when she found another fem with true verbal facility. This was her first experience of speech as self-expression with any degree of complexity, eliciting responses of similar quality. It gave her an extraordinary feeling of power, of reality.
>   That was the danger. (pp. 196–7)

This sense of power is a danger to Alldera because it is illusory, totally compromised by her existence in a social system inimical to women, a society in which 'a man's usage conferred existence' (p. 187). So Charnas describes both the power of language and its ideological function, and she writes particularly about the position of women in a male-dominated society, a society in which women only have existence in relation to men. This point was also made by Elgin in the final pages of *Native Tongue*. There the women of the linguist households have learned that the only way to live with the men without being destroyed by them is not to refuse to play their gender games, but to play them too well. These women are not unfeminine; they are too feminine. They play the game as they would don a mask, preserving their true, non-feminine, womanly selves underneath. The men perceive the reality of the situation, without understanding their own perception: '"The problem," he said, "is not difficult to summarize. It can in fact be done in three words, thus: WOMEN ARE EXTINCT."' (p. 288). That is, women as defined by men are extinct. In rebelling against their male-dominated order and constructing their own female order, female consciousness, as women, the female linguists have ceased to exist *as women* for the men. Both texts lead to the same conclusion: women in a male-dominated order have no existence as individual subjectivities; they are the unmen, the feminine, in relation to which men define themselves.

In the work of these three novelists access of women to knowledge and to power is intimately related to their use of and representation in language. The texts explore this problematic relationship of women to language from a number of perspectives, each inflecting SF conventions in the investigation of a conventional SF concern: the nature of *knowledge*. In each text knowledge was shown to be a male preserve, encoded in *language* which simultaneously encoded the exclusion, the negation, of women. And it is worth noting that the texts do not end hopelessly: Genly does learn to accept Estraven, and hence the female; the women of the Linguist households construct their subversive feminist consciousness along with their subversive language, Laadan; and Alldera escapes the brutalities of the male order and sets out into the wilderness to find a new life. And in the same way Anne McCaffrey's female harper, Menolly defeats the system which argues she cannot be a harper because she is female (McCaffrey, 1978 (B)). The great significance of her victory is that on Pern, the world in which the novel is set, a harper is a combination of folklorist, counseller, communications specialist and court advisor. It is, in other words, a position of great power. And harper songs are shameless propaganda; they encode the ideological discourses of Pern society. As a woman and a harper Menolly is now in a position to subvert the phallocentricity of those discourses. Feminist science fiction writers have analysed contemporary Western thought and its structuring medium of language and found it to be phallocentric. Their works utilize the conventions of SF to deconstruct that thought, philosophy, knowledge or science and its ideological practices and then to suggest the conditions for the renegotiation of meaning, of social reality. These writers are concerned primarily with the construction of a feminist reading position by which readers may re-evaluate and reconstruct their own postion within the present order and in so doing become part of the subversion and renegotiation of that order.

Feminist writers have also used the *science* of science fiction in more traditional ways in their texts, addressing the issues broached by Mary Shelley in *Frankenstein*: the relationship between science and technology and the society which produced it, and the relationship between scientific and gender discourses. Again different writers have their own particular approaches to these issues and their fictionalization. James Tiptree Jr., for example, has used scientific experiment as a template to write about gender relationships, and at the same time comment on those experiments. In 'The Screwfly Solution' (Tiptree, 1981 (B)) Tiptree writes about the outbreak of a new crime, femicide – the mass and indiscriminate slaughter of women. The story is told by a combination of narratives, the scientist Alan and later his wife Anne, and newspaper and scientific reports. Alan is away in South America working on a biological control program when he hears from his wife about the 'Sons of Adam' cult

composed of men who kill women on sight, creating what they call a
'Liberated Zone'. An army driver who is present during one of these
killings describes the experience:

> After a while the door opened and Mayor Blount came back in. He
> looked terrible, his clothes were messed up and he had bloody scrape
> marks on his face. He didn't say anything, he just looked at me hard
> and fierce, like he might have been disoriented. I saw his zipper was
> open and there was blood on his clothing and also on his (private
> parts).
> ...I saw Dr. Fay lying on the cot in a peaceful appearance. She was
> lying straight, her clothing was to some extent different but her legs
> were together. I was glad to see that. Her blouse was pulled up and I
> saw there was a cut or incision on her abdomen. The blood was coming
> out there, like a mouth. It wasn't moving at this time. Also her throat
> was cut open. (pp. 58–9)

This horrific murder is disturbing not only as a narrative event, but
also as a reference to contemporary society, to 'snuff' movies which
specialize in the sexual torture and mutilation of women. In the story
the murders are represented as obscene horrors and yet, in our own
society, their representation is also entertainment for some people.
Tiptree then describes the rationale for the murders: the driver relates
the Mayor's religious fundamentalist explanation:

> We discussed the book, how man must purify himself and show God a
> clean world. He said some people raise the question of how can man
> reproduce without women but such people miss the point. The point is
> that as long as man depends on the old filthy animal way God won't
> help him. When man gets rid of his animal part which is woman, this is
> the signal God is awaiting. Then God will reveal the new clean way,
> maybe angels will come bringing new souls, or maybe we will live
> forever, but it is not our place to speculate, only to obey. (p. 59)

The Manichaean hatred of the flesh represented in this explanation is
frequently associated with fundamentalism, where it almost invariably takes the form of a misogynic rejection of women. As the
survivors of the war in *Walk to the End of the World* blame their victims
for the war, so men have traditionally blamed women for their own
self-hatred, their own violence. In a world increasingly obsessed with
fundamentalist religions of all kinds Tiptree's text is a timely warning
of the consequences for women. Tiptree reinforces this connection
between religious ideology and misogyny in a note Alan recieves
from his friend, Barney:

> *UP/Vatican City 19 June.* Pope John IV today intimated that he does not

plan to comment officially on the so-called Pauline Purification cults
advocating the elimination of women as a means of justifying man to
God. A spokesman emphasized that the Church takes no position on
these cults but repudiates any doctrine involving a 'challenge' to or
from God to reveal His further plans for man.

Cardinal Fazzoli, spokesman for the European Pauline movement,
reaffirmed his view that the Scriptures define woman as merely a
temporary companion and instrument of man. Women, he states, are
nowhere defined as human, but merely as a transitional expedient or
state. 'The time of transition to full humanity is at hand,' he concluded.
(p. 65)

Not only does Tiptree here evoke the notorious unwillingness of the
Catholic Church to condemn social injustice, particularly where it
involves women (as the debate over contraception has shown), but
she also evokes a theological argument once a part of Catholic
teaching. In the ninth century the Vatican did rule that women were
nowhere given the status of human. This argument is another grim
truth for the reader. Though no longer official Church teaching, it is
recognizable in theology (for example, in the misogynic readings of
Paul's Letters) and in the Church's inaction over social injustice.
Misogyny is not just a function of fundamentalist religious practices
but ingrained in the practices of the West's oldest established Church.

Having established misogyny as a social practice endemic in the
West, sanctioned not only by its religious organization but as a form
of entertainment, Tiptree moves from the political to personal areas of
activity. Her narrator, Alan daydreams about his meeting with his
wife, fantasizing their first erotic encounter:

A terrible alarm bell went off in his head. Exploded from his dream, he
stared around, then finally down at his hands. *What was he doing with his
open clasp knife in his fist?*

Stunned, he felt for the last shreds of fantasy, and realized that the
tactile images had not been of caresses, but of a frail neck strangling in
his fist, the thrust had been the plunge of a blade seeking vitals. In his
arms, legs, phantasms of striking and trampling bones cracking. And
Amy [his daughter] –

Oh God, Oh God –

Not sex, blood lust. (pp. 67–8)

Appalled at his own actions Alan reads the last of the reports on the
femicide epidemic sent to him by Barney. An article from *Nature*, it
begins: 'A potential difficulty for our species has always been implicit
in the close linkage between the behavioral expression of aggression/
predation and sexual reproduction in the male' (p. 69). The article

concludes that this linkage is only a feature of male behaviour. Alan then reconsiders his own sexuality: 'Yes; much of their loveplay could be viewed as genitalized, sexually gentled savagery. Play-predation . . .' (p. 70). In Alan's narrative, then, Tiptree makes the connection between political and personal action; that personal activity is a mediated version of political ideology, transformed in its procedure but maintaining its fundamental motivation.

Anne's narrative finishes the story. She is hiding in Barney's wilderness cabin disguised as a man, but she knows she cannot survive much longer. Anne puts together the events of the story – the femicide epidemic, the visions the men have had of 'angels', the biological control experiments of her husband and his colleagues, and her own sighting of an 'angel'. She leaves a note for Barney:

> Let me repeat – it was *there*. Barney, if you're reading this, *there are things here*. And I think they've done whatever it is to us. Made us kill ourselves off?
>
> Why? Well, it's a nice place, if it wasn't for people. How do you get rid of people? Bombs, death rays – all very primitive. Leave a big mess. Destroy everything, craters, radioactivity, ruin the place.
>
> This way there's no muss, no fuss. Just like what we did to the screwfly. Pinpoint the weak link, wait a bit while we do it for them. Only a few bones around; make good fertilizer.
>
> Barney dear, good-bye. I saw it. It was there.
>
> But it wasn't an angel.
>
> *I think I saw a real estate agent.* (p. 75)

Tiptree employs a very familiar SF ending: the aliens who have come to take over the earth. Only in her text there is no battle: the aliens win, and they win because of the inability of humanity to deconstruct male agression, to work out the connection between male sexuality and violence. The screwfly experiment is the framework around which Tiptree constructs the story; biological control in the service of humanity becomes an allegory of the biological control, that is, devastation, of humanity. On one level the story constructs a critique of scientific practice. Given the appalling violence apparent when the experiment is translated into human terms, do we have any right to use such means against animals? On another level Tiptree uses this violence to reveal the institutionalization of violence in contemporary society, where it takes the forms of religious fundamentalism, official theology, personal love-play. So the scientific paradigm is used by Tiptree to reveal abuses and injustices within contemporary scientific and gender discourses and the practices they foster.

In other feminist SF stories the central problem is the relationship between technological or scientific achievement and *colonialism*. In colonialist invasions women invariably suffer not only the humilia- tion of the males of a conquered race, but also become the sexual prey of the conquerors. In the Tiptree story 'We Who Stole the *Dream'* (Tiptree, 1975 (B)) the Joilani, a physically feeble race plan the theft of a spaceship, the *Dream*, in which to escape from the brutish Terrans. One of the Joilani, Lal gives her life to help her people:

> Ahead of Lal lay only pain and death. She was useless as a breeder; her short twin birth channels had been ruptured by huge hard Terran members, and the delicate spongy tissue that was the Joilani womb had been damaged beyond recovery. So Lal had chosen the greater love, to serve her people with one last torment. (p. 92)

The callousness of the Terran invaders is represented most vividly in this abuse of the Joilani women:

> Now he wished to enter her. She was almost inured to the pain; her damaged body had healed in a form pleasing to this Terran. She was only the commander's fourth 'girl.' There had been other commanders, some better, some worse, and 'girls' beyond counting, as far back as the Joilani records ran. (pp.98–9)

The other mark of Terran brutality is their enjoyment of 'Stars Tears':

> Hate and disgust choked him, though he had seen it often: Terrans eagerly drinking Stars Tears. It was the very symbol of their oblivious cruelty . . . they could not be excused for ignorance; too many of them had told Jalun how Stars Tears was made. It was not tears precisely, but the body secretions of a race of beautiful, frail winged creatures on a very distant world. Under physical or mental pain their glands exuded this liquid which the Terrans found so deliciously intoxicating. To obtain it, a mated pair were captured and slowly tortured to death in each other's sight. Jalun had been told atrocious details which he could not bear to recall. (p. 95)

Only one act of violence happens aboard the *Dream* before it leaves with the Joilani: old Jalun kills these Terrans, one of whom had raped his granddaughter and murdered his grandson. He kills them with one of their own weapons. After a long flight in the *Dream* Joilani reach their home planet, where the Joilani are bigger and stronger than they, and technologically advanced. They receive the *Dream* passengers as part of living history, and arrange for them to be settled on a new planet, giving as their reason for this removal the technolo- gical ignorance of the travellers. One of the old Joilani elders, Jivadh is not impressed with his new-found relatives, however, citing evidence of poverty, exploitation and corruption in this advanced society. Perhaps, he suggests, the empire-building which accompanies technological advancement is the same no matter by whom it is performed:

> 'O my people,' he said sombrely, 'the *Dream* has not come home. It may be that it has no home. What we have come to is the Joilani Federation of Worlds, a mighty, growing power among the stars. We are safe here, yes. But Federation, Empire, perhaps it is all the same in the end. Bislat has told you that these so-called Elders kindly gave us to eat. But he has not told you what the High Elder offered us to drink.'
>   'They said it was confiscated!' Bislat cried.
>   'Does that matter? Our high Joilani, our people of the faith –'
> Jivadh's eyelids closed in sadness; his voice broke to a hoarse rasp. '*Our Joilani* . . . were drinking Stars Tears.' (pp. 114–15)

The connection between technological achievement and aggression seems unavoidable. Hence the significance of the only Joilani violence in the story, Jalun's murders and Sosalal's murder of the base commander; are all killed with their own weapons, the Terran technology which enabled their enslavement of the Joilani. Yet, as Jivadh suggests, it is not only the Terrans who are exploiters and enslavers; it seems that access to power may corrupt even the most peaceful races. Tiptree's story thus engages with the debate activated by Mary Shelley in *Frankenstein* about the relationship between social structure and technological power. Tiptree's story takes that debate a step further, into the consequences of technological mastery not only for the society itself – its brutalization, but also for societies in which it comes into contact – their enslavement. She deals with the implications for women as part of this exploited colonial society.

In *The Word for World Is Forest* Ursula LeGuin also writes about Terran colonizers, but she makes an even more direct connection between colonialist ideology and sexism (LeGuin, 1980 (B)). In Chapter One she introduces the major colonialist character, Captain Davidson:

> Two pieces of yesterday were in Captain Davidson's mind when he woke, and he lay looking at them in a darkness for a while. One up: the new shipload of women had arrived . . . the second batch of breeding females for the New Tahiti Colony, all sound and clean, 212 head of prime human stock. Or prime enough, anyhow. (p.11)

Davidson regards women simply as sexual objects for his use, an attitude which LeGuin relates directly to the frontiersman, colonialist mentality: 'Earth was a tamed planet and New Tahiti wasn't. That's what he was here for: to tame it' (p. 11). Davidson's musing on his role as subjugator directs his thoughts back to women:

> Can't keep us down, we're Men. You'll learn what that means pretty soon, you godforsaken damn planet, Davidson thought, and he grinned a little in the darkness of the hut, for he liked challenges. Thinking Men, he thought Women, and again the line of little figures began to sway through his mind, smiling, jiggling. (p. 11)

Instead the reverse happens: Davidson is defeated by the endemic population, the Athsheans whom he disparagingly calls 'Creechies'. The act which precipitates the rebellion of the peaceful Athsheans against the barbarous Terrans is the rape and murder of an Athshean woman by Davidson. This brutal act is merely one incident in a catalogue of violence against the native people, but it creates a new Athshean, a god. The Athshean woman's husband, Selver, brings death to the Athsheans as he leads them on an assault of the Earthmen's camp.

> We may have dreamed of Selver these last few years, but we shall no longer; he has left the dream time. In the forest, through the forest he comes, where leaves fall, where trees fall, a god that knows death, a god that kills and is not himself reborn. (p. 34)

Selver's own people have a simple and highly sophisticated technology. They do not tame their forest environment; they live in total harmony with it. Murder is unknown among them and this is tied by LeGuin to the psychic harmony of the male Athsheans. Dream is an important part of their lives; it is the mechanism by which the irrational is controlled and peaceful existence assured – until Davidson's murderous assault. Selver brings murder and at the same time loses his ability to dream. He becomes like the Terrans, who seem to his people to be insane, full of hatred and violence, for each other as well as the Athsheans. The insanity of the Earthmen is a consequence of their lust for power, and this is equally manifest in their gender and race ideologies. Throughout the book the colonialist abuse of the Athsheans is signified by their sexual violation: from the rape of Athshean women to the punitive castration of Athshean men. For LeGuin the same motivation operates in both cases, the desire for dominance, for control. The tragedy of *The Word for World Is Forest* is that, as the result of Davidson's brutality, the Athsheans, too, are brutalized; in responding to Terran violence they, too, become violent. And at the centre of the violence, the focus of the transformation, are the entwined ideologies of sexism and racism. Of the two technologies LeGuin describes in the book, the harmonious, sophisticated, integrated technology of the Athsheans and the antagonistic, brutal, divisive technology of the Terrans, it is not difficult to decide which is the progeny of Victor Frankenstein – though one suspects even he would be appalled at its inhumanity.

The other convention of science fiction specified by Darko Suvin in his description of SF as the literature of 'cognitive *estrangement*' is, of course, *estrangement*, and this is also used consistently and productively by feminist writers. Estrangement was developed theoretically as a fictional convention by Russian Formalist critics in the early twentieth century. Shlovsky, Tomashevsky and their colleagues regarded the ability to make the everday world look strange or new as one of the major functions of all art. The estrangement of science fiction is often far less subtle than the Formalist conceptualization. This is not a matter of constructing a nuanced representation of the everyday in order to show it as a particular kind of ideological construct, which is the Brechtian application of the Formalist concept. Instead the reader is involved in the construction of a society very different from her/his own, that difference being signified by its alien technology, often (but not always) far in advance of that of Earth. The technology might be amazing microcircuitry or highly-developed psychic power, but it is always different from that of Earth, though intelligible to the reader. And it is in the process of this intelligibility, in making this strange technology familiar, that the estrangement function operates.

As the reader translates the technology into everyday terms s/he can understand, the everyday begins to take on a different aspect; the reader is given a new perspective on her/his own society. In a lot of science fiction this estrangement process is a by-product of the writer's preoccupation with technology and in those cases the implicit comparison with contemporary society will have little impact. As in Verne's fiction conservative discourses will be coded into the text where they will operate naturalistically. The comparison with contemporary society will be null because the society evoked by the text, that is, by the discourses operating in the text, *is* contemporary society. So the society of *Star Wars* is, in all but the most banal senses, contemporary American society. The reading position constructed in these texts is that of a political conservative, who accepts the dominant ideological discourses (of gender, race, class) of contemporary society as unproblematic, commonsense and natural. In the work of politically aware writers, however, different reading positions are constructed – feminist, socialist or radical. In these non-conservative texts the difference between the society represented in the text and the reader's own society becomes the site of a political critique. The discourses mobilized in the text do not equate with dominant ideological discourses and that difference also constitutes the political critique. Readers are so positioned by these texts that the different society can only be comprehended if they operate non-conservative discourses and in so doing they are not only given a different view of the dominant ideology, but are also shown that it *is* an ideology, not a natural state. So the estrangement convention, operated by the reader in the process of constructing the alien world of the SF text, is crucial to the political activity of these texts, which is the deconstruction of dominant ideological discourses.

For feminist science fiction writers estranging the everday was a way of showing and deconstructing the operation of the patriarchal gender discourse of sexism. Sometimes, as in *The Word for World Is Forest*, sexism and racism are found to function in unison, with the control of superior technology shown to be their motivating force and enforcer. LeGuin establishes her story of Athshe as an estranged representation of the everyday not only through her repeated references to Earth, but also through her characterization of Davidson, the stereotypical colonialist. His attitude to the Athsheans is the attitude of all colonizers to the people they displace, and the attitude of sexist men to women:

> 'They're little, all right, but don't let 'em fool you, Ok. They're tough; they've got terrific endurance; and they don't feel pain like humans. That's the part you forget, Ok ... The thing is, Ok, the creechies are lazy, they're dumb, they're treacherous, and they don't feel pain. You've got to be tough with 'em, and stay tough with 'em.' (pp. 17–18)

Interestingly LeGuin does not describe in detail the Terran technology, but writes at length about the Athshean dreaming. In working to understand this technology the reader is led to a new understanding of the nature of technology, that its success is measured by its *lack* of intrusiveness (the Athshean technology) and that its exploitation as an agent of imperialism accords with the most virulent and unjust social practices (Terran technology). The 'new' everyday the reader sees after *The Word for World Is Forest* is a rapacious, colonialist society in which technological achievement has led to the exploitation and often cultural, if not physical, devastation of people in countries either less technologically advanced, or whose technology was so sophisticated that it could not be perceived by the colonizers, whose 'superiority' was merely a function of their weaponry. In this 'new' society women are treated as sexual toys by the representatives of the military-industrial complex. In *The Word for World Is Forest* LeGuin uses an off-world setting to represent and deconstruct the operation of ideological discourses – of technology, gender, race – which are fundamental to contemporary Western society.

In her short story, 'Sex and/or Mr Morrison' Carol Emshwiller has a less ambitious project, to show the prudery and prurience with which we treat human sexuality (Sargent, 1978 (B)). The narrator spends the whole story preparing to hide in Mr Morrison's room so she can see him naked – and finally succeeds:

> But I see him now. The skin hangs in loose, plastic folds just there, and there is a little copper-colored circle like a fifty-cent piece made out of pennies. There's a hole in the center and it is corroded green at the edges. This must be a kind of 'naked suit' and whatever the sex organs may be, they are hidden behind this hot, pocked and pitted imitation skin. (p. 190)

She then runs downstairs to her flat to await Mr Morrison's pursuit, but he does not come. Waiting there she reflects on her own sexuality: '"Goodness knows," I'll say, "if I'm normal myself." (How is one to know such things when everything is hidden?)' (p. 190). In the narrator's parenthetical statement Emshwiller presents the focus of her story: when everything is hidden, how can we ever know ourselves or others. From this ignorance comes prurience and obsession, the obsession of this narrator for Mr Morrison. The story itself is a voyeuristic fantasy, harmless except for the pathetic statement with which it ends: '"Why doesn't he come?"' (p. 190). Emshwiller's analysis is not profound but it does recognize the consequences of our societal coyness, individual loneliness. And the chief means she uses to expose that coyness is her factual description of male sex organs, estranged by its very realism.

Kit Reed, in her story 'The Food Farm,' presents an estranged view of the social demands on women to conform to a particular shape (Sargent, 1978 (B)). Her heroine is a fat woman ostracized because of her weight. Her family send her to expensive clinics in order to force her to lose weight and so become socially acceptable. There she meets and falls in love with a man who loves fat women. Her great tragedy is that she is unable to regain the weight she has lost at the clinic. Now she runs her own clinic to fatten girls up. The story is a ludicrous send-up of the tyranny under which women labour in contemporary society. They may choose not to attempt to fit those prescribed shapes, but they will then suffer social disapprobation which will damage them both personally and professionally. Again estrangement of the everyday is used by the writer to criticize everyday practices, here particularly involving women.

Without going into great detail it should be clear that the Hainish worlds of LeGuin's novels, Anne McCaffrey's Pern, the future world of *Native Tongue*, the settings of Tiptree's stories, and the post-nuclear landscape of *Walk to the End of the World* are all part of their author's strategy to produce in readers a new perception of their own society. Most of these works (excluding, perhaps, McCaffrey's) are only non-problematic if the reader adopts a feminist reading position; that is, if the reader views the events of the narrative from a perspective informed by feminist discourse. In adopting that reading position the reader is inevitably led to a very different perception of her/his own society. Often the societies of SF novels are thinly disguised versions of the reader's own society, in that familiar ideological discourses are employed in the composition of the narrative. In feminist SF, however, these other worlds often seem very different – until the feminist reading position is adopted. Brian Eno described in an interview how he had walked into a grove of seemingly randomly placed trees and yet, by moving a few feet sideways to a different viewing position, he had discovered that the trees were all planted in orderly, straight rows.[3] The same process occurs when the events of texts are viewed from a different reading position. Suddenly the horrific and barbaric events described are recognizable as barely exaggerated versions of everyday incidents, interactions and ideological practices. With a text like *Walk to the End of the World* this recognition may be profoundly disturbing. In feminist science fiction this estrangement procedure is especially important, given that the major aims of the writer include the deconstruction of contemporary ideological practices. Showing these practices in operation, showing that gender interactions do not happen in a naturally random way, but are heavily determined by ordering, delimiting, discourses such as sexism, is an important part of this deconstructive process.

Closely related to this estrangement convention is the convention of the *alien*, the character from another planet through whose eyes we are given a different view of our own society:

> the strange system of human society was explained to me ... I learned that the possessions most esteemed by your fellow-creatures were, high and unsullied descent united with riches. A man might be respected with only one of those advantages; but without either, he

was considered . . . as a vagabond and a slave, doomed to waste his
powers for the profits of the chosen few! (Shelley, 1977 (B), p. 124)

So the creature of Shelley's *Frankenstein* describes his understanding
of human society, the society of its author, early nineteenth-century
English society. Again Shelley establishes a convention used often in
politically aware SF as part of its social analysis, as well as in more
conservative texts where it is also a guide to the writer's ideological
position. The aliens of early and mid-twentieth century pulp were not
given an opportunity for incisive political comment before they were
blasted unmercifully from the sky. In fact, the blasting provides the
political comment. *Earth vs. the Flying Saucers* is an appropriate
(B-grade movie) comment on the consciousness of Americans living
in the Cold War 1950s under the shadow of the bomb, their very own
creation. The xenophobic hysteria of that movie was not unlike the
public disturbances which accompanied Orson Welles's 1938 radio
dramatization of H.G. Wells's *The War of the Worlds*, which a number
of Americans heard literally as a Martian invasion. The other use of
the convention has persisted, however, and has been used with
varying degrees of political commitment in texts such as *My Favorite
Martian, Star Trek, The Left Hand of Darkness* and 'Houston, Houston,
Do You Read?' In the 1960s television series, *My Favorite Martian*
Uncle Martin, the Martian, spends a lot of time finding out how
ridiculous Earth people are, and particularly how truly silly women
can be, through his interaction with a cast of stereotypes ranging
from his adoptive nephew, Tim, an all-American nice guy to his
absurd, but feminine and good-hearted landlady, Mrs Brown. Overt
political commentary was replaced by the familiar American moral-
ism almost mandatory in television shows aimed at a family audience.
Star Trek was more politically aware than most of its contemporaries
and made frequent use of aliens for the purposes of estrangement,
most notably with the character of Mr Spock. Although the political
commitment of particular episodes depended on the writer for the
week, the Spock character was frequently used to comment on the
organization of human society, his alien view showing it from a
different perspective, pointing out injustices or discrimination. Mainstream SF writers also continue to use this convention to great effect
in their work, among them contemporary feminists.

In *The Left Hand of Darkness* the convention of the alien finds
multiple expression. Genly Ai is the alien on the planet, Gethen.
Through his responses to its inhabitants LeGuin reveals the function
and pervasiveness of patriarchal gender ideology in human, that is,
the reader's own, society. As a Gethenian Genly's friend, Estraven, is

also an alien – to Genly's society, which is the reader's own, human society. LeGuin uses Estraven's questions to Genly about his society to comment further on the nature of contemporary society, and particularly on its gender ideology. Sonya Dorman, in her short story, 'When I was Miss Dow', also uses a non-human character to comment on the nature of human gender relations (Sargent, 1978 (B)). The Miss Dow of the title is a persona adopted by one of the aliens on a planet now supporting a Terran colony. The aliens adopt human shape in order to communicate more easily with their Terran co-workers, and they also use their adopted personae to investigate the colony. The Miss Dow character explains: 'we put on our faces, forms, smiles and costumes. I am old enough to learn to change my shape too' (p. 142), a provocative statement which might be read as a description of feminine behaviour (particularly the phrase, 'putting on a face' commonly used to describe the application of makeup). Miss Dow goes to work for a Terran scientist, Dr Proctor and observes his behaviour with puzzlement and some amusement. While x-raying her racing pet, for example, he makes a pass at her: 'Suddenly, he gives a little laugh and points the end of the wax pencil at my navel, announcing, "There. There, it is essential that the belly button onto the pelvis, or you'll bear no children"' (pp. 145–6). Confused, Miss Dow notes: 'Thoughts of offspring had occurred to me. But weren't we discussing my racer?' (p. 146). At first Miss Dow has trouble adjusting to the social role expected of her as a female Terran; she has to learn to be feminine. Her emotions as she sits watching Dr Proctor carving wood suggest to the reader that Miss Dow has learned the part, and she has learned it by her interactions with her boss/lover.

> He's absorbed in what he doesn't see there, but he's projecting what he wants to see ... I begin to suffer a peculiar pain, located in the nerve cluster between my lungs. He's not talking to me. He's not caressing me. He's forgotten I'm here, and like a false projection, I'm beginning to fade. In another hour perhaps the film will become blank. If he doesn't see me, then am I here?
> He's doing just what I do when busy with one of my own projects, and I admire the intensity with which he works: it's magnificent. Yes, I'm jealous of it, I burn with rage and jealousy, he has abandoned me to be Martha and I wish I were myself again, free in shape and single in mind. Not this sack of mud clinging to another. Yet he's teaching me that it's good to cling to another. I'm exhausted from strange disciplines. (p. 148)

These strange disciplines are the behaviours engendered by the gender role Miss Dow learns from her boss. She becomes what women under patriarchy are expected to be: only visible when a man acknowledges them. As Alldera notes in *Walk to the End of the World*, 'A man's usage conferred existence' (Charnas, 1978 (B), p. 187). Miss Dow has learned the role and is wearied by it. Through this character Dorman shows the operation of patriarchal ideology on women, how it operates on an interpersonal level, and its consequences for the emotional and intellectual life of the individual woman. It is important to note here that Dr Proctor is relatively harmless, not a Captain Davidson (the macho soldier of *The Word for World is Forest*), and yet his expectations and behaviour still have an enormously stressful effect on Miss Dow.

In Tiptree's 'Houston, Houston, Do You Read?' all the protagonists are human, a group of male astronauts aboard a spaceship projected into the future is met by a group of women aboard another spaceship (Tiptree, 1976 (B)). The men are soon to learn that a plague on earth has destroyed all the men, and most of the women. The earth is now sparsely populated by women, cloned from a genetic pool of genotypes. The women drug the men to free their inhibitions, so that they can observe their behaviour and collect sperm samples. The sexual behaviour exhibited by the man who attempts to mate with one of the women is extremely sexist. Without his inhibitions operating the man verbalizes his thoughts as he manhandles the woman he is intent on mating with.

> 'Well, first we wish each other well, like this.' He draws her to him and lightly kisses her cheek. 'Kee-rist, what a dumb bitch,' he says in a totally different voice. 'You can tell you've been out too long when the geeks start looking good. Knockers, ahhh –' His hand plays with her blouse . . . (p. 214)

The interchange continues with the man becoming increasingly abusive and violent. In his interaction with the aliens/women Tiptree presents a view of gender relations stripped of socialized modification; the exploitative nature of patriarchal gender ideology and its social practices is thereby demonstrated. Another of the men takes on the role of Pauline theologian:

> 'The head of the woman is the man,' Dave says crisply. 'Corinthians one eleven three. No discipline whatsoever.' He stretches out his arm, holding up his crucifix as he drifts toward the wall of vines. 'Mockery. Abominations.' He touches the stakes and turns, framed in the green arbor.
>
> 'We were sent here, Lorimer. This is God's plan. I was sent here. Not you, you're as bad as they are. My middle name is Paul,' he adds in a conversational tone . . .

'Oh Father, send me strength,' Dave prays quietly, his eyes closed. 'You have spared us from the void to bring Your light to this suffering world. I shall lead Thy erring daughters out of the darkness. I shall be a stern but merciful father to them in Thy name. Help me to teach the children Thy holy law and train them in the fear of Thy righteous wrath. Let the women learn in silence and all subjection; Timothy two eleven. They shall have sons to rule over them and glorify Thy name.'

He could do it, Lorimer thinks, a man like that really could get life going again. (pp. 220–1)

That is, a man like that could re-establish the patriarchal order. The collusion of Lorimer, until now the most reasonable of the men, in this aspiration demonstrates the power of this ideology given a religious inflection. Tiptree demonstrates in this story both the brutality of patriarchal gender relations and the means used to justify and maintain those relations, which consist in the subjugation and silencing of women. In this story, too, the role of alien is used in the deconstruction of contemporary gender ideology and, significantly, as in 'The Women Men Don't See', the women are the aliens.

This story also uses another SF convention with an established history, *extrapolation*, since Tiptree sets the events of the story in the future. Ever since Wells popularized time displacement with his time machine science fiction writers have enthusiastically employed this means of siting their marvellous technologies and new societies. In the novel, *The Time Machine*, time travel is used to comment on the nature and trajectory of Wells's own society. The time traveller finds first a society divided rigidly into upper and lower classes, existing symbiotically in conditions of terrible violence: the upper class, the beautiful Eloi, exploiting the labour of the fearsome Morlocks who live underground and feed, literally, on the Eloi. As the time traveller moves forward in time, he sees human society dwindle and regress back to the primeval slime from which it evolved. This course represents Wells's warning of the chaos and degradation faced by his own society if it maintained the class antagonism which is its defining characteristic. After Wells twentieth-century SF writers made time displacement almost mandatory for science fiction. In many ways it replaced the geographical displacement that had characterized adventure novels before this time. Most of the socially aware SF of the 1960s and 1970s uses this convention: the work of such writers as Philip K. Dick, Stanislaw Lem, Arthur C. Clarke, John Brunner, Ursula LeGuin, Samuel Delany. The future world is conventionally constructed by taking elements of contemporary society and projecting them to their il/logical extreme, as Wells did in *The Time Machine*. So Dick's *Do Androids Dream of Electric Sheep?* is a compendium of the social and technological ills afflicting contemporary society, pollution, alienation, religiosity, chemical dependence. The 'kipple' or trash into which the world is constantly decomposing signifying the entropic decay of this society, its fragmentation under the stress of technological and natural disasters it is socially too weak to encompass. For feminist writers this future setting offers a similar opportunity to project the future consequences of contemporary ideological practices, with particular focus on gender issues.

A number of the works already discussed employ this convention: LeGuin's *The Left Hand of Darkness* and *The Word for World Is Forest* set in the future when interplanetary travel is a commonplace for humans, *Walk to the End of the World* after the nuclear war which decimates the world we know, the Tiptree stories, 'Houston, Houston, Do You Read?' and 'We Who Stole the *Dream*', Dorman's 'When I Was Miss Dow' and McCaffrey's Pern novels are also set at times of interplanetary travel. Feminist works which deal with a devastated earth, society stripped back to its unsocialized fundamentals, as a way of showing the operation of contemporary ideological practices, are usually extrapolative. Another example is Chelsea Quinn Yarbro's 'False Dawn' in which a young woman battles against rape and murder in a society which has broken down (Sargent, 1978 (B)). The inhibitions which prevent sexist ideology being practised at its logical extreme no longer operate and women are objects, prey. A different perspective on the future is given by Josephine Saxton in her story, 'Big Operation on Altair Three', set in a Terran colony of the future (Green and LaFanu, 1985 (B)). In this colony some of the worst abuses of contemporary society are preserved, Saxton focusing on the use of women in advertising. The advertisement for a new car consists of a hysterectomy performed on the back seat while the car is in motion, to demonstrate the car's smooth suspension. As the narrator explains: 'the line was not sex but it had to be women. Female bodies sell everything to anyone, but we needed something a little different, to get the scientists, artists, doctors' (p. 12). Extrapolation is essentially another estrangement convention and is used by feminist writers to show the practices of gender ideology in our own society, by making the society and those practices seem new or strange or different. Most of the futurist texts employ a feminist reading position, that is, the works are only non-problematic if the reader adopts a feminist perspective, and this is one of the feminist writer's principal aims; from this new, feminist perspective the reader's own society is profoundly estranged, familiar social practices have new significance, new meaning, and the (ideological) means by which those practices are maintained are revealed as not natural or obvious or common-sense, but socially constructed in accordance with a particular set of discourses (sexist) defining a particular power relationship – men dominant, women dominated. Extrapolation is another SF convention used effectively by feminist science fiction writers.

Finally, a convention of science fiction with much potential for conservatism is its use of *narrative*. (As noted in the Introduction it is perhaps more correct typologically to classify science fiction as a particular subset of narrative fiction, but what is pertinent to this study is the fact that so much SF is structured by the linear, quest narrative that it effectively operates as a convention of the genre. It is, therefore, essential that the critic analyses the ideological practice of narrative as it is realised in science fiction – and here particularly feminist science fiction.) A lot of science fiction employs the quest narrative with its familiar conventions of the tough male hero and helpless, passive female victim/prize; so that a masculinist gender ideology is encoded in the text before the writer even begins telling the story. And, as I argued in Chapter 1, narrative is a mode of representation which tends to obscure the process of telling, so concealing the ideological discourses coded into its conventions. For the politically committed writer this necessitates constant vigilance, to prevent embedded ideological content subverting an intended political message. For the reader these conflicting ideological inputs may be experienced as conflict or discomfort – or not at all, particularly if the embedded conservative input predominates; then the text will read as entirely non-problematic. The feminist science fiction writer is confronted with a complex task which involves manipulating narrative to reveal what narrative conventionally conceals, and using a masculinist story-telling mechanism to tell a feminist story. The final lines of Sonya Dorman's poem, 'The Child Dreams' state the problem succinctly:

> The prince is a figment
> of our boring legend, he is
> the gravity her sleep-ship
> may escape from. Dressed
> in a red shift, she's always
> a world ahead of his weight. (Sargent, 1978 (B), p. 55)

Feminist science fiction exposes the prince of legend by showing how he is coded into the discourses which engender social practices inimical to women. In the discussion of 'The Women Men Don't See' at the beginning of this chapter the means by which Tiptree routed the prince (Fenton) were discussed. Tiptree used two intersecting narratives in order to produce a feminist reading position by which the Fenton narrative, the frontiersman-adventurer inflection of the quest narrative, was exposed as a construct of ideologies of gender and race antipathetic to women. Tiptree revealed the mechanisms of that narrative without being constrained by them; she used them and exposed them. In some other feminist SF, however, the quest narrative is not so clearly disempowered. In Anne McCaffrey's Menolly novels, *Dragonsong* and *Dragonsinger*, for example, the quest narrative is used to relate the story of Menolly's struggle to become a harper, something considered a male profession. This narrative is not problematized in any way with the result that the conclusion is, from a feminist perspective, severely compromised; Menolly becomes effectively an honorary man. This male persona is shown in Menolly's disdain for female clothing and her insistence on wearing the same uniform as the boys. Even more it is shown in Menolly's fictionalization of the incident which expedited her arrival at Harper Hall, her rescue of a fire-lizard clutch:

> *The little queen all golden*
> *Flew hissing at the sea.*
> *To stop each wave*
> *Her clutch to save*
> *She ventured bravely.*
>
> > *As she attacked the sea in rage*
> > *A holderman came nigh*
> > *Along the sand*
> > *Fishnet in hand*
> > *And saw the queen midsky.*
>
> > > *He stared at her in wonder*
> > > *For often he'd been told*
> > > *That such as she*
> > > *Could never be*
> > > *Who hovered there, bright gold.*
>
> > > > *He saw her plight and quickly*
> > > > *He looked up the cliff he faced*
> > > > *And saw a cave*
> > > > *Above the wave*
> > > > *In which her eggs he placed.*
>
> *The little queen all golden*
> *Upon his shoulder stood*
> *Her eyes all blue*
> *Glowed of her true*
> *Undying gratitude.* (McCaffrey, 1978 (B), p. 9)

In the song Menolly transforms herself into a man, the holderman. In the typical quest narrative the rescuer is a male role and so, Menolly as a girl, cannot occupy this role in the story. Similarly, in the novels, Menolly functions in the male role only on sufferance, constantly reminding the reader that this is actually a male role. When Menolly succeeds, the victory is for a girl who makes herself look and act as nearly as possible like a boy, who wears their clothes, plays their games, sits with them at table, and deprecates (perhaps correctly) the 'superficiality' of the girls (though with some understanding of the family, that is, social, pressures they suffer). Nevertheless, Menolly is a girl and she is a harper, her success constituting a familiar pattern in which members of marginalized groups or classes in a society succeed within the dominant group/institutions only by being far more competent than their colleagues. This success, though hard-won by the individual, is significant socially in that it prepares the way for other members of their own group/class to follow, who may be judged more equably than the pioneers who prepared the ground. So the Menolly novels are problematic, comprised to a certain extent, but not untenable for a feminist writer or reader. The reading position they construct is not so radically feminist as in some of the other texts discussed, but nor is it wholly conservative. It functions as does Menolly's success, challenging the reader's acceptance of conservative ideological discourses, rather than completely deconstructing them. Unlike the other texts discussed, however, McCaffrey's novels are best-sellers and it is useful to consider whether her less radical political stance, which is obviously a factor in her success, her texts being less problematic for (conservative) readers, is a useful compromise given the size of the audience she therefore reaches.

Feminist science fiction: a brief history

Mary Shelley first used science fiction to explore patriarchal gender ideology with her prototypal SF novel, *Frankenstein*. During the nineteenth and early twentieth century male writers dominated science fiction almost entirely, possibly because of the emphasis on technology, an area of knowledge to which women had little access. Instead feminist writers used such genres as realism and utopian fiction to explore their own society and its gender roles. In the 1930s C.L. Moore gained prominence as a writer of science fiction. Though not a feminist writer in the contemporary sense, she was an accomplished storyteller who created strong and complex female characters with which to people her fictional worlds, such as the Amazonian Jirel of Joiry. Moore was joined in the creation of strong female characters by Leigh Brackett whose work began to be published in the 1940s. Brackett's science fiction is often criticized for its conservatism, yet she did produce strong female characters at a time when women were being forced back into purely domestic roles, which were subsequently devalued, and when McCarthyism and Cold War politics were about to transform Western society. Another 1940s writer who did use science fiction for social and political analysis was Judith Merril. Her celebrated story, 'That Only a Mother' (1948) is a shocking indictment of the consequences of uncontrolled technological 'progress'. The mother in the story gives birth to an intellectually gifted baby which her horrified husband subsequently discovers is totally limbless. The mutation is a result of the parents' exposure to radiation and the disturbing point of the story is that the mother has not let herself recognize the deformity of her child. The story is important in that it gives voice to matters of close concern to women, childbearing in a nuclear age, but also typical of its time in having the mother adopt such a helpless and unrealistic role. The 1950s saw the publication of women writers such as Katherine MacLean, Zenna Henderson and Andre Norton whose success in the SF genre prepared the way for the more adventurous and feminist writers of the 1960s and 1970s, including Josephine Saxton, Kit Reed, Sonya Dorman, Joanna Russ, C.J. Cherryh, Pamela Zoline, Marion Zimmer Bradley, Anne McCaffrey, Carol Emshwiller, Tanith Lee, Suzette Haden Elgin, Vonda McIntyre, Suzy McKee Charnas, Elizabeth Lynn, Kate Willhelm, Joan D. Vinge, Joy Chant, Chelsea Quinn Yarbro, Octavia Butler, Ursula K. LeGuin and James Tiptree Jr., to name only some of the more well-known authors.

As I noted earlier, contemporary feminist science fiction received its greatest theoretical input from the Women's Movement of the 1960s and its increasingly sophisticated theorization in the 1970s and 1980s. Feminist science fiction reflects that increasing sophistication. The earliest woman-centred SF reflected the growing demands by women that they be treated equally to men and that women's work be revalued by producing the disparagingly named 'wet-diaper' SF of the 1940s and early 1950s and the role reversal fiction peopled by characters such as Jirel of Joiry. With the 1960s Women's Movement came a greater awareness of not only the kinds of roles which women and men are induced to adopt, but also the mechanisms by which those roles are structured and maintained. Stories such as 'The Food Farm' by Kit Reed and Katherine MacLean's 'Contagion' focus on the obsession with appearance which is such a destructive force particularly in the lives of women, where it operates as a form of social tyranny. Tanith Lee's story, 'Love Alters', dealing with a society in which homosexuality is the norm and heterosexuality a barely tolerated perversion suggests the arbitrariness of our sexual prejudices and relates them to environmental influence rather than nature. On a more complex level the novels of many of the writers listed above deal in great detail with the production and maintenance of patriarchal gender ideology and its social practices. The focal point for many of these works is the kind of incident described by Joanna Russ in her story, 'When It Changed', another story of Earthmen arriving on a planet totally occupied by women, here Russ's world of Whileaway.

> 'Where are all the people?' said that monomaniac.
> I realized then that he did not mean people, he meant *men*, and he was giving the word the meaning it had not had on Whileaway for six centuries. . . .
> 'Yes,' he said, catching his breath again with that queer smile, that adult-to-child smile that tells you something is being hidden and will be presently produced with cries of encouragement and joy, 'a great tragedy. But it's over.' And again he looked around at all of us with the strangest deference. As if we were invalids.
> 'You've adapted amazingly,' he said.
> 'To what?' I said. He looked embarrassed. He looked inane. Finally he said, 'Where I come from, the women don't dress so plainly.' (Ellison, 1972 (B), pp. 274–5)

The complete negation of women as viable individuals, their relegation as children or invalids, the obsession with their appearance by men, are all issues addressed in various ways by contemporary feminist writers. Through these issues the sexist discourse by which such practices are engendered is revealed and analysed. And very often the writer's practice involves the construction within the text of a feminist reading position by which readers experience a different, transgressive way of perceiving the society in which they live. By this means the political practice of the text is extended beyond the confines of the particular narrative. An integral part of this political awareness is the feminist writer's consciousness of the ideological function of textual convention. I have noted already the skill with which Tiptree subverts the quest narrative in 'The Women Men Don't See'. Joanna Russ exposes the various permutations of this narrative in traditional, male centred SF in her article, 'The Clichés from Outer Space'. They include 'The Weird-Ways-Of-Getting-Pregnant Story,'

'The Talking-About-It Story,' 'The Noble Separatist Story' and 'The Turnabout Story or I always knew what they wanted to do to me because I've been doing it to them for years, especially in the movies.' (Green and LeFanu, 1985 (B)). Feminist SF often uses the quest narrative structure, but avoids the cliché by building it (the cliché itself) into the story and deconstructing it as part of the text. The process of this deconstruction then becomes the process of construction of the feminist reading position, which is the major political strategy of the feminist science fiction text.

Science fiction offers the feminist writer a number of conventions which can be used to construct a story in which the writer denaturalizes institutionalized modes of behaviour, of representation and self-representation, in contemporary Western society. Conventions such as estrangement, enquiry into the nature of scientific knowledge and of technology, the alien and extrapolation can be used to represent contemporary society as seen through other eyes; that is, in terms of a discourse (feminism) which has only a marginalized, oppositional role in the discursive formation (*patriarchal*, bourgeois, white supremacist) which defines, describes and delimits contemporary society. On the other hand, conventional use of the linear, quest narrative is extremely problematic for feminist science fiction writers since it encodes a patriarchal discourse which contradicts the feminist discourse operating in the text and jeopardizes the construction of a feminist reading position. One means used to obviate this problem is the textual construction and contextualization of the quest narrative, which reveals its hidden (patriarchal) discursive content; as in 'The Women Men Don't See' this demystification is part of the construction of a feminist discourse and feminist reading position. Reading feminist science fiction can be a new way of seeing and understanding the nature and operation of contemporary society:

> 'Just tell me,' he says to Lady Blue, who is looking at the bullet gashes, 'what do you call yourselves? Women's World? Liberation? Amazonia?'
>
> 'Why, we call ourselves human beings.' Her eyes twinkle absently at him, go back to the bullet marks. 'Humanity, mankind.' She shrugs. 'The human race.'
>
> The drink tastes cool going down, something like peace and freedom, he thinks. Or death. (Tiptree, 1976 (B), pp. 225–6)

3
Feminist Fantasy

For fantasy is true, of course. It isn't factual, but it is true. Children know that. Adults know it too, and that is precisely why many of them are afraid of fantasy. They know that its truth challenges, even threatens, all that is false, all that is phony, unnecessary, and trivial in the life they have let themselves be forced into living. They are afraid of dragons, because they are afraid of freedom. (LeGuin, 1979 (C), p. 44)

Ursula LeGuin, in her essay 'Why Are Americans Afraid of Dragons?', explores the contemporary dislike and/or distrust of imaginative literature by those who regard themselves as most 'in touch' with the real. Those 'realists' reject fantasy as a worthless, escapist pastime, a gesture LeGuin relates to their repression of imagination. Undisciplined, this repressed imagination subsequently finds relief in the impoverished genres of pornography or naïve romance, which, in LeGuin's terms, are no more real than fantasy, and considerably less true. Fantasy, LeGuin argues, is not bound by the conventions of realism into something like a faithful reproduction of the contemporary 'real'. As a result it can explore areas of life that realist literature tends to deny or repress, concepts and ideas which fall outside the ideological compass of the contemporary (bourgeois) real. Fantasy can be used to discover the nature of the contemporary real, in the very process of its own definition. As Rosemary Jackson notes in her study, *Fantasy: the Literature of Subversion*, fantasy 'exists in a parasitical or symbiotic relation to the real' (Jackson, 1981 (C), p. 20). Fantasy is what the real is not, and so a fantasy text necessarily traces the limits of the real, the categories by which the real is described and known.

Anti-rational, it is the inverse side of reason's orthodoxy. It reveals reason and reality to be arbitrary, shifting constructs and thereby scrutinizes the category of the 'real'. Contradictions surface and are held antinomically in the fantastic text, as reason is made to confront all that it traditionally refuses to encounter. (p. 21)

The conventions of realism construct texts which encode the categories constitutive of the contemporary, bourgeois real; fantasy texts expose those categories as arbitrary constructs, not philosophical absolutes or commonsense inevitability, and so reveal them as ideologically determined. The contradictions concealed by realist conventions are highlighted in fantasy literature, held in impossible juxtaposition. Fantasy thereby shows the fragmentation of the real, revealing the real as a negotiation of conflicting discourses engendered by specific socio-economic conditions and denying the definition of the real commonly proposed in realist texts as an essentially unchanging product of an essentially unchanging 'human nature'. Like Jackson, LeGuin argues that the reader of fantasy has the opportunity to develop a critical understanding of the nature of her/his own society precisely because s/he is no longer confined by hegemonic discourses, no longer constrained by the subject position those discourses define. Fantasy reveals the existence, and sometimes the nature, of oppositional ideologies and the subject positions they construct. 'Those who refuse to listen to dragons are probably doomed to spend their lives acting out the nightmares of politicians (LeGuin, 1979 (C), p. 11).

The real, LeGuin argues, is no less arbitrary than the fantastic; it is the product of socio-economic conditions, the nature of which is determined by political leaders, 'the nightmares of politicians'. If individuals are prepared to use their imaginations, to see beyond the real as it is (ideologically) re-presented, 'to listen to dragons', then they may be freed from the tyranny of that real. They will be able to make some choices about the values by which they live, the assumptions which govern their actions, and the institutions with which they interact. Those choices may be conservative and leave the contemporary social formation fundamentally unchallenged, or they may conflict with dominant discursive positionings and so constitute an oppositional position and a subversive act. In the latter case the individual is transformed from puppet or actor, 'acting out' a script prepared by other hands, and instead acts to reject the role of passive recipient, writing her/his own script, constructing her/his own real from a position of understanding and political awareness.

Both LeGuin and Jackson present a case for fantasy as a potentially subversive literary form, subversive not only of other literary forms, but also of the means by which we construct and verify the real. Those means are the discourses which are encoded in the narrative and generic conventions of texts and which categorize experience in crucial ways, validating or denying it in relation to dominant ideologies. In a patriarchal society the experience of women is commonly denied, invalidated, by reference to the dominant gender discourse of sexism; the sphere of activity open to women is severely circums- cribed, while women's experience of injustice is denied a voice. Women, the experiential subjects rather than the idealist construct, are not only invisible; they are entirely imperceptible. Feminist fantasy explores the problems of being for women in a society which denies them not only visibility but also subjectivity. It scrutinizes the categories of the patriarchal real, revealing them to be arbitrary, shifting constructs: the subjugation of women is not a 'natural' characteristic, but an ideological process. Feminist fantasy explores the contradictions elided by the (patriarchal) real; for example, that women are both inside patriarchal ideology, as the essential Woman, and outside it, as the (repressed and denied) experiential subjects. In this encounter women as active subjects become perceptible, and the feminine construct of patriarchy, Woman, is revealed as a negotiation inimical to women as subjects. Those who choose to converse with dragons are no longer doomed to spend their lives acting out the Draconic fantasies of patriarchy.

Feminist fantasists have used three different kinds of fantasy to write about the experience of women in contemporary Western society: 'secondary' or 'other' world fantasy, fairy-tale, and horror. None of these forms is specific to feminist fantasy; rather all have the propagandist virtue of being extremely popular literary forms, so affording the feminist fantasist the opportunity to reach a wide and varied audience. The most common form of contemporary fantasy among both feminists and their non-feminist colleagues is secondary world fantasy.

Secondary world fantasy

But that is why the Free Amazons exist, in the final analysis. So that every woman may, at least, know there is a choice for them ... that if they accept the restrictions laid upon women, on Darkover, they may do so from choice and not because they cannot imagine anything else.

Bradley, *The Shattered Chain*

In the most common form, the secondary world fantasy, a writer textually constructs another world which is implicitly and sometimes explicitly a comment on the writer's own society. This estrangement technique, whereby the (contemporary) reader is positioned to examine critically her/his own society from a different, other world, perspective, is also used extensively by politically aware science fiction writers. The alien worlds of SF are often given a 'rational', (pseudo) scientific, explanation: unfamiliar causal relationships are related to specific social or natural conditions, bizarre creatures (like Anne McCaffrey's dragons) given their own natural history. Fantasists are bound by no such demand for rationalization; their secondary worlds simply are. Consequently the fictional world of fantasy may seem extremely strange to the reader, far removed from the representation of the 'real' to which s/he is accustomed. As a result readers may see even more clearly the constructedness of their own society, the inflection of discourses which constitutes the contemporary hegemonic bloc. They may see their own society with eyes freed from the constraints of a particular set of ideological blinkers. This is not to say that feminist fantasists would claim some kind of immunity from ideology; clearly their own work operates from the premises of feminist ideology. However, unlike those who occupy the dominant hegemonic ideological bloc – the complex of discourses that defines the contemporary, dominant, conservative positioning (i.e., patriarchal, Anglo-Saxon, middle-class, Protestant) – feminist writers acknowledge their ideological status. They do not mystify their own position or pretend to an objectivity or naturalness or commonsense which is itself an ideologically-defined stance. So when Ursula LeGuin writes, 'For fantasy is true, of course. It isn't factual, but it is true', the truth to which she refers is not some kind of absolute knowledge, but rather the truth that every position available to the individual within a society is a construct of particular ideological discourses. Fantasy can reveal that truth, that there is no neutral, objective, natural, commonsense position or perspective because of its overt play with the conventions by which we define and describe the real, conventions which are themselves constructed by particular discourses.

On the other hand, the opposite response can occur; the techniques used to construct the secondary world of the text may alienate, rather than estrange, some readers. The secondary world may become a kind of compensatory dream or wish fulfilment which enables readers to avoid engagement with the real. The secondary world fantasy in which this reading position is not only available, but favoured, commonly presents an *appearance* only of strangeness. The discourses by which the text is constructed are those of the dominant hegemonic bloc, a cursory play with the conventions of realism serving merely to underline or confirm the deception of the eye by the dominant ideological positioning. Realist convention is commonly used to naturalize ideological discourses, aligning ideological practices with conventionally accepted and produced representations of the real, an alignment of mind and eye characteristic, as Rosemary Jackson notes, of a society in which 'I see' means 'I understand' (Jackson, 1981 (C), p. 45). Fantasy may be used to disrupt that particular nexus, so producing some doubt or concern about the limits of the real. But it may not. Fantasy which is superficially fantastic, as *Star Wars* is superficially alien or futuristic, may yet be a composition of hegemonic discourses, as *Star Wars* is a substantial, but not literal, representation of contemporary US society.

> Oh, damn these Amazons, they are making me question everything: myself, Gabriel, my very life!
>
> Bradley, *The Shattered Chain*

Feminist fantasists negotiate this contradictory potential of the fantasy text in their secondary world fiction. As with feminist SF, the texts which work as feminist fantasy are those which situate the reader in a feminist reading position; that is, a reading position in which the deconstruction of patriarchal discourse is a fundamental strategy. In Marion Zimmer Bradley's *The Shattered Chain*, for example, the patriarchal society on the secondary world, Darkover, is shown through the eyes of the Free Amazons, a network of women who reject the patriarchal practices of their society:

THE OATH OF THE FREE AMAZONS

From this day forth, I renounce the right to marry save as a freemate. No man shall bind me di catenas [in chains] and I will dwell in no man's household as a barragana [kept woman].

I swear that I am prepared to defend myself by force if I am attacked by force, and that I shall turn to no man for protection.

From this day forth I swear I shall never again be known by the name of any man, be he father, guardian, lover or husband, but simply and solely as the daughter of my mother.

From this day forth I swear I will give myself to no man save in my own time and season and of my own free will, at my own desire; I will never earn my bread as the object of any man's lust.

From this day forth I swear I will bear no child to any man save for my own pleasure and at my own time and choice. (Bradley, 1978 (C), p. 5)

The reader is shown the reality of life for women (and men) under patriarchy. Most striking is the representation of marriage in a patriarchal society, as seen by the Free Amazons: 'By Dry-Town custom, each woman's hands were fettered with a metal bracelet on each wrist; the bracelets were connected with a long chain, passed through a metal loop on her belt, so that if the woman moved either hand, the other was drawn up tight against the loop at her waist' (p. 16). This is the 'de catinas' marriage rejected in the Amazon oath. On Darkover it is the marriage form practised by the most overtly sexist sub-group, the Dry-Town people. It is also the catalyst for the action of the story. When Melora, a woman kidnapped and married (that is, raped under legal sanction) by a Dry-Town overlord, realizes the inevitable fate for her own daughter, she makes a superhuman effort to contact her kinswoman, Rohana and plead for rescue:

> 'Did I tell you why I suddenly knew I must escape, get Jaelle away, or kill her myself before this child was born?'
> 'No dear, you didn't tell me – '
> 'When I found her – playing with Jalak's other little daughters – they had all of them, even Jaelle, tied ribbons about their hands, playing at being grown up, and in chains – ' (p. 69)

Rohana does not live in chains, but both she and her husband wear marriage bracelets which symbolize the 'de catinas' chains. To the Free Amazons she is as unfree as the Dry-Town women and, if anything, her thralldom is more complete, more insidious, because it is less visible. When Rohana and the Amazon leader, Kindra discuss the Dry-Town women, Kindra observes:

> 'I feel no very great sympathy for them. Any single one of them could be free if she chose. If they wish to suffer chains rather than lose the attention of their men, or be different from their mothers and sisters, I shall not waste my pity on them, far less lose sleep or appetite. They endure their captivity as you of the Domains, Lady, endure yours; and truth to tell, I see no very great difference between you. They are, perhaps, more honest, for they admit to their chains and make no pretense of freedom; while yours are invisible – but they are as great a weight upon you.' (p. 17)

From the perspective of the Free Amazon invisible chains are made visible. From a feminist reading position the role of women in a patriarchal marriage is revealed to be un-free, whether the chains are visible or not. The traditional marriage rings of contemporary society are metaphorically represented by the Domain bracelets, both seeming refinements of the 'de catinas' chains. Yet there are subtle differences: both bracelets and rings are (sometimes) worn by men, indicating an acceptance by the male partner of restrictions imposed by this patriarchal institution on his individual behaviour. Even so, the Free Amazons are scornful of an institution so obviously designed to accommodate patriarchal practices, particularly those relating to/engendered by the contemporary economic system. Rohana is influenced by their doubts:

> At first the world in which the Amazons lived had seemed hard and comfortless, strange and lonely. Then she had realized that most of the strangeness was not the physical lack of comfort at all. It was quite different. It was easy to get used to long hours of riding, to unfamiliar and ugly clothes, to bathing as one could in stream or river, to sleeping in tents or under the sky.
>
> But it was not nearly so easy to give up the familiar support of known projections, known ways of thinking. Until she came on this journey, she had never quite realized how much all her decisions, even small personal ones, had been left to her father and brothers, or, since she married, to her husband . . .
>
> A strange, painful, almost traitorous thought kept returning: Now that I know how to make my own decisions, will I ever be content again to let Gabriel decide for me?
>
> Or, if I do go back, is it only because it is so much easier to do exactly what it is expected of a woman of my caste? (p. 83)

Rohana outlines the contemporary, conservative position for women under patriarchy and her dilemma is a part of the textual strategy by which a feminist perspective is constructed. As Rohana recognizes her own lack of choice, and her abdication of any demand for choice, so the contemporary reader is positioned to perceive the lack of choice commonly experienced by contemporary women. Under an ideology which interpellates women not as active subjects, but as passive objects, choice is denied them. When Rohana later chooses to return to her family, she does so at her own volition:

> Rohana knew, now, that she was living that life by choice; not because her mind was too narrowly bounded to imagine any other life, but because, having known another life and weighed it, she had decided that what was good in her world – her deep affection for Gabriel, her love for her children, the responsibility of the estate of Ardais, that demanded the hand of its lady – outweighed what was difficult, or hard for her to accept. (pp. 90–1)

As Kindra observed in Chapter One, 'that is why the Free Amazons exist . . . So that every woman may, at least, know there is a choice for them' (p. 21). *The Shattered Chain* is a feminist fantasy novel which argues the need for women to have choice about the kind of life they lead. And in demanding choice for women, the novel necessarily demands also that women be treated as autonomous subjects, not passive objects, which is a fundamental challenge to patriarchy.

Bradley relates this debate specifically to the world we know by introducing a major character who is a Terran. Magda Lorne has been raised on Darkover, but is of Terran parentage. Her narrative comprises the second major section of the book. Lorne's ex-husband, Peter Haldane, has been kidnapped by a Darkover bandit, Rumal di Scarp, and, because of his uncanny resemblance to a Domain aristocrat, is being ransomed on penalty of torture and death. Lorne elects to deliver the ransom and, under advice from Lady Rohana, disguises herself as a Free Amazon. On the trail to the bandit's stronghold, however, she meets a band of Free Amazons who recognize her as an imposter and require her, as recompense, to take the Free Amazon oath.

Magda Lorne, like Lady Rohana, makes a choice after her time with the Free Amazons. Through her interactions with these women Lorne undergoes a period of self-discovery, as had Rohana. She realizes that her marriage was based not on personal intimacy, but on a shared ideological placement; that she and Peter Haldane were both raised on Darkover and so share many of the values and assumptions of that society, rather than of their Terran parents. Once she begins to see other possibilities, other perspectives, her connection with Haldane is broken. Lorne also finds that an oppositional stance is possible, that she is not confined by the patriarchal gender ideology with which she has been raised. From this point Lorne's education constitutes another step in Bradley's textual deconstruction of patriarchal gender practices, begun in the Rohana Ardais narrative immediately preceding. Paradoxically, contemporary readers are positioned to identify the gender practices of the Darkover-raised Lorne and Haldane, rather than those of Terran society, as those of their own time; in *The Shattered Chain*, though not in its sequel *Thendarra House*, the gender ideology of future Terran society is depicted as far more liberated than that of Darkover.

Bradley continues this process with the narrative of Jaelle n̄ ha Melora, Free Amazon. Jaelle was the little girl whose rescue from bondage provided the catalyst for the first narrative. Again Bradley writes about choice, that an oppositional stance should also be chosen freely; Jaelle should not regret her choice, made at the age of fifteen, to join the Free Amazons rather than live as a Domain aristocrat. This section also works to counteract negative assessments of a non-patriarchal lifestyle. Bradley uses the Jaelle narrative to demonstrate that women who refuse to operate as patriarchal subjects (i.e. as objects) are not excluded from heterosexual relationships; rather that they reserve the right to play an active role (as subjects) in those relationships. Jaelle falls in love with Haldane after Lorne secures his rescue from Rumal di Scarp. During Jaelle's recuperation in the Ardais household from wounds received during a roadside battle she and Haldane become lovers, much to the disgust of Rohana's son and Haldane's double, Kyril Ardais. Kyril attempts to treat Jaelle as a chattel, in line with the sexist ideology common on Darkover. With Kyril and Haldane as virtual mirror images Jaelle's interactions with the two exemplify different possibilities available to female/male relationships: the subject/object, owner/chattel relationship characteristic of patriarchy, rejected by Jaelle, and the subject/subject, egalitarian relationship acceptable to the Free Amazon as a freemate choice.

The Jaelle narrative of *The Shattered Chain* affirms the choices made earlier in the book by all three major female characters. Rohana's choice to remain a married Domain noblewoman is vindicated by the wisdom with which she manages both the Ardais lands and the Ardais family, her love for her husband Garbriel at least partly compensating for the demands he makes of her. Lorne's choice to honour her Free Amazon oath provides her with the choice she needed to avoid rekindling the relationship with Haldane, based, as it was, more on convenience than mutuality. And Jaelle chooses to exercise her Amazon option to take a freemate rather than denying her desire for a male lover. So Bradley uses an interweave of three narratives – of a Darkovan noblewoman, a Terran and a Free Amazon – to construct a novel which examines patriarchal practices from a number of perspectives and which, particularly with its recurring image of the 'de catinas' chains, positions readers oppositionally in relation to practices which are subsequently revealed as fictionally transformed representations of contemporary gender roles and behaviours. 'Women who come to us . . . usually learn self-respect, not self-hate' (p. 89).

Another reason feminist writers use fantasy is that it seems to impose fewer restrictions on characterization, specifically on female characters. In her 'Introduction' to the first volume of *Women of Wonder* stories Pamela Sargent specified this as a potential of both SF and fantasy, that they 'can show us the remarkable women as normal where past literature shows her as the exception' (Sargent, 1978 (B), p. 48). In realist fiction the remarkable woman is conventionally presented as unusual, as some kind of aberration, rather than as the potential (fulfilled) of most women. This is precisely because much realist fiction is ideologically bound to the dictates of patriarchy: in a patriarchal society exceptional women are not only unusual, they are dangerous. In patriarchal societies women are actively prevented from becoming exceptional, accomplished, or heroic. If they do, they are clearly a threat to the established order. This situation is most commonly represented fictionally by the emotional fulfillment of the heroine who accepts a subordinate or somehow circumscribed role and the downfall, usually emotionally and then financially and/or physically and/or intellectually of the female character who is presented in an oppositional stance. Good girls get their man; bad girls are thrown out into the cold. Fantasy has the potential to construct a new kind of heroine. In a letter to the feminist journal, *Frontiers*, Pamela Sargent noted:

> Within the context of most human societies to date, women of strength and achievement are exceptions to the rule. This is reflected in novels about the past or present. Science fiction and fantasy, on the other hand, allow one to imagine and write about worlds where strong independent women *are* the rule,[1] or to construct a society whose features can illuminate the workings of our own.[1]

This characterization of women is notable in Elizabeth Lynn's fantasy novel, *The Northern Girl* (Lynn, 1981 (C)). This novel resists sexist stereotypes by portraying female characters who are physically strong and tough, lesbian relationships which have integrity and commitment. Strong women who are also sensitive and intelligent, intelligent women who are emotionally secure and tender. The most recent feminist fantasy, including work by Ursula LeGuin, Suzy McKee Charnas, Vonda McIntyre, Kate Willhelm, Tanith Lee, Marion Zimmer Bradley, Barbara Hambly and Joy Chant constructs strong, but subtle, female characters who are more effective and less easily appropriated than the earlier Amazonion warrior queens of writers such as C.L. Moore. Her Jirel of Joiry stories are most notable for the sheer brutality of the female warrior, Jirel. Jirel is even more macho than most men. The problem with this kind of role-reversal is that it does not challenge the nature of the role itself. In making the role available to a female character role-reversal writers offer a challenge to patriarchy, but that challenge is too easily appropriated as the role is preserved at the cost of the individual character. Jirel becomes a kind of honorary man, so long as she occupies this role; its masculine gender coding is barely threatened. Nevertheless these stories were useful as ground-breaking exercises, not dissimilar to the consciousness raising exercises of the early 1960s. In an Introduction to her own work Marge Piercy wrote about this necessity to re-make roles:

We must break through the old roles to encounter our own meanings in the symbols we experience in dreams, in songs, in vision, in meditation. Some of these symbols are much older than capitalism, and some contain knowledge we must recover; but we receive all through a filter that has aligned the stuff by values not our own.

What we use we must remake. Then only we are not playing with dead dreams but seeing ourselves more clearly, and more clearly becoming. The defeated in history lose their names, their godesses, their language, their culture. The myths we imagine we are living (old westerns, true romances) shape our choices.[2]

Fairy-tale reworked

Piercy's words are an appropriate introduction to the next section of this chapter, which deals with feminist rewriting of fairy-tale. Feminist critics have written at length about fairy-tale because of its role in the acculturation of gender ideology. In an essay entitled ' "Some Day My Prince Will Come": Female Acculturation through the Fairy Tale' Marcia Lieberman analyses the gender roles portrayed in fairy-tale, noting:

> Among other things, these tales present a picture of sexual roles, behavior, and psychology, and a way of predicting outcome or fate according to sex, which is important because of the intense interest that children take in 'endings'; they always want to know how things will 'turn out'. A close examination of the treatment of girls and women in fairy tales reveals certain patterns which are keenly interesting not only in themselves, but also as material which has undoubtedly played a major contribution in forming the sexual role concept of children, and in suggesting to them the limitations that are imposed by sex upon a person's chances of success in various endeavors. (Zipes, 1986 (C), p. 187)

She then analyses the kinds of behaviour associated with female characters in a range of fairy stories. The good women, the heroines, are invariably beautiful, passive and powerless while female characters who are powerful are also evil and very often ugly and ill-tempered.

> Being powerful is mainly associated with being unwomanly.
> The moral value of activity thus becomes sex-linked. The boy who sets out to seek his fortune, like Dick Whittington, Jack the Giant-Killer, or Espen Cinderlad, is a stock figure and, provided he has a kind heart, is assured of success. What is praiseworthy in males, however, is

rejected in females; the counterpart of the energetic, aspiring boy is the scheming, ambitious women ... Women who are powerful and good are never human; those women who are human, and who have power or seek it, are nearly always portrayed as repulsive. (p. 197)

Feminist writers express the same findings about traditional fairy-tales by rewriting them. Judith Viorst's poem, 'And Then the Prince Knelt Down and Tried to Put the Glass Slipper on Cinderella's Foot' is one example.

> I really didn't notice that he had a funny nose.
> And he certainly looked better all dressed up in fancy clothes.
> He's not nearly as attractive as he seemed the other night.
> So I think I'll just pretend that his glass slipper feels too tight. (Zipes, 1981 (C), p. 73)

The title of the poem is as important, and almost as long, as the poem itself. It contains all the elements of the traditional story. The prince's search for Cinderella is complicated by his apparent obliviousness to her as a person, as a subject. She exists for him only as a combination of physical characteristics (though this does not include her face!). Her dainty feet, worthy of the finest shoes, signify that determining female characteristic, beauty. In fact, Cinderella is so dainty that, in accordance with the object status she has as a woman, he has to put her shoe on for her. Cinderella is entirely passive and helpless; the Prince is the active subject. The narrative form of the title follows the quest trajectory of the original title: the quest of Cinderella is to be confirmed as passive object and rewarded for her malleability, of the Prince to find the object which defines him as subject. But the poem does not quite work this way. Cinderella is immediately critical of the Prince, and is therefore active. Rather than passive object, she takes an active role in her destiny. This Cinderella acts as an independent, autonomous subject. Worse (or better) she rejects the Prince both as a marriage prospect and as a meal ticket. She is also prepared to lie to rid herself of his attentions, which is most decidedly unwomanly. The Cinderella of the poem differs fundamentally from the traditional fairy-tale character in exercising choice, and it is precisely this option which is omitted from the original story. Yet, as Lieberman records, the Cinderella story has a male version in the Norwegian tale of Espen Cinderlad:

> Cinderella's male counterpart, Espen Cinderlad, the hero of a great many Norwegian folk tales, plays a very different role. Though he is the youngest of the three brothers, as Cinderella is the youngest sister, he is a Cinderlad by choice. His brothers may ridicule and despise him, but

no one forces him to sit by the fire and poke in the ashes all day; he elects to do so. All the while, he knows that he is the cleverest of the three, and eventually he leaves the fireside and wins a princess and half a kingdom by undertaking some adventure or winning a contest. (p. 192)

Cinderlad fulfils the role of hero. If his strategy initially involves the adoption of a subordinate (feminine) role, even this is a matter of his own choice. Cinderella, by contrast, has no choice; her role is entirely passive. In his study of folk and fairy-tales, *Breaking the Magic Spell*, Jack Zipes raises a series of questions about the Cinderella story which leave little doubt about its contemporary ideological function:

> Though it is difficult to speculate how an individual child might react to Cinderella, certainly the adult reader and interpreter must ask the following questions: Why is the stepmother shown to be wicked and not the father? Why is Cinderella essentially passive? . . . Why do girls have to quarrel over a man? How do children react to a Cinderella who is industrious, dutiful, virginal and passive? Are all men handsome? Is marriage the end goal of life? Is it important to marry rich men? This small list of questions suggests that the ideological and psychological pattern and message of Cinderella do nothing more than reinforce sexist values and a Puritan ethos that serves a society which fosters competition and achievement. (Zipes, 1979 (C), p. 173)

Zipes notes earlier in the same study that the central issue of most folk and fairy tales is power and that the ideology of power most commonly propagated is 'a primitive or feudal ideology of "might makes right"' (pp. 20–40). It is hardly necessary to observe here that women are excluded from holding power in this ideological scheme, their power can only be a reflection of that of husband or father. Female characters, encoded with the ideological positioning of women, are accordingly passive, objectified, positioned as prize or reward for consumption by an active, aggressive male subject. Zipes notes:

> The immanent meaning of the tales has little to do with providing suitable direction for a contemporary child's life. From a contemporary perspective, the tales are filled with incidents of inexplicable abuse, maltreatment of women, negative images of minority groups, question-able sacrifices, and the exaltation of power. (p. 170)

Tanith Lee rewrites Cinderella in her story, 'When the Clock Strikes', published in the volume tantalizingly titled *Red as Blood, or Tales from the Sisters Grimmer* (Lee, 1983 (C)). In Lee's story the main female character, Ashella, adopts passivity strategically, as does Espen

Cinderlad. She is the sole remaining member of the family bloodily ousted by the father of the reigning prince; her descent is reckoned matriarchally and so not recognized by her society. Ashella hides her birth and her beauty behind a facade of ugliness and madness:

> People forgot her beauty. She was at pains to obscure it. She slunk about like an aged woman, a rag pulled over her head, dirt smeared on her cheeks and brow. She elected to sleep in a cold cramped attic and sat all day by a smoky hearth in the kitchens. When someone came to her and begged her to wash her face and put on suitable clothes and sit in the rooms of the house, she smiled modestly, drawing the rag or a piece of hair over her face. 'I swear,' she said, 'I am glad to be humble before God and men.'
>
> They reckoned her pious and they reckoned her simple. Two years passed. They mislaid her beauty altogether, and reckoned her ugly. They found it hard to call to mind who she was exactly, as she sat in the ashes, or shuffled unattended about the streets like a crone. (p. 54)

When the ball to celebrate the prince's name day is announced, no one thinks to tell Ashella. With the help of her satanic powers she attends the ball and, when the prince is bewitched by her beauty, she curses him in the name of her whole family. The prince is condemned to spend the rest of his life searching for the woman whose foot fits the glass slipper Ashella leaves behind. He never finds her:

> Is it really surprising? The shoe was sorcerous. It constantly changed itself, its shape, its size, in order that no foot, save one, could ever be got into it. (p. 63)

The prince is soon reduced to the level of passivity voluntarily adopted by Ashella: 'His clothes were filthy and unkempt. His face was smeared with sweat and dust ... it resembled, momentarily, another face' (p. 64). Eventually the prince is killed by intriguers who are themselves soon ousted from power by external enemies. There is no happily ever after; Ashella simply disappears, her quest complete. Lee's narrative confronts the popular fairy tale at every turn. Ashella is active, aggressive with a quest passed to her by her satan-worshipping mother. She does not marry the prince, but transforms him into a mirror image of Cinderella. And just as the narrative of the fairy tale Cinderella ends with her subjective annihilation, her assimilation into the identity of the prince as his object/prize, his princess, so the prince is annihilated as his ability to perform his role as active subject is destroyed by Ashella's curse.

Lee's rewriting of the Cinderella fairy-tale reveals by negation the assumptions encoded in the more familiar version, primarily the passivity of Cinderella and the annihilation of her subjectivity, her being as the conclusion of the narrative quest. These invidious practices are coded into 'Cinderella' for consumption by the passive reader. And, as Jackson notes, fairy-tales are so constructed that their reading position is peculiarly passive:

> As narrative forms, fairy tales function differently from fantasies. They are neutral, impersonalized, set apart from the reader. The reader becomes a passive receiver of events, there is no demand that (s)he participate in their interpretation. Structurally, too, fairy tales discourage belief in the importance or effectiveness of action for their narratives are 'closed'. Things 'happen', 'are done to' protagonists, told to the reader, from a position of omniscience and authority, making the reader unquestioningly passive. (Jackson, 1981 (C), p. 154)

So fairy-tales not only encode conservative ideological discourses, but they also operate according to the mystificatory tactics of ideology, inflecting narrative to naturalize the discourses they carry. The reader is positioned passively by these narratives to receive these discourses and their constituent power relations as inevitable or commonsense or natural. Feminist revisions of these stories position readers actively to re-evaluate the nature of fantasies represented ideologically as harmless – by implication, value-neutral – childhood amusements. Feminist writers present not one authoritative narrative, but two narratives – the revised version of the traditional narrative and its discursive referent, the traditional narrative. Tanith Lee continually emphasizes this metanarrative function of her story by direct reader address:

> I hazard you have begun to recognize the story by now. I see you suppose I tell it wrongly. Believe me, this is the truth of the matter. But if you would rather I left off the tale . . . (p. 56)

> Did you intend to protest about the shoe? Shall I finish the story, or would you rather I did not? It is not the ending you are familiar with. Yet, I perceive you understand that, now. (p. 62)

Lee's readers are positioned at a point of dialogue between the two stories, 'Cinderella' and 'When the Clock Strikes'. Her rewriting of episodes and characters elicits a continual comparison between the two versions: the text on the page and its absent referent. In the differences the reader discovers Lee's identification of the discourses encoded in the familiar story, primarily the passivity of the role of Cinderella. And most importantly the reader discovers that fairy-tale is not the value-free collection of childhood fantasy which it is (ideologically) reputed to be. Rather fairy-tales are revealed as carriers of conservative ideological discourses which prepare the child reader to be not active, critical subjects, but passive recipients of those same discourses.

Angela Carter's revisions of fairy-tales in her collection, *The Bloody Chamber and other stories*, function similarly (Carter, 1979 (C)). Carter rewrites the stories of Bluebeard, Beauty and the Beast, the vampire, the Elf-king, Puss-in-Boots and Red Riding Hood. Her stories seem as much a fictional/critical reply to Bruno Bettleheim's analyses of the stories in *The Uses of Enchantment* as direct responses to the stories themselves (Bettleheim, 1978 (C)).

His analyses are conservative applications of Freudian theory, apparently without any critical examination of the gender ideology of that theory. Bettleheim's analysis of 'Little Red Riding Hood' concludes:

> Little Red Riding Hood lost her childish innocence as she encountered the dangers residing in herself and the world, and exchanged it for wisdom that only the 'twice born' can possess: those who not only master an existential crisis, but also become conscious that it was their own nature which projected them into it. Little Red Riding Hood's childish innocence dies as the wolf reveals itself as such and swallows her. When she is cut out of the wolf's belly, she is reborn on a higher plane of existence; relating positively to both her parents, no longer a child, she returns to life a young maiden. (p. 183)

For many critics the 'higher plane of existence' to which Bettelheim refers is nothing other than the patriarchal order, the gender ideology of which dominates Western society. Red Riding Hood has, on this reading, been brutally inserted into the patriarchal order as a result of rape or the threat of rape, represented by the wolf, from which she is rescued by the patriarchal figure of the hunter, who, in some versions, is also her father. Zipes quotes Susan Brownmiller's assessment of the story in her book, *Against Our Will*:

> Red Riding Hood is a parable of rape. There are frightening male figures abroad in the woods – we call them wolves, among other names and females are helpless before them. Better stick close to the path, better not be adventurous. If you are lucky, a good friendly male may be able to save you from certain disaster. (Zipes, 1986 (C), p. 232)

Zipes himself conducted a chilling semiotic analysis of illustrations of the tale from the early nineteenth-century to the present day (Zipes, (1986), (C), pp. 227–60). Zipes finds that 'most illustrations imply that she willingly makes a bargain with the wolf, or, in male terms, "she asks to be raped".' (p. 239) He concludes:

> Ultimately, the male phantasies of Perrault and the Brothers Grimm can be traced to their socially induced desire and need for control – control of women, control of their own sexual libido, control of their fear of women and loss of virility. That their controlling interests are still reinforced and influential through variant texts and illustrations of Little Red Riding Hood in society today is an indication that we are still witnessing an antagonistic struggle of the sexes in all forms of socialisation, in which men are still trying to dominate women ...
>
> In the case of the Red Riding Hood illustrations and the classical texts by Perrault and the Grimms, the girl in the encounter with the wolf gazes but really does not gaze, for she is the image of male desire. She is projected by the authors Perrault and Grimm and generally by male illustrators as an object without a will of her own. The gaze of the wolf will consume her and is intended to dominate and eliminate her. The gaze of the wolf is a phallic mode of interpreting the world and is an attempt to gain what is lacking through imposition and force. Thus, the positioning of the wolf involves a movement toward convincing the girl that he is what she wants, and her role is basically one intended to mirror his desire. In such an inscribed and prescribed male discourse, the feminine other has no choice. Her identity will be violated and fully absorbed by male desire either as wolf or gamekeeper. (pp. 257–8)

Zipes's work deserves lengthy quotation not only for its critical acuity, but also as a response to Bettelheim. As Zipes's pictorial study shows, 'Little Red Riding Hood' is a patriarchal fable, expressive of male fears of active female sexuality and instrumental in the conditioning of women (and men) to circumvent confrontation with this fear. The feminist rewritings of the tale constitute fictional analyses which complement the critical work of Zipes. In *The Bloody Chamber* Carter has written three wolf stories, two of which, 'The Werewolf' and 'The Company of Wolves', are based directly on the Red Riding Hood Story. Both feature a very active and assertive little girl. In the first story her confrontation with wolf leaves him rather the worse for wear:

> It [the wolf] was a huge one, with red eyes and running, grizzled chops; any but a mountaineer's child would have died of fright at the sight of it. It went for her throat, as wolves do, but she made a great swipe at it with her father's knife and slashed off its right forepaw.
>
> The wolf let out a gulp, almost a sob, when it saw what had happened to it; wolves are less brave then they seem. It went lolloping off disconsolately between the trees as well as it could on three legs, leaving a trail of blood behind it. (p. 135)

This Red Riding Hood uses the tools of patriarchy, assertiveness and

power (her father's knife), to defend herself against attack, figurative-
ly castrating her would-be assailant. When she reaches her grandmother's house, she finds the old lady in bed with a fever – its cause,
a severed right hand. With the neighbour's help she kills her
werewolf grandmother: 'Now the child lived in her grandmother's
house; she prospered' (p. 136). This alternative Red Riding Hood
operates with the tools of patriarchy, driving out the woman who,
through her co-option by patriarchy, has been operative in attempting to insert her granddaughter into that order as passive object. In
refusing that role the girl usurps the power and influence of the male
(active subject) role; she owns property, and prospers.

In 'The Company of Wolves' Carter focuses on the wolf as an image
of active sexuality. Her Red Riding Hood is visualized as newly
pubescent:

> Her breasts have just begun to swell; her hair is like lint, so fair it hardly
> makes a shadow on her pale forehead; her cheeks are an emblematic
> scarlet and white and she has just started her woman's bleeding, the
> clock inside her that will strike, henceforward, once a month.
>
> She stands and moves within the invisible pentacle of her own
> virginity. She is an unbroken egg; she is a sealed vessel; she has inside
> her a magic space the entrance to which is shut tight with a plug of
> membrane; she is a closed system; she does not know how to shiver.
> She has her knife and she is afraid of nothing. (p. 141)

When this girl ventures into the forest, the space of desire, she has no
fear, confident as she is with her own sexuality. Carter notes that she
begins her adventure when her father is away, otherwise he 'might
forbid her' (p. 141). On the other hand, her mother colludes in her
journey: 'her mother cannot deny her' (p. 141). In the forest she meets
a handsome young huntsman with whom she is clearly taken. They
separate temporarily and he reaches grandmother's house before her,
where he reveals himself as a wolf and disposes of the old lady. When
the girl arrives, he is disguised as her grandmother but she soon
recognizes him and her danger. Instead of running from him,
however, she matches his desire with her own:

> The firelight shone through the edges of her skin; now she was clothed
> only in her untouched integument of flesh. This dazzling, naked she
> combed out her hair with her fingers; her hair looked white as the snow
> outside. Then went directly to the man with red eyes in whose
> unkempt mane the lice moved; she stood up on tiptoe and unbuttoned
> the collar of his shirt.
>
> What big arms you have.
> All the better to hug you with.

Every wolf in the world now howled a prothalamion outside the window as she freely gave the kiss she owed him.

What big teeth you have!

She saw how his jaw began to slaver and the room was full of the forest's Liebestod but the wise child never flinched, even when he answered:

All the better to eat you with.

The girl burst out laughing; she knew she was nobody's meat. She laughed him full in the face, she ripped off his shirt for him and flung it into the fire, in the fiery wake of her own discarded clothing. (pp. 146–7)

Again Carter depicts a girl who outwolfs the wolf, who takes the weapons of patriarchy into her own hands and succeeds: 'See! sweet and sound she sleeps in granny's bed, between the paws of the tender wolf' (p. 147). In this story Carter reworks the sexual significance of the traditional story. Instead of being intimidated into passivity by the sexual potency of the aggressive male, and so being eaten (i.e. destroyed) like her granny, the girl asserts herself sexually and so is freed from the wolf's domination; they live peacefully together. In 'The Company of Wolves' Carter transforms a tale which dramatizes the brutal subjugation of women by a patriarchal order, and the expression of male fears of assertive female sexuality, into a story of the sexual maturation and potency of a woman who rejects male domination.

Tanith Lee also rewrites 'Little Red Riding Hood' in her story, 'Wolfland' (Lee, 1983 (C)). In this story a woman deliberately becomes a werewolf in order to deal with a brutal husband. She passes this power of transmogrification on to her granddaughter in order to avoid any punishment at her death – although she adds that the indications of this power were already evident in her granddaughter. When the girl protests at her grandmother's murder of her husband, the old woman questions her alternatives:

'You should have appealed for help.'

'To whom? The marriage vow is a chain that may not be broken. If I had left him, he would have traced me as he did the child. No law supports a wife. I could only kill him.' (p. 134)

In Lee's story the power assumed by the woman as werewolf is more justifiable, even more natural, than the appalling cruelty of her husband. The wolf identify here signifies the assumption of power, of self-determination, within a social formation which denies that power, those rights as subject, to women.

The 'Little Red Riding Hood' rewrites, like the revisions of 'Cinderella', operate via an implicit comparison with the traditional tale, or more accurately the nineteenth-century version, as an absent referent. In the differences of characterization and incident between the feminist and traditional versions feminist writers reveal the discourses encoded in the traditional tales, which are thereby shown as ideologically determined rather than value-free. Recent collections such as Jack Zipes's *Don't Bet on the Prince* record the feminist revisions of traditional stories by a wide variety of writers including Carter, Lee, Jane Yolen, Anne Sexton, The Merseyside Fairy Story Collective, Olga Browmas and Margaret Atwood. Some of these stories are accessible to young readers and might even be used as substitutes for the traditional stories. However, the primary function of these revisions is, as stated above, to operate as metafictions which, while significant in themselves of particular gender relations, rely on the constant comparison with traditional narrative to construct a feminist reading position from which the anti-woman ideology coded in traditional fairy-tale becomes visible.

Horror

Feminist horror fiction is not a major sub-genre of feminist fantasy, but at least one feminist writer, Suzy McKee Charnas, has used horror conventions effectively to deconstruct the nature of contemporary gender relations, and to comment on the nature of contemporary horror fiction. In her dystopian novel, *Walk to the End of the World* (Charnas, 1978 (B)) she employs many of the horror conventions of contemporary literary and cinematic pulp: the psychopathic male guards, the Rovers who kill women on sight, the barbaric slave-like conditions under which women live, the burning of women as ritual sacrifice in a homocentric society, the breeding pens by which the species is propagated, in order to not only reveal the nature of patriarchal gender practices, but also to comment on the cultural products to which they give rise – from the nineteenth-century horror of *Dracula* to contemporary texts such as *Hallowe'en* and *Nightmare on Elm Street*.

One horror convention used by a number of feminist writers is the vampire; Tanith Lee's *Sabella*, Jody Scott's *I, Vampire* and Charnas's *The Vampire Tapestry*[3] all feature vampire protagonists. Charnas's text, however, constructs the most fundamental interrogation of the vampire convention, and popular fiction as a whole, as a carrier of patriarchal ideology (Charnas, 1980 (C)). Her text consists of five interrelated narratives, all featuring the vampire protagonist living in the identity of the distinguished academic, Dr Edward Weyland. The text charts the gradual breakdown of Weyland's subjectivity and it is in the description of this process of dissolution that Charnas shows the constitution of the male patriarchal subject.

In the first narrative, 'The Ancient Mind At Work' the vampire is shot and grievously wounded by a woman from a society as barbaric and predatory as he is himself, white South Africa. Katje de Groot works at the same university as Weyland and she recognizes him as a vampire because of early training in hunting predators. Weyland prepares to murder de Groot recognising the danger of exposure, without realizing that he has an enemy with training in hunting similar to his own. Even when armed, de Groot at first hesitates to defend herself. Her ideological positioning as passive recipient, as victim, by the patriarchal order, represented in all its barbarity and (ideologically constructed) seductiveness by the vampire, militates against any action on her own behalf. Ironically Charnas earlier has de Groot reject the necessity for active involvement in both race and gender politics, de Groot believes that she can exist independently of both race and gender positioning, outside society. Her confrontation with the vampire dramatizes the fallibility of that belief. De Groot shoots Weyland, but only after she identifies with him: *'But I am myself a hunter!'* (p. 50)

The significance of this episode must be traced by reference to the traditional semiosis of the vampire text, in which bloodsucking, the feeding practice of the vampire, equates with sexual intercourse. Charnas makes this connection in the text when de Groot's co-worker, Nettie, naively describes Weyland's sexual magnetism in precisely those terms. Nettie has offered to act as an experimental subject for one of Weyland's sleep experiments: 'He leaned over me to plug something into the wall, and I said, "Go ahead, you can bite my neck any time." You know, he was sort of hanging over me, and his lab coat was sort of spread, like a cape, all menacing and batlike' (p. 31). Further Charnas has de Groot read the original *Dracula* for clues about how to approach her enemy: *'Dracula* was a silly book. She had to force herself to read on in spite of the absurd Van Helsing character with his idiot English – an insult to anyone of Dutch descent' (p. 35). Just as Van Helsing precipitated the destruction of the original vampire, the ur-patriarch, so the Afrikaaner de Groot begins the process which leads to the eventual destruction of his modern successor. The significance of her identification with the vampire, then, lies with her assumption of the aggressor role reserved under patriarchy for the male. De Groot matches the vampire as hunter, and wins; a woman adopts the aggressive 'male' role and vanquishes her attacker. Traditionally a woman who assumes the masculine role, like the vampire women in Dracula's castle and Lucy Westenra after her assult by Dracula, are doomed to mutilation and death by men who represent the patriarchal order. Phallically staked through the heart and then ritually mutilated, they are reinserted into the phallic order from which their assertiveness, their expression of active subjectivity, had removed them.[4] Katje de Groot suffers no such fate.

In the following narrative the seriously wounded Weyland is found by a group of petty thugs who put him on display for the (sexual) gratification of their devil-worshipping friends. Weyland is forced to feed publicly in a displaced sexual display. The young boy, Mark who tends the vampire during the day makes this connection: 'It isn't just eating to the ones who come here. They make it dirty' (p. 98). Weyland is also subjected to a degrading oral/genital examination by the leader of the devil cult, Reese:

> Reese bent and clamped the vampire's head hard against his thick thigh with one arm. Seizing him by the jaw, he wrenched his mouth open . . .
>
> 'It's true there are no fangs, but here – see that? A sort of sting on the underside of the tongue. It probably erects itself at the prospect of dinner, makes the puncture through which he sucks blood, and then folds back out of sight again.'
>
> 'Sexy,' Roger said with new interest. (pp. 77–9)

In this episode the vampire is reduced to the level of (sexual) object. Like women in a patriarchal society he is defined by his difference from the (phallic) norm, which becomes the means of his control and exploitation. Weyland escapes with the help of the boy, Mark, who is not yet fully socialized into the degree of exploitation and brutality evident in Reese's barely suppressed sadism or Roger's casual indifference. Mark feeds the starving vampire and his response to the experience is a naïve indictment of the macho sexuality of patriarchy:

> To have someone spring on you like a tiger and suck your blood with savage and single-minded intensity – how could anyone imagine that was sexy? He would never forget that moment's blinding fear. If sex was like that, they could keep it. (pp. 116–17)

With the boy's help Weyland escapes, and then performs the action which signifies the continuing disintegration of his subjectivity: he lets the boy go free. Mark knows Weyland's identity: as an effective predator, Weyland should destroy him, but he does not.

The next episode, 'The Vampire Tapestry' is central to the disintegration of the vampire's identity. Weyland is accepted back to his
university position on the understanding that he undergoes psychiatric treatment for his delusion that he is a vampire. The psychologist,
Floria Landauer asks Weyland to describe his hunting practices and
to specify his victims. His subsequent report is an exposition of the
sexual repressiveness of patriarchal society. As a masculine (patriarchal) subject, a respectable member of the establishment, Weyland's
(sexual) prey are those whose own desires are not recognized by
patriarchy, who are denied the right to assert their own sexual needs,
women and gay men. Landauer then asks Weyland to empathize
with his prey. Weyland refuses:

> 'I will not. Though I do have enough empathy with my quarry to enable
> me to hunt efficiently. I must draw the line at erasing the necessary
> distance that keeps prey and predator distinct.' (p. 146)

Weyland's response signifies a refusal of emotional engagement. If
the hunter fully engages with the prey, the hunt is no longer possible.
So Weyland is disturbed by the growing emotional understanding
between himself and Landauer: 'The seductiveness, the distraction of
our – human contact worries me. I fear for the ruthlessness that keeps
me alive' (p. 169). Eventually Landauer seduces Weyland, an act
which is a turning point for the patriarchal hunter. In recognizing her
(sexual) needs and engaging with her Weyland rejects the sexist
discourse which positions her as object, as essentially unreal, without
subjectivity: 'How did you grow so real? The more I spoke to you of
myself, the more real you became' (p. 183). Weyland's new-found
empathy marks the beginning of his dissolution.

In the next episode, 'A Musical Interlude' this empathy is explored
further. The vampire has learned the empathy which will now enable
him to appreciate not only human beings, but also human culture
(Weyland had specifically rejected the value of human art during his
sessions with Landauer). He can now empathize, but he does not
have the 'civilized' detachment, the generic training, which enables
him to separate performance from subject-matter. Consequently
attendance at a performance of Tosca constitutes an almost unbear-
able ordeal. Empathizing closely with the story Weyland finds
himself plunged back into a time which was a part of his past: roused
by its barbarity and by the music which dramatizes the cruelty of the
story, Weyland kills unnecessarily, 'without need, without hunger'
(p. 220). Weyland's response is used by Charnas to question our

'sophisticated' detachment from and enjoyment of artworks which encode discourses we might otherwise, in another format or representation, find unacceptable. Again Charnas positions readers reflexively, to question the politics of her own and other texts, from the pulp vampire novels which are the generic context of *The Vampire Tapestry* to high-art forms such as opera. What kinds of discourses are encoded in these texts? How do they position us as audience? And Charnas offers another possibility to us as audience, in the subversive re-reading of the opera given by another of Weyland's party. She describes the murder of Scarpia, the villain, by Floria Tosca as appropriate assertive behaviour. Responding to the description of the opera as rubbish she observes:

> 'Other people do [reject it] too; they honestly feel that *Tosca*'s just a vulgar thriller . . . I think what shocks them is seeing a woman kill a man to keep him from raping her. If a man kills somebody over politics or love, that's high drama, but if a woman offs a rapist, that's sordid.' (pp. 226–7)

Charnas relates the two Floria stories here, that of the operatic heroine and of the psychologist. Both have acted assertively and in their own defence to destroy the patriarchal rapist/aggressor. Like Scarpia Weyland is destroyed by the encounter.

The final narrative, 'The Last of Dr Weyland' describes the annihilation of the vampire. Unable to hunt, to prey (sexually) on those rendered powerless by patriarchal society, the vampire is forced to withdraw, his subjectivity or identity as Weyland destroyed. Before he leaves this society, however, Weyland kills Reese, the sadist who had exploited and degraded him when he was helpless. In preparation for this encounter Weyland temporarily reconstitutes his identity as predator:

> If he could release his grip on his human surface and sink back into the deeper, darker being at his core, his root-self . . . this was not so simple as in simpler times. He suffered a frightful moment of imbalance and disorientation. Then something hot and raw began coiling in his body.
>
> I am strong, I am ready bent on departure, and I am hungry; why should I not hunt the hunter in my own house tonight? (p. 287)

Weyland meets Reese on equal terms, both exploitative male patriarchal subjects. Weyland kills Reese and, in so doing, defeats a part of himself, the 'root-self', the part that has allowed him to survive as that archetypal masculine subject. In killing Reese Weyland destroys the discursive positioning which constitutes the identity of Weyland, the masculine patriarchal subject, the dominant male. His victory also serves those victimized by heterosexism, those with whom Weyland is identified in the second narrative by his helplessness and subsequent exploitation, and in the third by his growing empathy. Weyland defeats the representative of patriarchy, as did de Groot in the opening narrative, by assuming the role of patriarchal aggressor and so subverting the role from within.

In *The Vampire Tapestry* Charnas reworks the convention of the vampire, the macho hunter/lover, to reveal its encoded gender ideology and the procedures, of exploitation and aggression, by which it is sustained and which constitute the masculine subject position under patriarchy. Simultaneously she positions readers to challenge the politics of all texts. *The Vampire Tapestry* consists of five interconnected narratives and the narratives they discursively indicate, *Dracula* and the vampire literature which has followed the original and *Tosca* and the high art narratives of which it is an example. So her narratives not only relativize each other, but also operate as metafictions which deconstruct the gender ideology of other popular texts, high and low brow. This example of feminist horror therefore functions similarly to the feminist revisions of fairy-tale, revealing the gender ideology of familiar texts and showing that those texts are not value-free or neutral – and in her narrative 'A Musical Interlude' Charnas specifically directs the reader to the need for both the critical analysis of all fiction and its subversive rereading.

History of Gothic horror

Horror and 'other world' fantasy can be traced back to the Gothic fiction of the eighteenth century. Not all Gothic is necessarily subversive; as David Punter illustrates in his study, *The Literature of Terror*, Gothic fiction

> enacts psychological and social dilemmas: in doing so, it both confronts the bourgeoisie with its limitations and offers it modes of imaginary transcendence, which is after all the dialectical role of most art. Gothic fiction demonstrates the potential of revolution by daring to speak the socially unspeakable; but the very act of speaking it is an ambiguous gesture. (Punter, 1980 (C), p. 417)

In *The Mysteries of Udolpho* (1794) Ann Radcliffe expresses the powerlessness of women in a patriarchal society, their confinement within the walls of the bourgeois household, through the story of the perils of her heroine, Emily St. Aubert. Yet the fantastic or supernatu-

ral elements of the narrative, which contribute so much to the sense
of menace that pervades the story and dramatize so effectively the
invidious position of women under patriarchy, are eventually explained away as the hysterical imaginings of the highly sensitive
Emily. So, even though Radcliffe does criticise in the novel the
education which produced Emily's extreme susceptibility, there is a
sense in which Emily, signifying the upper middle-class woman, is
responsible for her own distress. More importantly her distress is
explained away textually, leaving only a few comments about the
nature of female education for the reader to ponder and on which to
exercise her/his own analytical powers. The labyrinthine structure of
Gothic too easily recontains the subversive critique at its heart:

> When fantasy has been allowed to surface within culture, it has been in
> a manner close to Freud's notion of art as compensation, as an activity
> which sustains cultural order by making up for a society's lacks. Gothic
> fiction, for example, tended to buttress a dominant, bourgeois, ideolo-
> gy, by vicarious wish fulfilment through fantasies of incest, rape,
> murder, parricide, social disorder. Like pornography, it functioned to
> supply an object of desire, to imagine social and sexual transgression.
> (Jackson, 1981 (C), p. 175)

The Mysteries of Udolpho features all of the above fantasies, except
parricide, and, as Jackson suggests, they function as a contradictory
subtext to Radcliffe's demand for a more appropriate female education. As Jackson goes on to note, fantastic elements or conventions
which disrupt the realist surface of narrative and so challenge the
inability or naturalness of that realism and the categories by which it
is constructed, 'have been constantly reworded, re-written and recovered to *serve* rather than to *subvert* the dominant ideology' (p. 175).

Nevertheless, Gothic fiction opened up possibilities which were
later exploited by writers from a variety of ideological allegiances.
Mary Shelley employs many of the motifs of Gothic in *Frankenstein*
(1818) and it is apparent that science fiction, too, finds its roots in
Gothic fiction. The convention which is common to both science
fiction and fantasy is estrangement, the use of setting, event and
character to distance the reader from the assumptions of realism,
from the categories by which the real is conventionally constructed.
This estrangement may be achieved by setting the novel in another
time; early Gothic was often set in the past when superstition and
belief in the supernatural were more credible to the rationalist
eighteenth-century reader. Early English Gothic was also often set in
another place, usually the Continent, where superstition was be-

lieved to be rife and all manner of strange events and characters were not only credible, but even assumed. From here it was a small step to the 'other world' fantasies of writers such as Poe, Kingsley, MacDonald, Morris, Carroll, Machen, Stoker, Kipling, Haggard. Nineteenth-century rereading and reworkings of Arthurian legend, of classical mythology and the Icelandic Eddas, as well as popular interest in sensational fiction (horror, ghost stories, tales of the supernatural) and recently translated collections of German folk-tales (including Grimm's *Marchen* (1823)) provided the literary background for their more or less radical questioning of the nature of the 'real'. This work includes stories set in another 'real' place and/or time (Kipling, Haggard, Morris, Poe), stories set in contemporary society into which intrude elements of the supernatural (Machen, Stoker, Poe), and stories set in a wholly other, sometimes faery, world (MacDonald, Kingsley, Carroll, Morris). Contemporary fantasy, including feminist fantasy, uses the last two settings extensively. The fantasy shelves of booksellers are heavily stocked with 'other world' stories: Tolkien's tales of Middle Earth, Stephen Donaldson's *The Chronicles of Thomas Covenant, the Unbeliever*, Patricia McKillip's *Riddle-Master of Hed* series, LeGuin's *Wizard of Earthsea* trilogy, Terry Brooks' Tolkien-inspired Shannara books, the prolific writings of Tanith Lee, Andre Norton's *Witchworld* series, Guy Gavriel Kay's *Fionavar Tapestry*, Barbara Hambly's *Darwath* trilogy, Elizabeth Lynn's *Chronicles of Tornor* and the *Darkover* novels of Marion Zimmer Bradley.

The works which deal with the intrusion of the supernatural into everyday life generally fall into the category of horror, which also traces its roots as a novelistic genre back to the Gothic fiction of the late eighteenth century. Its antecedents there include *The Mysteries of Udolpho*, in which the uncanny events of the narrative are naturalized, given a simple everyday explanation, and *The Castle of Otranto* (1764), in which they are not. In *The Mysteries of Udolpho* Radcliffe writes about differences of perception: Emily St. Aubert thinks she sees ghosts and rotting corpses, but is mistaken; she thinks her lover is imprisoned with her, but is mistaken; she thinks her aunt has been murdered by her uncle and, once again, she is mistaken. The novel dramatizes the problem of differing perceptions of the 'real', but in the end resolves the problem in favour of one 'commonsense' view. Radcliffe's novel thereby functions as an exemplary model of co-option or containment; a subversive non-hegemonic view is expressed, but is ultimately revealed as a mistaken understanding of the dominant subject position. All is resolved when that (patriarchal) subject position is adopted. With *The Castle of Otranto*, however, the reader is offered no such resolution. The enormous helmet which suddenly appears in the courtyard of the castle at the beginning of the book is never explained away; realist assumptions are undermined as Walpole signifies the breakdown of the established social order. In *The Castle of Otranto* the problem of perception remains.

Nineteenth-century horror fiction continued this equivocal inter-rogation of the real, with macabre events more often than not given a rational explanation. Again this resolution commonly signified the narrative reassertion of dominant discourses – Anglo-Saxon, middle-class, patriarchal, Protestant. Bram Stoker's *Dracula* is the obvious example. In texts such as *Dracula* socially subversive elements, including active female sexuality and the aristocratic remnants of the pre-bourgeois social order, are given voice in order to be silenced. As Rosemary Jackson notes:

> Very clearly with *The Lair of the White Worm*, but equally so with *Dracula*, Stoker reinforces social, class, racial and sexual prejudices. His fantasies betray the same tendency as many Victorian texts: they manipulate apparently non-political issues into forms which would serve the dominant ideology ... In the guise of its 'unnameable' absolute otherness, social realities are deformed and dismissed. The shadow on the edges of bourgeois culture is variously identified, as black, mad, primitive, criminal, socially deprived, deviant, crippled, or (when sexually assertive) female. Difficult or unpalatable social realities are distorted through many literary fantasies to emerge as melodrama-tic shapes: monsters, snakes, bats, vampires, dwarfs, hybrid beasts, devils, reflections, *femmes fatales*. Through this identification, trouble-some social elements can be destroyed in the name of exorcising the demonic. (Jackson, 1981 (C), pp. 121–2)

With literary horror, then, it is crucial to analyse not only the disruption of realist convention, but also the (discursive) nature of the disrupting elements, incidents and characters – and then to trace the resolution of the disruption. The very act of representing disruption is not, in itself, subversive, particularly when it becomes a means of containing and neutralizing discourses which are disruptive of domi-nant ideological discourses and the subject position they construct. When much twentieth-century horror, such as the work of contem-porary doyen, Stephen King, is subjected to this kind of analysis, its conservatism becomes clearly visible. Many of these texts, literary and cinematic, centre on a rape fantasy (*Hallowe'en*, *Cujo*, *Nightmare on Elm Street*), which is a contemporary expression of the fear of female sexuality dramatized earlier by Stoker. And just as Stoker's text was a response to the increasing volubility and visibility of the late nineteenth-century Women's Movement, so much contemporary horror, with its images of destructive female sexuality (*Fatal Attraction*) and/or potent male power (*Hallowe'en*), express the fear of contemporary masculine subjects at the increasing autonomy and self-determination of women repositioned by their acceptance of feminist discourse.

Contemporary feminist fantasy

Contemporary feminist fantasy is specifically concerned with the way gender ideologies construct 'reality' for the individual. For women living under patriarchy this (ideological) reality often has only tenuous links with their experiential reality. Patriarchal denials of discrimination against women, for example, find little support from the daily experience of most women. The reality of the men (and women) who accept that (patriarchal) discourse, therefore, differs substantially from that of the women who experience its constant contradiction. Similarly sexist discourse asserts that men and women are equal but different; yet, in practice, this discourse maintains men in positions of power and dominance and women in subordinate roles. Under patriarchy men and women are not equal but different; rather, men are dominant, women subordinate. Women are not autonomous subjects under patriarchy; they are the opposite or negation of men. The male/female dichotomy of patriarchy is deconstructed as male/not-male. Women are not subjects, not agents, not active; they are the negation by which men describe themselves as male. Femininity is the male construct which defines, not women, but masculinity. De Lauretis cites Lucy Irigaray in her formulation of the feminist response to this patriarchal real:

> I believe that to envision gender (men and women) otherwise, and to (re)construct it in terms other than those dictated by the patriarchal construct, we must walk out of the male-centred frame of reference in which gender and sexuality are (re)produced by the discourse of male sexuality – or, as Lucy Irigaray has so well written it, of hom(m)osexuality. (De Lauretis, 1987 (A), p. 17)

Feminist fantasists use fantasy literature as a means by which 'to envision gender (men and women) otherwise'. They avoid the reference frame of patriarchy by constructing textually a feminist reading position in which the male-centred categories of this patriarchal 'real' are deconstructed, in which the hom(m)osexuality of patriarchy no longer operates. Feminist fantasy fulfils Jackson's definition of the fantastic in that it 'draws attention to the relative nature of these [patriarchal] categories' by which the real is constructed and so 'moves towards a dismantling of the [patriarchal] "real"'. Suzy McKee Charnas discusses feminist fantasy in these terms:

> Feminist fantasy goes ... into areas of thought that allow us to think of ourselves in new ways (at its best it does this, anyway). And the funny thing is that this kind of thinking is actually a lot closer to the spirit of the Brontë sisters, who more or less put the oomph into Gothic fantasy which has lasted it till this day, then the crud that the 'women's' fantasists – many of them male – claim to be mining from the Brontë vein. *Jane Eyre* is *not* Sweet Savage Shit; it is, for its time, a bold assertion of the truth of certain aspects of women's interior lives – and exterior lives too, for that matter. This is what feminist fantasy continues to attempt, particularly in exploring hopes and fears and dreams we have that are still mainly in the realm of the mind; ideas about the future, ideas about the past.[5]

And, one need hardly add, about the present.

Feminist revisions of fairy-tale can also be traced to a nineteenth-century literary genre, the fairy-tale as popularized by the translation of folk-tales collected by the brothers Grimm. Since that time folk- and fairy-tales have been represented as suitable moral guidance for children and yet, as Zipes records in *Breaking the Magic Spell*:

> the folk tales were often censored and outlawed during the early phase of the bourgeoisie's rise to power because their fantastic components which encouraged imaginative play and free exploration were hostile to capitalist rationalization and the Protestant ethos. Once the bourgeoisie's power was firmly established, the tales were no longer considered immoral and dangerous, but their publication and distribution for children were actually encouraged toward the end of the nineteenth century. The tales took on a compensatory function for children and adults alike who experienced nothing but the frustration of their imaginations in society ... Like other forms of fantastic literature ... the tales no longer served their original purpose of clarifying social and natural phenomena but became forms of refuge and escape in that they made up for what people could not realize in society. (Zipes, 1979 (C), p. 174)

More significantly the tales were encoded with dominant ideological discourses – such as patriarchal gender ideology – and their function of 'clarifying social and natural phenomena' was enlisted in the construction of the subject position of patriarchal capitalism. This does not mean that the radical, imaginative function of the tales was lost, but that it existed in contradictory combination with a fundamentally conservative discursive practice which operated to contain and neutralize the subversive power of imagination. Contemporary feminist writings of these tales reveal their co-option by hegemonic ideologies and their role in the construction of the patriarchal subject, in the process constituting a feminist reading position which is fundamentally subversive of the subject position of patriarchal capitalism.

The final word on the subject of women and fairy-tale belongs to Carolyn Steedman. In *Landscape for a Good Woman* Steedman claims that (traditional) fairy-tales persist even in the social analysis of commentators such as Richard Hoggart and Jeremy Seabrook:

> Women are, in the sense that Hoggart and Seabrook present in their pictures of transition, without class, because the cut and fall of a skirt and good leather shoes can take you across the river and to the other side: the fairy-tales tell you that goose-girls can marry kings. (Steedman, 1986 (A), pp. 15–16)

The blindness of Hoggart and Seabrook to women's experiential reality is a function of their unquestioning acceptance of patriarchal gender ideology. These analysts of class ideology fail to perceive their own heterosexism. As a result they accept a mythical or ideological vision of the intersection of class and gender which is a propaganda tool of both patriarchal and bourgeois discourses: be a good girl, be attractive and dress nicely, and you will be privileged to cross that turbulent divide into the security, civility and power of the middle class. This bourgeois fairy-tale denies the autonomy and value of non-hegemonic class positioning, of working-class culture, in its assumption that the goose-girl wants to marry the king in the first place. Furthermore it conceals the economic inequality between the classes, the access to capital of the middle class which determines and defines its social dominance, just as effectively as did the 'Self Help' propaganda of the nineteenth (and late twentieth) century. The right cut of skirt comes from Pierre Cardin or Jean Muir, the shoes are hand-crafted Italian leather, the price is prohibitive.

Steedman raises a complex of issues around the ideology of gender, beginning with its interdependence with class ideology. Commentators who fail to recognize the relationship between these discourses in the case of women reduce women to Woman, denying the formation of female subjectivity as a negotiation of many discourses (for example gender, class, race) and instead substituting an idealist concept constructed in terms of sex-gender. At the same time such commentators reveal their vulnerability to bourgeois ideology which supresses the economic basis of class difference: just as any goose-girl can marry a king, any boy [sic] can be president. Significantly Steedman then evokes one of the means by which this gender-blindness is acculturated into individual subjectivity, the fairy-tale. It is in this area of the relationship between gender ideology, individual subjectivity and cultural production that feminist fantasy writers have attempted to intervene. As de Lauretis noted in *Technologies of Gender*, contemporary feminist writing no longer constructs the subject in terms of gender alone, but instead deals with 'a subject en-gendered in the experiencing of race and class, as well as sexual, relations' (1987 (A), p. 2). While little feminist fantasy directly addresses issues of race and class, the reading position constructed in these texts opposes the existing hegemonic order and its constitutive subject position. By constructing a feminist reading position via the inflection of feminist, rather than patriarchal, gender discourses, feminist fantasy necessarily involves readers in a renegotiation of their familiar, patriarchal capitalist, subject positioning. This intervention in the interpellation of the subject by hegemonic discourses plays a significant role in the undermining, the disempowering, of those discourses and goes some way toward answering Terry Lovell's critique of Jackson's work:

> Two different kinds of subversion have been elided in the 'fantastic as subversion' thesis: subversion of a socially constructed class society in which women are systematically subordinated to men; and subversion of a precarious psychic order which secures a viable personal identity for the individual within that social order. (Lovell, 1987 (A), p. 67)

The maintenance of a particular social formation is largely dependent on the interpellation of the individual subject by the discourses (of class, gender, race, etc.) which constitute and describe that formation. If fantasy literature can reposition readers to evaluate critically and oppose hegemonic discourses, so modifying their own subject position, then a modification of the social formation is inevitable: goose-girls may decide that regency jobs aren't all they're cracked up to be.

4

Feminist Utopias

I'll tell you how I turned into a man.
First I had to turn into a woman.
Joanna Russ, *The Female Man*

James Tiptree Jr. once wrote a charming E.T. type story called 'Angel Fix' about a terrifically good-natured alien called, for the sake of Earth-persons' convenience, Joe Smith (Tiptree, 1981 (D)). Joe has come to give to Earth's 'good guys' a device which enables them to travel to an uninhabited Earth-type planet for 'refreshment' from the unending battle with the 'bad guys'. The 'good guys' can take their friends with them, but never a 'bad guy' because then the gateway will close forever. Of course the 'good guys' he contacts – a boy named Marty, Whelan, a ranger and ecologist, a doctor, Marion Legersky, a Chippewa lawyer named Cleever, and a black university professor, Dr Lukas – are all especially pleased to find they have access to a non-polluted, uncolonized, unexploited wilderness. And the alien is happy, because he is a real estate agent, and the story ends with a rapturous conversation between Joe and his fellow aliens in different parts of the world:

> 'You can't guess what I ran into,' the voice chattered in his own language. 'A whole town full of heavy *disarmament* types! From all over. Place called Geneva. One of them's already planning to move his family out. How'd you do? Hey, is the *fremth* this good where you are?'
>
> 'Fantastic,' said the alien known as Joe. 'My group went beautifully, such nice people. I feel sure that they and their friends will decide to leave this planet permanently after a few visits.'
>
> 'Mine, too,' the voice chuckled. 'And as we always say, when all the good guys go, good-bye planet. How's Shusli doing? If he's having the same luck we'll have this place ready to go in no time.'

'Shusli here . . . Absolutely ripe. I tell you there won't be a sane mind left on this planet in a couple of their ridiculously short generations.'

'Yeah,' said Joe happily. 'I just hope the sickies don't mess the place too badly before they wipe themselves out . . . Listen, guys, we better start thinking about our sales brochures.' (p. 27)

Tiptree's story raises the central problem of utopian writing: is it merely an escape from an unpleasant reality or does it serve some political function? If the 'good guys' all remove themselves, one way or another (i.e. physically and/or imaginatively), from their own society, does this mean that the 'bad guys' will take over and destroy the society? And, if the 'good guys' do all go, then does that matter? Of course the real life possibility of such a complete departure is low; even separatist communities live within the boundaries of the dominant culture. Yet the question stands: since utopian texts are characterized by their textual construction of a society more perfect than the writer's and contemporary reader's own, which we might call the utopian figure (Marin, 1976 (D)), then does this utopian figure simply deflect the reader's attention from the very real inadequacies in her/his own society and so constitute an imaginative escape from that society, the political consequence of which is lack of engagement, of involvement, by the individual and the abandonment of the mechanisms of power to the exploitative, the corrupt, the 'bad guys'? Or can the utopian figure be used as part of a more complex textual and political strategy by the politically-committed writer to stimulate engagement by the reader with the inadequacies and injustices of her/his own society and so function as a challenge to those power mechanisms, both how they operate and/or who controls them?

Questions about the political efficacy of utopian writing became a part of socialist debate at the end of the nineteenth century, particularly after the publication of Friedrich Engels's pamphlet, *Socialism: Utopian and Scientific* (1882; English translation 1892). Engels was concerned that utopian writing, which had burgeoned during that century and received great impetus from Edward Bellamy's controversial utopian novel, *Looking Backward* (1887),[1] might divert readers from active intervention in the class struggle into wish-fulfilment fantasies and so effectively abandon the political arena to the bourgeoisie. Engels's objections to utopian writing focused on the impracticability of the utopian figure elaborated, and on the failures of the utopian communities established in the nineteenth century as a response to the kind of social vision presented in these writings:

The solution of the social problems, which as yet lay hidden in undeveloped economic conditions, the Utopians attempted to evolve out of the human brain. Society presented nothing but wrongs; to remove these was the task of reason. It was necessary, then, to discover a new and more perfect system of social order and to impose this on society from without by propaganda, and, wherever it was possible, by the example of model experiments. These new social systems were foredoomed as Utopian; the more completely they were worked out in detail, the more they could not avoid drifting off into pure phantasy. (Engels, 1954 (D), p. 40)

Engels's denunciation of the utopian figure focuses on its use as a blueprint for a future society. As a blueprint, Engels suggests, the utopian figure becomes increasingly fantastic – that is, impractical – as more detail is added. What Engels does not consider, however, is that the utopian figure may have another function in the text altogether, a function employed in his own time by William Morris in his utopian novel, *News from Nowhere*, and more recently theorized and fictionalized by critics such as Fredric Jameson, Louis Marin and E.P. Thompson[2] and by writers such as Joanna Russ, Marge Piercy, Ursula LeGuin and Samuel Delany. In the work of these writers and critics the utopian figure is viewed as part of a textual strategy aimed at politicizing readers through the deconstruction of dominant ideologies and the positioning of the reader as active subject. The notion of the utopian figure as blueprint is simply not relevant to their work and in fact constitutes a serious misreading of any but the most naïve utopian texts.

Generic history of utopian fiction

The seminal text of the utopian genre was Thomas More's *Utopia* (1516), written as the report in two books of the conversations between the traveller, Raphael Hythlodaeus and Thomas More, Citizen and Sheriff of London (More, 1964 (D)). In the first book More presents a debate about the nature of councillorship as the character More attempts to persuade Hythlodaeus to adopt this as a profession. This debate becomes an analysis of the state in More's own time, assisted by Hythlodaeus's interventions on the comparative social strategies of various countries he has visited in his travels. Only in Book Two does the reader encounter the island occupied by the Utopians, whose society avoids many of the injustices of More's (and the contemporary reader's) own society. This structuring of the text belies the notion of the utopian figure, here the island state of Utopia,

as a blueprint for a more just English society. Rather Book One
establishes the pattern of debate by which the text operates, as the
character More indicates: 'To be sure, just as he called attention to
many ill-advised customs among these new nations, so he rehearsed
not a few points from which our own cities, nations, races, and
kingdoms may take example for the correction of their errors' (p. 15).
In Book One the function of the text as an analysis by comparison of
Tudor English society is established, along with a textual apologetic
for the criticisms presented: they are the dutiful observations of the
honest and concerned councillor. In Book Two, then, More simply
follows his established pattern of debate, using the Utopian society as
a comparison by which to engage his own honest and concerned
critique of Tudor England. So, even in this earliest work of the genre
the utopian figure, Utopia itself, should not be read simply as the
blueprint for More's vision of a future or alternative England. Rather
it is a textual strategy employed by More to engage readers (in More's
time a select, educated minority) in a critical analysis of the customs
and institutions, the dominant ideological practices, of their own
time.

More's text provided the framework for subsequent utopian texts,
though the textual conventions used by More were modified to
account for changed social and political conditions. One of the major
conventions of utopian fiction, in common with other generic forms
such as science fiction and fantasy, is estrangement. Another world,
the utopian figure, is constructed in the text and the reader, in the
process of (re)constructing this figure, is positioned to see her/his
own society from a different perspective. Tom Moylan notes in his
excellent critical study *Demand the Impossible*:

> Opposed to other fantasy forms, utopias and science fiction practise an
> estrangement that is cognitively consistent with nature as it is known
> or with the imagined natural laws in the particular text. That is, the
> estranged world of utopia must appear realistic, must not partake of the
> impossibilities of the supernatural or the naturally undoable. (Moylan,
> 1986 (D), pp. 33–4)

This cognitive consistency, this realism, of the utopian figure is no
doubt the reason for its interpretation as a blueprint. However, if the
utopian figure is placed within the political practice of the text, then
its blueprint realism may be seen as serving an entirely different
function, that of reinforcing the constant direction of the reader back
to the realities of her/his own society. As each detail of the social
structure of the utopian figure is logically described, the implicit

comparison with that of the reader's own society is made. In this way a detailed (re)vision of the reader's society is constructed within the text – and this is the focus and function of the utopian text; the value of the utopian figure as alternative town planning is not an issue.

Other estrangement conventions include the geographical and temporal placement of this alternative society. In More's text the utopian figure is displaced only geographically from the contemporary reader's own society; the Utopian state is represented as operating simultaneously with the reader's own society, so reinforcing the comparison between the two states. Both are monarchies; both operate with a political infrastructure of councillors and bureaucrats; similar class structures function in both; but laws, domestic and social arrangements, political philosophy differ in complex and subtle ways. The reader is thereby positioned to question the mechanisms of her/his own society, because another social structure with apparent advantages over her/his own, but also many similarities, is shown operating simultaneously. In other words, the sense of inevitability, of naturalness, about the contemporary social order is challenged; the reader is positioned to see contemporary society differently.

Another estrangement convention More uses in *Utopia* is the traveller/guide Hythlodaeus. The details about the state of Utopia are given to the reader via the dialogues between Hythlodaeus and More – More representing the civilized and educated man of his time and Hythlodaeus the intelligent, critical and estranged commentator on More's (the contemporary reader's) society. Hythlodaeus's descriptions of other states, and particularly of Utopia itself, are the means by which the view of Tudor England as a natural state, an inevitable or commonsense political and social formation, is challenged. The educated sixteenth-century reader was positioned to appreciate the philosophical/political debate between these two characters, the sheriff and the reluctant, but well-qualified, councillor, and to include the points of argument in her/his own conjectures about the nature of the state. Hythlodaeus's arguments against the role of councillor do, of course, signify his suitability for, and fulfilment of, that role. More's own qualifications as sheriff and good citizen were widely known and accepted. In incorporating both the roles the reader is positioned as scholar and philosopher, just councillor and citizen. More's text is not a revolutionary intervention; it does not call for the overthrow of the monarchy or the eradication of classes. It does, however, position the reader as an active subject, or as one with the intelligence and wisdom to contribute to the reorganization of English society. In this respect *Utopia* has a role in the revolutionary change of English society from a feudal to a bourgeois state; the reader is positioned as bourgeois subject.

The characters of traveller/guide and contemporary citizen, their detailed conversations about alternative (including utopian) social formations, the construction of the utopian figure, its geographical displacement from the writer's (and contemporary reader's) own society are all estrangement conventions which were used by More's successors, so constituting the literary genre of utopian fiction. After 1516 utopias appeared at a steady rate but the next burst of utopian writing accompanied another major change in the political paradigm. As Ernst Bloch records in his book, *On Karl Marx*: 'Thomas More inaugurated a series of utopias in the bourgeois modern period, while Fourier marked the beginning of a trend to socialism as it became possible' (Moylan 1986 (D), p. 23).

The nineteenth century saw an extraordinary output of utopian writing, from the political and philosophical work of Fourier, Saint Simon and Owen to the more literary texts of Bellamy and Morris. In his article, 'Themes in utopian fiction in English before Wells' Lyman Tower Sargent estimates that between 1516 and 1895 about 400 utopias were published in English, of which approximately 320 appeared in the nineteenth century (Sargent, 1976 (D)). Sargent also notes that the catalytic effect of Bellamy's novel was so great that about half this number for the nineteenth century were written before 1887 and the other half between 1887 and 1896. There are several reasons for the impact of *Looking Backward*: the 1880s was a period of intense political activity in Western countries still negotiating the enormous social changes which accompanied the Industrial Revolution. In the 1880s political conflict involved not only socialist and labour groups versus the bourgeois state, but also internal dissension within the ranks of labour and socialist activists about the most efficient and/or ethical forms of opposition. Bellamy's text is a contradictory compendium of bourgeois and socialist attitudes and desires, and an expression of wonder and delight both in technological achievement and in the city. *Looking Backward* was condemned as both capitalist and communist, futuristic and retrogressive; it expressed a consciousness aware of the injustices of the capitalist state, but not prepared to reject that state, perhaps because of the added richness and complexity that the capitalist economic system seemed to have given to life. Bellamy's most influential critic was the English political activist, artist and writer, William Morris. Morris wrote a damning review of *Looking Backward* in which he traces Bellamy's entrapment within contemporary bourgeois ideology:

This temperament may be called the unmixed modern one, unhistoric and unartistic; it makes its owner (if a Socialist) perfectly satisfied with modern civilisation if only the injustice, misery, and waste of class society could be got rid of; which half-change seems possible to him. The only ideal of life which such a man can see is that of the industrious *professional* middle-class men of to-day purified from their crime of complicity with the monopolist class, and become independent instead of being, as they are now, parasitical. (Morris, 1889 (D), p. 194)

Morris went on to write his own utopian novel, *News from Nowhere*, which is, at least in part, a response to *Looking Backward*. Morris constructs a more self-conscious text than Bellamy, in both literary and political senses, but together the two texts represent the development of utopian writing to the end of the nineteenth century. Their modifications of the conventions introduced by More and their use of new conventions are indicative of changes in social and political thought and of an awareness of the role of fiction in the construction and maintenance of ideological discourses. These are the conventions with which contemporary feminist writers began to work, and this awareness of the ideological role of fiction became a fundamental proposition of feminist textual theory and practice.

As with *Utopia* estrangement is a fundamental characteristic of late nineteenth-century utopias. The work of both Bellamy and Morris engages the reader in a (re)construction of her/his own society, in *Looking Backward* late nineteenth-century America and in *News from Nowhere* late nineteenth-century England. However, in both these texts the displacement of the utopian figure is not geographical but temporal. Bellamy does not construct another society which operates at the same time as nineteenth-century Boston; rather his utopian figure is geographically located as Boston, but in the year 2000 AD. Similarly, Morris constructs a utopian figure on the site of nineteenth-century London, but projects it forward into the twenty-first century. The utopian figure of these texts is not another place by which the injustices of the reader's own society are revealed; rather it is the reader's own society purged of those injustices. Several reasons might be suggested for this change in textual strategy. The nineteenth century was a time of expanding travel, mostly as a result of imperialism. The notion of a society existing elsewhere on earth with such a radically different, but also similar, organization to that of the reader's own was no longer so acceptable: the blank spaces on the maps of imperialist powers, such as Britain and the United States, were rapidly being filled/colonized. A geographical Utopia at this time would be in imminent danger of invasion. Temporal displacement of the utopian figure solved this problem and had the added advantage of impressing very firmly on the reader that the focus of the text was her/his own society; after all, no other society was represented in these reworked utopian texts.

Another reason was the interest in historical process, perhaps most clearly exemplified at this time in the writings of Karl Marx. It was no longer sufficient to have a utopian figure simply be; it had to have a history. One of the most noted features of *News from Nowhere*, for example, is Morris's description of the revolution which led to the communist state of twenty-first century England. Again, however, the textual strategy is rarely one of naïve realism. Morris is not giving a blueprint for revolution any more than he is presenting a town plan for reconstructed (communist) London. Instead his historically placed utopian figure directs the reader to the processes of historical change, processes in which s/he may play an interventionist role as a socialist or radical activist. So long as a society is seen to be universal or permanent or impervious to the actions of individuals, it will seem irresistible. To make it seem so is the task of dominant ideological discourses, which position the reader as passive subject. The social critic who is concerned to effect change must alter the status of the individual subject from passive to active. In texts such as *News from Nowhere* the construction of a utopian figure which is temporally displaced and historically situated is essential to the production of an activist reading position.

The overdetermination of the utopian figure's geographical location is also essential to this process. Fredric Jameson notes of the utopian text:

> In the case of the Utopian narrative, the place of the Real ... may be identified by the obsessive references to actuality which seem part of the conventions of such texts, the perpetual play of topical allusion throughout the narrative which, intersecting the more properly diegetic interest, is constantly on the point of fragmenting the text into an anecdotal and discontinuous series of vertical indicators. (Jameson, 1977 (D), p. 7)

Both Bellamy and Morris constantly refer their readers to the location of their utopias, *News from Nowhere* reading as a virtual travelogue of London and its environs. Morris takes his reader on a suburb by suburb cart-ride through twenty-first century London, past well-known landmarks such as the Houses of Parliament and the Stock Exchange, and then on a trip up the Thames into Oxfordshire. As Jameson notes, the references to the reader's own 'reality' are

continuous and relentless, so that the narrative is always on the point
of fragmentation, its temporal development constantly interrupted.
Since the temporal unfolding of the narrative has a major role in its
naturalization procedures, and hence its ideological practice, the (late
nineteenth-century) utopian text can be read as a revaluation of
narrative practice, and hence of its ideological function. Utopian
narrative does not offer the comfortable, resolved reading position
often associated with narrative texts, because of this continual inter-
ruption, this continual referral of the reader to a problematic, often
alienating and hostile, real. This convention of the utopian text works
against a passive reading position and for the construction of an
engaged, activist reader, a reader not constrained by the narratives
which structure everyday events, beliefs and values, but one who
actively questions those ideological positions.

Another estrangement convention of the utopian text used by both
Morris and Bellamy is the utopian traveller or guide, though again the
nineteenth-century utopia writers modify the convention inherited
from More. Both replace the traveller-guide exemplified by Hythlodaeus with two separate characters, a utopian traveller who is a
member of the (contemporary) reader's own society and a guide who
is a member of the utopian society. The philosophical debate of *Utopia*
is replaced by a narrative in which a representative of the (contemporary) reader's society is guided through the utopia by one of its
citizens. The actantial roles of More and Hythlodaeus are redistri-
buted to produce a contemporary character with whom readers may
empathize (not necessarily such a well-known and respected character as More, but an average citizen instead) and a utopian character
who embodies in an individualist sense the values of the utopia. The
utopian citizen describes not only the present features of the utopian
state, but also its history – how it developed from the society of the
utopian traveller or visitor to its present, comparatively idyllic state.
The traveller or visitor embodies the common problems of the
reader's own society, its injustices, unwitting prejudices, antisocial
attitudes. Through this (empathetic) character readers are positioned
to confront their own similar injustices, prejudices, attitudes; this
character is one of the principal means by which the dominant
ideologies of the reader's own society are exposed *as ideology* and then
analysed. This character's reactions to the utopian citizen's description of the history of his/their society is also the reader's own and,
again, this is a means of positioning the reader; her/his objections to
the changes described are predicted and then forestalled.

As noted earlier, the purpose of this description of social change is not to provide a blueprint for the future, though the kinds of changes depicted are an essential part of the deconstruction of ideology which occurs in the text. Rather the confrontation of the utopian visitor with the process of change is a means of showing that such change is possible, that the social formation in which the reader is situated is not natural or obvious or inevitable, but a construction of particular parameters (economic, social, political) and therefore liable to transformation. For disaffected, alienated readers this message in itself might be encouraging and it is one of the reasons given by Morris for writing his utopian romance. It may also suggest to the reader that her/his own political position contributes to the maintenance, and therefore also to the transformation, of her/his own society. When this revelation of political responsibility, and therefore power, is allied with the demystifying operation of the fragmented utopian narrative, the reading position produced is active, engaging the reader in a revaluation of contemporary ideological practices and of the role of the individual subject.

The reading position of the nineteenth-century utopia was also partly determined by the mechanism used by the writer to transport the utopian visitor to the utopian state. This was a new utopian convention, necessitated by the realignment of actantial roles and the practice of displacing the utopian state in time rather than, as in More's *Utopia*, in space. The usual explanation for the visitor's temporal displacement was some kind of dream or dream-like state. In *Looking Backward* Edward Bellamy used a mesmeric trance to transport his visitor, Julian West, to Boston in the year 2000 AD. West's trance is represented as a pathological episode; once awakened he is stranded in the future. There was at least one precedent for Bellamy's use of the mesmeric trance. A utopia first published in 1883 as *The Diothas: or, a Far Look Ahead* and reissued in 1890 as *Looking Forward, or the Diothas* by J. MacNie uses a trance to transport the visitor, Thiusen into the future (MacNie, 1889 (D)). In MacNie's text, however, the mesmeric trance is finally broken and Thiusen finds himself back in nineteenth-century America. Morris uses dream in the same way as MacNie, returning his visitor, Guest, to nineteenth-century London at the conclusion of his journey through twenty-first century Oxfordshire. By leaving West in the future Bellamy situates a point of closure within the text which effectively removes his visitor (and the empathizing contemporary reader) from engagement with the ideological practices of nineteenth-century society. Though estrangement techniques have been used throughout the text, so positioning readers to see their own society differently and to re-evaluate it, this closing strategy seems to undermine those functions of the text which produce an active reading position. Bellamy resolves his text in the future; readers can passively enjoy with West the delights of a life removed from nineteenth-century social injustice. In this sense *Looking Backward* fulfils Engels's worst fears about the utopia; that it is, in Engels's sense, fantastic, removed from the realities of everyday life. Bellamy's readers are offered the opportunity, against which Engels protested, of removing themselves imaginatively from their own society; they thereby become passive subjects of the bourgeois state. Morris's text, on the other hand, situates its point of closure at Guest's return to the harrowing conditions of nineteenth-century Britain, embodied in an old man:

> As I turned round the corner which led to the remains of the village cross, I came upon a figure strangely contrasting with the joyous, beautiful people I had left behind in the church. It was a man who looked old, but whom I knew from habit, now half-forgotten, was really not much more than fifty. His face was rugged, and grimed rather than dirty; his eyes dull and bleared; his body bent, his calves thin and spindly, his feet dragging and limping. His clothing was a mixture of dirt and rags long over-familiar to me. As I passed him he touched his hat with some real goodwill and courtesy, and much servility. (Morris, 1970 (D), p. 181)

The book ends with Guest musing on the utopians' last message to him and on his own commitment to activism:

> 'Go back and be the happier for having seen us, for having added a little hope to your struggle. Go on living while you may, striving, with whatsoever pain and labour needs must be, to build up little by little the new day of fellowship, and rest, and happiness.'
> Yes, surely! and if others can see it as I have seen it, then it may be called a vision rather than a dream. (p. 182)

His last statement spells out the difference between *News from Nowhere* and *Looking Backward*. Bellamy's text is a dream because it ends by disengaging the reader from the social critique presented, however proficiently, in the text. *News from Nowhere* continues throughout the political and textual reflexivity which is the strategy of the utopia, and ends characteristically by confronting readers with an image of the social injustice which is the focus of the book, the antithesis of the utopian figure, and then delivering a final warning that, unless the utopian figure is a part of readers' political activism, it will be nothing more than a dream, Engels's 'phantasy'.

Another convention introduced into the utopia in the nineteenth century was the love story. The form of closure used in the text was often determined by the treatment of the love story, and once again Bellamy and Morris are in direct opposition. Bellamy's West and Morris's Guest both fall in love in the course of their narratives but their relationships end very differently. In the final chapter of *Looking Backward* Julian West dreams about the nineteenth century, a horrific nightmare from which he returns to the twenty-first century and his love, Edith Leete: 'Kneeling before her, with my face in the dust, I confessed with tears how little was my worth to breathe the air of this golden century, and how infinitely less to wear upon my breast its consummate flower' (p. 119). With this conclusion of his romance Bellamy confirms the closure of the narrative in the utopian society; the utopian figure is thus given a status within the text formerly reserved for the text's absent referent, the writer's and contemporary reader's own society. Louis Marin wrote of the utopia: 'utopia as a figure within discourse refers to that which is not *of* that discourse: it opens onto the very end of discourse itself. It does not *signify* reality, but rather indicates it discursively' (Marin, 1976 (D), p. 72). Bellamy's conclusion diverges from this practice, resolving narrative conflict in terms of the utopian figure, and situating the reader unproblematical-ly, that is, passively, in relation to the utopian text. In *News from Nowhere*, on the other hand, the love story ends unhappily. Guest and his love, Ellen are not only separated; she forgets his existence entirely: 'I returned to Ellen, and she *did* seem to recognize me for an instant; but her bright face turned sad directly, and she shook her head with a mournful look, and the next moment all consciousness of my presence had faded from her face' (p. 181). Soon afterwards Guest finds himself back in his own time, distressed by the social injustices among which he lives, but determined to work for change. Through Guest Morris establishes the utopian figure as a political strategy; its absent referent is established as Guest's/Morris's/the reader's own society. By returning Guest to the only real indicated in the text, the (contemporary) reader's own society, Morris prevents an unprob-lematic resolution of the utopian narrative. In fact Guest explicitly problematizes the reader's relation to both the text and her/his own society. By breaking the romance convention of the happy ending Morris reinforces his rejection of both the naturalizing function of narrative and the ideology which situates the reader passively in relation to contemporary society. The reading position Morris pro-duces in *News from Nowhere* is that of a nineteenth-century socialist, actively interrogating contemporary dominant ideological discourses and the means by which those discourses are naturalized in everyday life.

Morris's textual reflexivity has already been noted, but its frequency is worth emphasizing. In fact this explicit reflection on textual practice is so effectively integrated with the practice of the utopian text that it seems a convention in itself. In *News from Nowhere* Morris precedes his description of the revolution which changed Britain to a communist state with a chapter dealing with the value and function of works of art. Dick Hammond, Guest's guide through the utopia, and his grandfather, Hammond the historian, champion the value of imaginative art-forms, fantasy and myth, against realist art on the ground that realism rarely addresses the everyday – as Old Hammond explains:

> It is true that in the nineteenth century, when there was so little art and so much talk about it, there was a theory that art and imaginative literature ought to deal with contemporary life; but they never did so; for, if there was any pretense of it, the author always took care ... to disguise, or exaggerate, or idealise, and in some way or another make it strange; so that, for all the verisimilitude there was, he might just as well have dealt with the times of the Pharaohs. (pp. 86–7)

In other words, realist art is an ideological construct by which the realities of everyday life were effectively disguised; art, itself, is ideological. Later in the story Ellen, Guest's love, offers a similar denunication of realism:

> But I say flatly that in spite of all their cleverness and vigour, and capacity for story-telling, there is something loathsome about them. Some of them, indeed, do here and there show some feeling for those whom the history-books call 'poor,' and of the misery of whose lives we have some inkling; but presently they give it up, and towards the end of the story we must be contented to see the hero and heroine living happily in an island of bliss on other people's troubles; and that after a long series of sham troubles (or mostly sham) of their own making, illustrated by dreary introspective nonsense about their feelings and aspirations, and all the rest of it; while the world must even then have gone on its way, and dug and sewed and baked and built and carpentered round about these useless – animals. (pp. 129–30)

The juxtaposition of the description of revolution with an evaluation of the ideological function of art positions the reader to perceive that description not as realism of any kind, not as a blueprint, but as a textual strategy in a work which focuses not on a blueprint, but on her/his own society. Ellen's comment constitutes an aberrant or subversive reading of the realist novel and again what it draws to readers' attention is the strategic operation of the text, the textuality or constructedness of the text, and the ideological determinants of that construction. By refusing a simplistic resolution to the novel, constantly referring readers to the narrative mechanism, characteristically directing readers to their own society, the discursive referent of the utopian figure, Morris constructs a reading position for an active, interrogative reader: the nineteenth-century socialist subject.

The status of the utopian text at the beginning of the twentieth century was represented by both Bellamy and Morris, Bellamy's work being indicative of the politically and textually naïve writer about whom Engels expressed concern. Though Morris also received Engels's scorn, his writing is innovative and sophisticated, politically and textually self-conscious. In *News from Nowhere* can be found the antecedents of many of the strategies employed by politically conscious twentieth-century writers of utopias, including feminist writers. Contemporary feminist utopias have another well-known antecedent, however, and that is Charlotte Perkins Gilman's *Herland*, written in 1916 (Gilman, 1979 (D)).

Herland is an interesting mixture of old and new utopian conventions. The displacement of the utopian state of Herland, for example, is geographical rather than temporal. In this the text looks back to More's *Utopia*. Yet this depiction of a society cut off from the rest of the world was not without contemporary precedent; Arthur Conan Doyle's *The Lost World*, about a prehistoric world isolated from evolutionary change on a remote mountain top, was first published in 1912 and, in 1914, with *At the Earth's Core*, Edgar Rice Burroughs began his series of novels set at the centre of the world. In fact *Herland* owes as much to the genre of science fiction as it does to the utopia proper. Gilman replaces the debate or question and answer sessions which characterize the interaction between utopian visitor and guide(s) with the narrative of discovery common in SF texts. Her utopian visitors, Terry, Jeff and Vandyck, fly into the all-woman country of Herland with very different expectations and behaviour patterns. Terry is rich, an adventurer and a playboy. His attitude toward women is cavalier; they are objects for his use. Terry envisages Herland as a summer resort, 'just Girls and Girls and Girls' (p. 7). Terry's behaviour has a sinister side, however, as revealed in his response to the native guide's fear of this country of women: 'No place for men? Dangerous? He looked as if he might shin up the waterfall on the spot' (p. 5). Terry's exploitative behaviour is a function of his male supremacist ideology, his sexism, which results in not only a total inability to comprehend the difference of Herland from his own society (Terry is totally blinkered by his ideology), but also violence which ranges from common assault to attempted rape. Terry has no conception of women as individuals; as Vandyck later explains:

> When we say *men, man, manly, manhood,* and all the other masculine derivatives, we have in the background of our minds a huge vague crowded picture of the world and all its activities ... That vast background is full of marching columns of men, of changing lines of men, of long processions of men; of men steering their ships into new seas, exploring unknown mountains, breaking horses, herding cattle, ploughing and sowing and reaping, toiling at the forge and the furnace, digging in the mine, building roads and bridges and high cathedrals, managing great businesses, teaching in all the colleges, preaching in all the churches; of men everywhere, doing everything – 'the world.'
> And when we say *women,* we think female – the sex. (p. 137)

This same inability to perceive women as individuals, as subjects, is evident also in the idealist and dreamer, Jeff.

Jeff idealizes women and looks forward to Herland as a country 'just blossoming with roses and babies and canaries and tidies, and all that sort of thing' (p. 7). As Gilman goes on to show, this attitude is equally culpable and possibly even more insidious, in that it is not directly offensive but rather subversive of women's fight for self-determination. Jeff, too, denies women the status of subject; they are the objects by which he defines himself as subject. Vandyck, the narrator, is a sociologist, an observer, but his observations are filtered through the lens of his sexism. As the men first fly over Herland, Vandyck declares: 'But they look – why, this is a *civilized* country! ... There must be men' (p. 11). Gilman's use of Vandyck as narrator is provocative, a male character being shown through a feminist state, but her definition of his prejudices serves a specific purpose. Terry and Jeff are common masculine types, the adventurer and the romantic dreamer, and they treat women according to the dominant stereotype of whore/virgin; women are either good (in which case they will be virgins and eventually, within the confines of marriage, mothers) or bad (in which case they are just whores). Gilman's text shows not only how these stereotypes determine the interactions between women and men, but also that they are two sides of the one coin, dependent on each other, and so equally dangerous to women. Vandyck is slightly different. As a sociologist he claims objectivity in his observations of behaviour: 'I held a middle ground, highly scientific, of course, and used to argue learnedly about the physiological limitations of the sex' (p. 9). As noted above, Gilman subsequently reveals that Vandyck's 'objectivity' is compromised by the sexist ideology he has inculcated. This explanation of the way that ideological discourses permeate scientific disciplines, including the relatively new discursive field of sociology, is crucial for feminism, given the influence of such disciplines on the lives of women, via their input into government policy, and business practice.

Vandyck is also the authoritative male narrator, like Fenton from 'The Women Men Don't See', and, like Fenton, he is seriously flawed. Fenton is not the he-man stereotype after which he, like Terry, patterns his behaviour, and Vandyck is not the detached social observer he claims to be. Gilman, like Tiptree, thereby challenges this narrative role, although Gilman simultaneously preserves the role; we only hear about Vandyck's sexist behaviour and his subsequent re-education from Van himself. The reason for Gilman's maintenance of the male narrator as (self-critical) authority probably lies with contemporary literary and social prejudices, which, paradoxically, arise from the sexism her utopia works to deconstruct. Yet Gilman manipulates the role in such a way that a reflection on its practice is incorporated into the text. Even with a male narrator the reading position constructed in this text is feminist.

Unlike Terry, Vandyck and, to some extent, Jeff, learn from their experience in Herland. They begin to understand that femininity is not a physiological characteristic, but an ideological construct, as is masculinity. In terms that later find an echo in LeGuin's *The Left Hand of Darkness* (LeGuin, 1981 (B), p. 86) Jeff complains: 'They don't seem to notice our being men. They treat us – well – just as they do one another. It's as if our being men was a minor incident.' Terry, Jeff and Vandyck are the means by which Gilman exposes the sexism in early twentieth-century US society. Again this is not a utopia as a blueprint; Gilman is not arguing for the development of parthenogenesis and the killing of all men. The absent referent of this utopian figure is the writer's and contemporary reader's own society.

Gilman also uses the love story convention. Terry, Jeff and Vandyck all fall in love in the course of the narrative but the outcomes of their relationships are very different. Vandyck and Jeff have successful relationships, though it remains doubtful whether Jeff's attitude has changed completely. It is therefore highly significant that Jeff does not leave Herland with Terry and Vandyck, but remains with his wife, Celis. Jeff is not yet able to sustain his feminism in the context of his own, sexist society. Vandyck leaves Herland with his wife, Ellador, she to consider the wisdom of Herland opening communication with the outside world, he to consolidate what he has learned in Herland by interaction with his own society. Terry, on the other hand, is expelled from Herland without his wife, Alima. He has learned nothing about women; he is still unable to perceive them as individual subjects. When Alima does not respond immediately to his sexual advances:

> Terry put in practice his pet conviction that a woman loves to be mastered, and by sheer brute force, in all the passion and pride of his intense masculinity, he tried to master this woman.
> It did not work. (p. 132)

Terry does not understand Alima's refusal to accept his domination, because of his uncritical acceptance of the power relationship between women and men specified by the dominant gender ideology of his own society. Terry attempts to rape her and, as Vandyck ruefully notes, 'In a court in our country he would have been held "quite within his rights"' (p. 132). In Terry's behaviour Gilman reveals the violence endemic to sexism. Between them the three love stories represent the kinds of relationships possible in early twentieth-century society: the violence of sexist relationships based on domination by the male partner, the unreality of relationships based on idealization (Gilman suggesting that such relationships cannot survive the conditions of twentieth-century society), and the socially aberrant or subversive egalitarian relationship. As in *Looking Backward* and *News from Nowhere* the conclusions of the love stories mark the conclusion of the narrative. By ending *Herland* with the imminent departure for the US of the most successful couple, Ellador and Vandyck, Gilman avoids containment of the narrative within the utopian figure which, as noted with *Looking Backward*, has political consequences. Instead the final chapter of *Herland* contains lengthy meditations on the nature of the society to which Vandyck is to return:

> 'Why should I want to go back to all our noise and dirt, our vice and crime, our disease and degeneracy?' [Jeff] demanded of me privately. We never spoke like that before the women. 'I wouldn't take Celis there for anything on earth!' he protested, 'She'd die! She'd die of horror and shame to see our slums and hospitals.' (p. 133)

The novel concludes with Ellador and Vandyck preparing to engage with these conditions, as must the reader. Like the communist society

of Morris's *News From Nowhere* the utopian figure of Herland is a
strategy in this engagement with the real, the discursive referent of
that figure.

One other feature *Herland* shares with *News from Nowhere* is a
revolutionary past. Herland was once a country of polygamous,
slave-owning people. Cut off from the outside world by a volcanic
eruption at a time when most of the country's fighting men were
away, the country was left in the hands of a few men, many slaves
and the women.

> [the slaves] now seized their opportunity, rose in revolt, killed their
> remaining masters even to the youngest boy, killed the old women too,
> and the mothers, intending to take possession of the country with the
> remaining women and girls.
> But this succession of misfortunes was too much for those infuriated
> virgins. There were many of them, and but few of these would-be
> masters, so the young women, instead of submitting, rose in sheer
> desperation and slew their brutal conquerors. (p. 55)

This expression of the anger of women treated as possessions is
indicative of an active subject position, women demanding to be
treated as subjects rather than accepting their relegation as objects.
Like Morris's description of the revolution which transformed England into a communist state, Gilman's revolution is not a blueprint for
the future, but a deconstruction of the conservative ideological
position that the contemporary social formation is natural or obvious
or inevitable. Gilman suggests that it is not natural, obvious or
inevitable that women are objectified, exploited and abused; it is a
function of a particular ideology which women (and men) can choose
to oppose.

Gilman's *Herland* employs many of the estrangement techniques of
the traditional utopia: the utopian figure displaced geographically
from the writer's and contemporary reader's own society; the utopian
travellers, here three representative males, the playboy, the artistic
dreamer, and the scientist; the utopian guide(s), various utopian
citizens who instruct the men about the history and operation of their
society. As in the late nineteenth-century utopias the representatives
of contemporary society reveal in their actions and opinions the
ideological discourses of their own society. Most importantly they
reveal those discourses *as* ideological constructs, not biological or
historical inevitabilities. Gilman's use of the nineteenth-century convention of the love story and her sustained use of the quest narrative,
typical of much contemporary science fiction, aid this deconstructive

process. In fact Gilman's text innovatively elides the two related genres, making maximum use of the estrangement conventions characteristic of both and employing the SF narrative to break through the prolonged debate conventional in the utopia but decidedly outmoded by realism. *Herland* is one of the earliest feminist utopias to exhibit political and textual sophistication and to construct a feminist reading position as a strategy in the production of a feminist subject.

In the next half-century dystopias replaced utopias as a popular form. Where utopias feature the textual representation of a society which is somehow better than the writer's and contemporary reader's own, dystopias feature a society apparently worse than the writer's/reader's own. Yevgeny Zamyatin's *We* (1923), Aldous Huxley's *Brave New World* (1932) and George Orwell's *Nineteen Eighty-Four* (1949) replaced the utopian visions of Morris and Gilman. As suggested earlier, it may be that the instability in Western society during this period – which included two world wars and a major depression – may account at least in part for the paucity of utopias. While utopias and dystopias share many conventions, primarily that of estrangement, there are also crucial differences between them. The essential difference between the utopian and dystopian figure is that the former discursively indicates the real, the latter signifies the real. Zamyatin, Huxley and Orwell were not writing about their own societies using another society displaced geographically or temporally; they were presenting a displaced view of their own societies. Their dystopias are not projections of the future of their own societies; they were representations of the present of those societies. Dystopian narratives usually feature a member of the dystopian state as main character. In describing her/his life the text details the horrific nature of the state. The textual strategy of the dystopia combines empathy with this main character and recognition of the contemporaneity of the social formation described to produce a critique of the writer's/reader's own society. The problem with dystopias is that readers commonly fail to recognize the dystopian society as a representation of their own real (though the banning of *We* in Russia in 1923 suggests that state officials understood Zamyatin's text well enough). If readers do not make this connection, they commonly turn back in relief to the relative ease of their own state, paradoxically the subject of the dystopia. Tom Moylan notes of the dystopia:

> the dystopian narrative itself has all too easily been recruited into the
> ideological attack on authentic utopian expression: commentators cite

the dystopia as a sign of the very failure of utopia and consequently urge uneasy readers to settle for what is and cease their frustrating dreams of a better life ... they [dystopias] serve as an artificially negative utopian zone employed by the hegemonic system to absorb resistance. (Moylan, 1986 (D), p. 9)

When utopias began to appear again, therefore, they had behind them both the recent developments within the utopian genre and the ambiguous political achievement of the companion genre of dystopia which had preoccupied writers and readers for the preceding 40 to 50 years.

As noted earlier, the literary genre of utopia is a response to changes in economic and political ideologies. As with all texts, the ideologies embedded in the utopian text, constitutive of that text, are those of the society in which the text was produced, though utopias articulate marginalized discourses more frequently than less politically concerned texts. However, utopias are also concerned specifically with the process of change itself; they focus not so much on the content of the changes occurring in society, as on the fact that change occurs, that it is possible. It was noted that More's *Utopia* is an exercise in the formation of the bourgeois subject and that many nineteenth-century utopias intervene in the construction of the socialist subject. In *Demand the Impossible* Moylan discusses the conditions of production of the utopia in a post-modern society:

> The romance and the utopia practice a narrative figuration centred around social structure and conflict, between good and evil or what is and what is not yet, that is especially suited to transitional moments such as our own in which two distinct modes of production coexist and contend: for us, the shift from monopoly to transnational capitalism, from industrial/mechanical society to post-industrial cybernetic society, from modern to post-modern culture, from democratic participation to bureaucratic management. (p. 43)

Moylan also notes that contemporary utopian thought is the product of what he terms an 'anti-hegemonic bloc' comprising three main areas of political debate: 'feminism, ecology, and self-management both of the workplace and of the sphere of daily life' (p. 27). The particularity of these debates demanded the abandonment of notions of an all-encompassing social or political theory, and this is one of the characteristics of the postmodern consciousness formed in this time of economic change. Some recent utopias, such as Samuel Delany's impressive novel, *Triton* (Delany, 1976 (D)) address the formation of postmodern consciousness via the articulation of many of these political debates. At the same time Delany subverts the naturalizing narrative structure with a framing critical apparatus which challenges the operation of narrative itself. This deliberate blurring of the boundaries between the two discursive operations, fiction and criticism, with its implicit challenge to notions of authority, is also characteristic of postmodernism. Ursula LeGuin's utopia, *The Dispossessed* (LeGuin, 1974 (D)) investigates different socio-economic systems and their consequences for the individual, LeGuin building a critique into her utopian figure which justifies the book's subtitle, 'An Ambiguous Utopia'. The majority of recent utopias, however, are explicitly feminist: Dorothy Byant's *The Kin of Ata Are Waiting for You* (published first as *The Comforter* in 1971), Joanna Russ's *The Female Man* (1975), Mary Staton's *From the Legend of Biel* (1975), James Tiptree Jr.'s 'Houston, Houston, Do You Read?' (1976), Marge Piercy's *Woman on the Edge of Time* (1976), Suzy McKee Charnas's *Motherlines* (1978) and Sally Miller Gearhart's *The Wanderground* (1978). While these books are part of the constitution of the postmodern consciousness and use many of the techniques of postmodern writing, their primary political concern is with patriarchal gender ideology and its social and political practice. Russ's book was perhaps the most influential of these, being known in the science fiction community for some years before its publication. Moylan notes that although completed in 1971 the book was '[u]nable to find a publisher because the feminist polemic and experimental narration put off editors in the male-dominated world of science fiction publishing' (p. 57). The literary and political intelligence of *The Female Man* found an appropriate successor in Piercy's *Woman on the Edge of Time*, and these two books serve as the focus of my analysis of contemporary feminist utopian fiction. Before starting this analysis it is worth noting and commenting on the feminist dystopia which was also written during the 1970s: at this time of great political optimism and activism by the members of the 'anti-hegemonic bloc.'

Feminist utopian and anti-utopian fiction

Suzy McKee Charnas's dystopia, *Walk to the End of the World* (Charnas, 1978 (D)) articulates many of the gender issues addressed in the feminist utopias. Charnas's dystopia is set in a post-nuclear war society ruled by the descendants of the generals and politicians who had access to nuclear shelters. The men were unable to accept their responsibility for the war, however, and so devolved it on to the functionaries who accompanied them into the shelters, their secretaries, who were women. The society is therefore divided on gender lines with men continuing their oppressive pre-holocaust regime, with their hatred, distrust and fear of women institutionalized. The narrative is divided between four characters: Kelmz who is Captain of a team of Rovers, men who have so inculcated *machismo* that they kill women on sight and have to be kept drugged and manacled, the ultimate heavy-metal warriors; Servan D Layo, a kind of hippie outcast who implicitly supports the post-holocaust society of Hold-fast by supplying its members with the drugs needed to endure their appalling society; Eykar Bek, a man who thinks he is enlightened, that he understands something of women's oppression, but who still cannot allow women autonomy or the independence to state their own case and resorts finally to rape as a means of consolidating his power position; and Alldera, a woman who is intelligent and strong enough to have survived this brutal society and who eventually escapes into the devastated 'Wild' to join the itinerant bands of women known as the Free Fems. Charnas's narratives thus represent a range of ideological positions available in the 1970s: the man whose subjectivity is constituted entirely in terms of his society's hom-(m)osexuality; the man who, like women, operates in a marginal role in his own society, but who is still privileged with one right by patriarchy, the power to exploit women; the man who perceives that this ideology is unjust but is unable to deny the power that ideology offers him; and the activist woman who decides to reject the victim role in which she is placed by her society's dominant gender ideology.

By dividing her narrative Charnas prevents a simplistic identification with any one of these characters, achieving the distancing and estranging effect conventional with the utopia. The process of comparison with the writer's and reader's own society is thereby initiated so that familiar social and ideological practices are exposed *as ideology* and analysed accordingly. The reader is positioned by a feminist discourse in terms of which the gender ideology of this society is made visible. Characteristically this oppressive ideology and the invidious social practices it engenders are revealed as those of the (contemporary) reader's own, not as worse than contemporary society. The ideological practices represented are those of the reader's own society divested of their familiar justifications, biological, psychological, religious, social. Charnas represents a brutalized society not as a future projection of her own society, but as the demystified reality of that society. The characteristic problem with the dystopia, that readers might be so pleased that the dystopian society is superficially dissimilar from their own that they miss the critique it generates, is obviated to some extent by Charnas's use of multiple narrators and her avoidance of textual closure within the boundaries of the dysto-pian figure; her text ends optimistically with Alldera free and about to begin, not end, her journey:

> A tune began in her head, weaving itself into the beginnings of a step-song for the journey: 'Unmen, the heroes are gone . . .' Without another glance back she started uphill with the slow gait of a runner warming up for a long, hard run.' (p. 246)

In company with the independent women of the 'Wild' Alldera and her daughter will find a life which, although not free from conflict or ideal, is superior to the brutalization endemic to the male-dominated society into which Alldera was born. The story is continued in Charnas's utopia, *Motherlines*.

Recent feminist utopias use many of the conventions of the late nineteenth-century utopias such as *News from Nowhere*, utilizing similar textual strategies in the construction of an activist reading position. Feminist writers also introduce modifications of the conven-tions appropriate to their own gender ideology. As noted earlier, the two works on which this analysis focuses are Joanna Russ's *The Female Man*, (Russ, 1985 (D)), as controversial and influential as Bellamy's *Looking Backward* in its time, and Marge Piercy's *Woman on the Edge of Time* (Piercy, 1979 (D)), another major work of the genre which shares many innovations with *The Female Man* but also features significant differences, both literary and political.

Both Russ and Piercy significantly modify the character of the utopian traveller and/or guide. In *The Female Man* Russ features four main characters: Joanna, the writer of the book, who is from the present; Jeannine from our world if the 1930s depression had not ended and the Second World War not happened, a society in which women are pressured into unfulfilling, exploitative roles which involve economic and emotional dependence on men; Janet from the planet Whileaway, a future version of earth on which there have been no men for hundreds of years, the utopian figure of this complex text; and Jael, the female warrior from another earth where men and women live in open combat. Jael expresses the anger of women who have had to play the 'female' games of sexist society; from the utopian displacement of Whileaway Janet exposes the absurdity and brutality of those games and of the definition and delimitation of women in our society; Jeannine tells us where we came from, how economic dependence engenders emotional dependence, physical limitation, political passivity; and Joanna is the contemporary woman attempting to negotiate the conflicting ideological discourses which characterize contemporary society and to evaluate them experientially. These four characters are essentially one character, the contemporary woman, fighting for autonomy in a sexist society against the institutionalized domination by men and her own inculcation of enervating discourses which position her as victim, object, prize. Through the interaction of the four Js Russ constructs a dialogue, the resolution of which is the need for feminist activism. And, since one of the four Js is a representative of contemporary society, that activist consciousness is also textually located in the present. The reading position of the text as the site at which this dialogue is intelligible and resolved is, therefore, one of feminist activism.

Marge Piercy constructs a similar reading position in *Woman on the Edge of Time*. Piercy uses two main characters, who occupy the conventional positions of utopian visitor or traveller, here Connie Ramos, a Chicana woman hospitalized as mentally disturbed by an intolerant, repressive society, and utopian guide, Luciente. As Moylan notes, the personal histories of the two characters reveal Luciente as the 'utopian analog of Connie':

> similar in appearance to Connie, though slimmer and healthier, who has lovers who match Connie's young husband, Eddie, and old lover, Claud, who has a daughter the age of Connie's lost daughter Angelina, who is psychologically sensitive like Connie, and who has gone on to be a scientist as Connie might have in a more just society. (Moylan, 1986 (D), p. 141)

In other words, Luciente is what Connie might have been in a different, just and equitable, social structure. The comparison between the two, their physical appearance and emotional vitality, the trajectory of their lives, their relationships with lovers and child, their professional achievement, is a terrible indictment of Connie's world, which is contemporary US society. The problematic invoked by the comparison is how Connie might become Luciente, not in a utopian future, but here and now. Textually the solution is political activism:

> 'Can I give you tactics?' Bee turned his chin back toward him. 'There's always a thing you can deny an oppressor, if only your allegiance. Your belief. Your co-opting. Often even with vastly unequal power, you can find or force an opening to fight back. In your time many without power found ways to fight. Till that became a power.' (p.328)

> 'Oh, yes.' She forced a stiff smile. 'I want to get well now.' War, she thought, I'm at war. No more fantasies, no more hopes. *War*. (p. 338)

'We can imagine all we like. But we got to do something real,' Connie said plaintively . . . (p. 343)

Never had she done such a thing, grabbed at power, at a weapon. She did not intend to go Skips' way. Yes, she had stolen a weapon. War, she thought again. She would fight back. (p.363)

'Power *is* violence. When did it get destroyed peacefully? We all fight when we're back to the wall – or to tear down a wall.' (p. 370)

'I just killed six people,' she said to the mirror, but she washed her hands because she was terrified of the poison. 'I murdered them dead. Because *they* are the violence-prone. Theirs is the money and the power, theirs the poisons that slow the mind and dull the heart. Theirs are the powers of life and death. I killed them because it is war . . . I'm a dead woman now too. I know it. But I did fight them. I'm not ashamed. I tried.' (p. 375)

Connie fights the institutionalized violence of the welfare and asylum systems with a crude physical violence which is a demystification of her own treatment by her society. Piercy is not thereby arguing for the violent overthrow of the social and political institutions of American society; Connie's actions are not a blueprint for political activism. However, Piercy does argue for engagement in the struggle with oppressive ideologies and their social practice. Connie's story reveals the violence endemic to the ideologies of gender, race and class dominant in her society; those ideologies must be revealed, analysed, and eradicated so that their violence is also removed.

A modification of utopian convention featured in both utopias is the use of a representation of contemporary society with which is contrasted the temporally displaced utopian figure. Traditionally contemporary society was the absent referent of the utopian figure; in these two innovative feminist utopias contemporary society speaks for itself. In *The Female Man* most of the story takes place in the present, with brief visits to the utopian Whileaway and dystopian Womanland/Manland used to reinforce the ideological analysis constructed in the text. In the conventional utopian sense Whileaway is a place of peace and rationality where women grow up strong and secure without the constant threat of violence by which contemporary society works to ensure women's compliance in their own domination.

There's no being *out too late* in Whileaway, or *up too early*, or *in the wrong part of town*, or *unescorted*. You cannot fall out of the kinship web and become sexual prey for strangers, for there is no prey and there are no strangers – the web is world-wide. (p. 81)

Like Herland Whileawayan society practises parthenogenesis, reproduction by cloning, so that men are superfluous to their existence.
Like the first male visitors to Herland, contemporary men assume
they will be received as heroes in Whileaway, their *hubris* revealed
constantly by their negation of women as individual subjects. This
analysis of sexism is reinforced by the male response to Janet during
her visit to contemporary society. The utopian visitor and utopian
guide are once more recombined, as they were in Hythlodaeus;
however, where Hythlodaeus was a contemporary character who had
visited Utopia and so was able to explain the utopian society to his
contemporaries, Janet is a member of a utopian society who visits the
decidedly less than utopian society of the writer's and reader's own
time and gives her own, estranged, responses to that society. The
political function of this reversal is that, as in *Woman on the Edge of
Time*, the estranged consciousness, the ability to see and analyse
ideological discourses such as sexism, is located in the present, not a
utopian future.

The Female Man also features a dystopia, the Womanland/Manland
nightmare world of Jael. Conventionally it is a displaced representation of contemporary society, which horrifies the other Js by its naked
violence. This inclusion of utopian and dystopian figures in the same
text is another recent feminist innovation, found also in *Woman on the
Edge of Time*. Jael's world is a graphic representation of sexism in
practice:

> 'You're a woman,' he cries, shutting his eyes, 'you're a beautiful
> woman. You've got a hole down there. You're a beautiful woman.
> You've got real, round tits and you've got a beautiful ass. You want me.
> It doesn't matter what you say. You're a woman aren't you? This is the
> crown of your life. This is what God made you for. I'm going to fuck
> you. I'm going to screw you until you can't stand up. You want it. You
> want to be mastered ... All you women, you're all women, you're
> sirens, you're beautiful, you're waiting for me, waiting for a man,
> waiting for me to stick it in, waiting for me, me, me. (p. 181)

Jael responds by killing this man, but, as with Connie's violence, this
is no blueprint for the vanquishing of sexism, but a statement of the
need for engagement with sexist discourse and its inherently violent
social practice. This need for engagement, for political activism, is
later confirmed by Jael's demystification of the process by which
Whileaway came about, not as the Whileawayan myths state by
biological means (a disease which killed only men), but by her
agency, as Jael tells Janet:

that plague you talk of is a lie. *I know.* The world-lines around you are not so different yours or mine or theirs and there is no plague in any of them, not any of them. Whileaway's plague is a big lie. Your ancestors lied about it. It is I who gave you your 'plague,' my dear, about which you now pietize and moralize to your heart's content; I, I, I, I am the plague, Janet Evason. I and the war I fought built your world for you, I and those like me, we gave you a thousand years of peace and love and the Whileawayan flowers nourish themselves on the bones of the men we have slain. (p. 211)

So utopia itself is conditional on political intervention; it will not develop naturally (even pathologically) from the present.

That present is represented in *The Female Man* through the intertwined narratives of the four Js, through the estranged responses of Janet and Jael, the pre-liberated timidity of Jeannine and the exasperation of the contemporary Joanna. It is the topography traced by the montage of passages that, along with the Js narrative, constitutes the text:

VIII
Men succeed. Women get married.
Men fail. Women get married.
Men enter monasteries. Women get married.
Men start wars. Women get married.
Men stop them. Women get married.
Dull, dull. (see below) (p. 126)

V
Burned any bras lately har har twinkle twinkle A pretty girl like you doesn't need to be liberated twinkle har Don't listen to those hysterical bitches twinkle twinkle twinkle I never take a woman's advice about two things: love and automobiles twinkle twinkle har May I kiss your little hand twinkle twinkle twinkle. Har. Twinkle. (p. 49)

VIII
There are more whooping cranes in the United States of America than there are women in Congress. (p. 61)

This textual construction of the present constantly affirms it as the focus of the activism which is the resolution of the narrative(s). The gender ideology of patriarchy and its social practice is scrutinized in this text by a variety of strategies: a montage of demystifying statements (such as those above), the interactions of the Js with modern males, the utopian figure, the dystopian figure. Moylan endorses the appropriateness of this complex textual/political strategy: 'The complexity of the current situation also calls for diverse tactics of opposition since a single, approved approach would only be an ineffective imitation of linear, authoritarian, male politics.' (Moylan, 1986 (D), p. 76)

Piercy's *Woman on the Edge of Time* also employs a variety of strategies, including a detailed representation of contemporary society, a utopian figure and a dystopian figure. The utopian figure, the society of Connie's 'utopian analog', Luciente, is an environmentally-sound, co-operative, non-sexist community. It is also highly advanced technologically, so much so that the technology does not intrude on the lives of the inhabitants. It also plays a crucial role in their method of reproduction which, as in *Herland* and *The Female Man*, avoids the entrapment of women in the nuclear family structure. In the place of parthenogenesis Piercy substitutes the brooder, an artificial womb into which the fertilized ova are placed:

> Connie gaped, her stomach also turning slowly upside down. All in a sluggish row, babies bobbed. Mother the machine. Like fish in the aquarium at Coney Island . . . Languidly they drifted in a blind school. (p. 102)

The genetic materials are mixed so that no notion of ownership exists between parent and child, and so that racism cannot survive: 'we broke the bond between genes and culture, broke it forever' (p. 104). Luciente explains to the disapproving Connie the reasons for this reproductive technology:

> 'It was part of women's long revolution. When we were breaking all the old hierarchies. Finally there was that one thing we had to give up too, the only power we ever had, in return for no more power for anyone. The original production: the power to give birth. Cause as long as we were biologically enchained, we'd never be equal. And males never would be humanized to be loving and tender. So we all became mothers. Every child has three. To break the nuclear bonding.' (p. 105)

In Piercy's description of this society traditional female/male gender roles are systematically eliminated, and nowhere is this so effective or so provocative than in its definition of the family. As with other aspects of the utopian figure the function of this representation is not predictive but analytical; the nature of contemporary gender ideology is examined and its practice in the constitution of the family analysed. The liberation of women from sole responsibility for child-bearing and rearing means that they are able to contribute socially in ways which suit their particular physical and intellectual capabilities, while the greater inclusion of men in this responsibility gives them much increased emotional awareness and freedom. The children, too, seem more independent and secure, freed of the complex psychological stresses of the nuclear family. Piercy emphasizes this elimination of traditional gender roles by her use of the non-specific possessive 'per' in the place of the sex-specific 'her' and 'his', and the noun 'person' instead of the pronouns 'she' and 'he'. The initial clumsiness of these neologisms is an indication to the reader of the pervasiveness of the gender ideologies which structure our society. Again their function is not predictive or a blueprint for the future, but an analysis of contemporary constructions of gender. Piercy's utopian figure also graphically articulates non-racist, ecologically aware, socially co-operative discourses which constitute the social and political environment in which the egalitarian gender discourse operates.

For Connie Ramos, the utopian traveller, the problems of survival in her own (contemporary Western) society are not only a function of gender, but also of race and class; Connie is treated as a criminal in the American society of the book because she is a woman *and* non-white *and* working class. This conjuction of ideological positionings almost guarantees her failure in a system which functions optimally for white, middle-class men. Yet Connie is highly intelligent and that might have been her way out of poverty, except that she is impregnated by her white, middle-class employer. Connie's gender, race and class identity facilitated her exploitation and combine to prevent her recovery, economically, socially or emotionally. Piercy's utopian figure therefore deals not only with the status of women as a group, but with the differences between women which make women of particular races or classes susceptible to different pressures, different kinds and degrees of exploitation. As de Lauretis writes of *Born in Flames*, this book gives an 'image of a heterogeneity in the female social subject, the sense of a distance from dominant cultural models and of an internal division within women that remain, not in spite of but concurrently with the provisional unity of any concerted political action.' (de Lauretis, 1987 (A), p. 139) The primary strategy Piercy uses to construct this image is the constant comparison of the utopian figure with Connie's wretched reality. And it is that comparison which confirms the marginalization of Connie by an uncaring, endemically violent system and so necessitates its active opposition by all who desire social justice: 'We can imagine all we like. But we got to do something real' (p. 343).

Connie's real is constructed differently from that of Joanna and her visitors in *The Female Man*: montage is replaced by realist narrative. Where Russ rejects the normalizing, conservatively-oriented realist narrative in favour of a disruptive montage that is a postmodern analogue of the constantly fragmented utopian narrative of the nineteenth century, Piercy develops a detailed realist narrative. She then counterpoints this narrative with a utopian figure which acts as an internal, textual gloss on the narrative. Moylan writes of *Woman on the Edge of Time*:

> By countering realism, with its tendency to reinforce the limits of the status quo, with utopian discourse, Piercy subverts realism from within by her use of a female and revolutionary protagonist and defeats it from without as the power of utopian imagination breaks open the realist text to a radically alternative future. (Moylan, 1986 (D), p. 126)

As Moylan notes, the construction of a main character who is not male, white or middle class is in itself a subversion of realism; this is not the kind of 'real' sanctioned by dominant ideological discourses. Connie's story, therefore, reveals the ideological function of realist narrative itself, its role in maintaining a particular version of the 'real.' The utopian figure glosses this demystification as did Morris's discussion of art immediately prior to his description of revolution in *News from Nowhere*. Thus it is also significant that the revolutionary action of this text occurs not only in the utopian figure, in the battles against the remnants of phallocratic capitalism, but also in Connie's real, reinforcing the text's activist message: an unjust 'real' can and must be changed, transformed, revolutionized.

The penalty for political passivity or apathy is the dystopia with which Connie accidentally connects after the death of one of the other 'patients.' It is another future possibility for Connie's society, one in which the battle between Luciente's ancestors and those who want to preserve the old ways (i.e. contemporary conservative ideologies) has been won by the latter. The result is a high-tech, severely polluted, class divided, exploitative, sexist society where Connie contacts not Luciente, but Gildina. Both these names suggest light, but with Gildina it is a garish, tinsel light. Gildina is another analogue of Connie:

> They were about the same height and weight, although the woman was younger and her body seemed a cartoon of femininity, with a tiny waist, enormous sharp breasts that stuck out like the brassieres Connie herself had worn in the fifties – but the woman was not wearing a brassiere. Her stomach was flat but her hips and buttocks were oversized and audaciously curved. She looked as if she could hardly walk for the extravagance of her breasts and buttocks, her thighs that collided as she shuffled a few steps. (p. 288)

Gildina has been surgically altered to suit the sexual desires of her employer who later tells Connie: 'She's just a chica, exactly like you look to be' (p. 299). Gildina *is* Connie, Gildina's physical mutilation a metaphor for the mental or psychological mutilation to which Connie is subjected as part of the hospital's behaviour modification experiments. In the realist narrative the doctors insert an electrode into Connie's brain by which particular areas can be stimulated or suppressed, thus controlling her behaviour; she will then be trained to act appropriately, to distort herself to fit the norms (including the physical) of the society in which she lives. Connie's understanding of this training programme is shown in the tactics she uses as she plans her ill-fated escape: 'Taking a shrewd and wary interest, volunteering for every task defined as women's work, cleaning, sweeping, helping with the other patients, picking up clothes, fetching and carrying for the nurses' (p. 339). In Gildina's society, Connie learns, everyone has electronic implants; everyone is controlled and monitored. The electronic implants are an apt representation of the function of ideology which operates on the individual both externally, via social and political institutions, and internally, as the structure of discourses negotiated by the individual in the construction of her/his subjectivity. As de Lauretis writes of gender: *'The construction of gender is the product and process of both representation and self-representation.'* (de Lauretis, p. 9) Gildina's society, the dystopian figure, *is* Connie's society, the society of the writer and contemporary reader, and it, too, serves as a gloss on the realist narrative which structures the text.

In *Woman on the Edge of Time* three intersecting narratives – realist, utopian, dystopian – construct a complex text in which Piercy deconstructs dominant ideological discourses, examines the interpellation of the individual in ideology and one of the principal means by which ideology is naturalized into the lives of individuals, the realist narrative. The development which informs these narratives is the formation of an active subject, self-consciously situated in relation to the dominant ideologies of her society and prepared to fight for the elimination of those oppressive, reactionary ideologies. Piercy positions the reader to understand the reasons for Connie's maltreatment in terms of the ideologies of gender, race and class and to recognize the need for political intervention in order to produce a society in which such abuse of the individual cannot occur; the reading position of this text is both feminist and activist.

The Female Man and *Woman on the Edge of Time* follow the late nineteenth-century utopias with several other conventions: the dream-like state by which the utopian traveller is conveyed to the utopian figure; the love story; point of closure of the narrative(s); and textual reflexivity. The dream-like state is particularly important in Piercy's utopia as it is the means by which Connie makes contact with her other selves, Luciente and Gildina. As with the nineteenth-century texts this use of dream locates the utopian, and here dystopian, narratives in the consciousness of the utopian traveller, who is the representative of contemporary society. So the activist consciousness constructed in/by this character is located in the present, as available to contemporary readers, a product of the articulation of marginalized discourses. Russ makes the same point by having her four characters, the four Js, constitute the one charac-ter, a member of contemporary society. Both utopias also feature love stories and, like Morris, the writers use their stories as part of their subversive propaganda. In *The Female Man* Janet's love-making with Laura is part of Russ's elaboration of the marginalized gender discourse of lesbianism, as are her descriptions of personal rela-tionships on Whileaway. Similarly her descriptions of Jeannine's degrading love affair and of the relationship between Jael and Davy, and the Manlander men and their sex-changed consorts, are decon-structions of dominant (heterosexist) gender ideology. Connie's loves in *Woman on the Edge of Time* deconstruct heterosexist ideology and elaborate the marginalized discourse of egalitarian partnerships. Neither book ends with the resolution of the love story, a narrative which is far more problematic for women than for men because of the gender ideology at its core. However, both books end in the present and with a description of activist intervention. In *The Female Man* the final section contains a summary of the utopia's analysis of gender ideology, particularly of its interpellation of the female subject: for example:

V

Learning to
despise
one's
self (p. 207)

And it contains the first act of subversion, the first denial of the heterosexist female role:

I committed my first revolutionary act yesterday. I shut the door on a man's thumb. I did it for no reason at all and I didn't warn him; I just slammed the door shut in a rapture of hatred and imagined the bone breaking and the edges grinding into his skin. (p. 203)

Similarly *Woman on the Edge of Time* ends with Connie's poisoning of the doctors and nurses carrying out the implantation surgery, and with her subsequent readmission to the maximum security psychiatric hospital. In other words, both texts return the reader to the unsatisfactory present, avoiding escapist closure within the utopian figure, and both end with the first subversive act by the feminist consciousness constructed in/by the text.

Both texts are also self-reflexive, as the analysis above has repeatedly shown. The intersecting narratives of *Woman on the Edge of Time* produce a text which constantly reflects on the mechanism of the realist narrative, which is one of its own mechanisms. Piercy also discusses the role of art explicitly in the text, in the debate over a hologram made by Bolivar, one of the utopians:

> The old person with the glittery black eyes, Sojourner, shook her head. 'Every piece of art can't contain everything everybody would like to say! I've seen this mistake for sixty years. Our culture as a whole must speak the whole truth. But every object can't! That's the slogan mentality at work, as if there were certain holy words that must always be named.'
>
> 'But do we have to be satisfied with half truths?' Barbarossa asked.
>
> 'Sometimes an image radiates many possible truths,' Bolivar said. 'Luciente appears to fix too narrowly on content and apply our common politics too rigidly.' (pp. 210–11)

Piercy here directs readers against the blueprint model of the utopia, the literal reading of the utopian figure, and instead proposes a more perceptive reading which attends to the text's signifying practices as well as its apparent content. *The Female Man* constantly draws attention to the text's signifying practice by its montage format which disrupts the narrative of the four Js with descriptions and analyses of gender relations and identities in the reader's own society. Moylan summarizes the operation of *The Female Man*:

> By means of a style that cuts through the binary oppositions of now and not yet, that explores the present as a multiplex and contradictory assemblage of closures and possibilities, and sets forth a vision of a better future as well as the activism needed to reach that set of possibilities, Russ's text in its very form disrupts the limits of the present ideological system. It uses the expansive possibilities of science fiction to express a utopia as well as an agenda for getting there that resists the traditional closure of narrow utopian systems, and hence their cooptation by the historical systems that they criticize. The fragmented, disconcerting, deconstructing, multiplex text – with its equally outrageous anger and humor – is a critical expression of the politics of opposition and a vision of a not yet realized society. (Moylan, 1986 (D), pp. 64–5)

These two texts exemplify the use of the utopian genre by contemporary feminist writers. In the late nineteenth century the utopia was enlisted by propagandists for and against socialism, who modified the conventions of the utopia to suit their political aims and the expectations of the contemporary reader. Recent feminist writers have followed a similar path, modifying the conventions they in turn inherited from their nineteenth-century, pro- or anti-socialist predecessors, and I would suggest that the socialist utopias, particularly *News from Nowhere*, are the major influence on their work. *Herland* was another major influence, of course, particularly in its extended use of narrative, which was a response to the increasing popularity of science fiction writing. Both *The Female Man* and *Woman on the Edge of Time* also modify the utopian narrative to accord with contemporary expectations shaped, at least in part, by other estranged forms such as fantasy and science fiction. Russ uses a number of intersecting narratives, constantly disrupted by a montage of contemporary references, in a postmodernist rewriting of the nineteenth-century utopia; Piercy uses three narratives in three different genres, realist, utopian, dystopian, which are essentially all the same narrative, and so sets up an internal process of reflection and demystification designed to challenge the normalizing function of the realist narrative. The political awareness of both writers therefore includes or necessitates textual reflection on their own literary/political practice. Marin's reflection that 'the utopian critique is ideological to the degree to which its critique is presented as natural or unproblematic *qua* ideology, rather than being reflected in a discourse about its own production '(Marin, 1976 (D), p. 71) finds a specific feminist response in these texts, which do not claim in any sense to be non-ideological (in itself an impossibility), but instead construct texts which only read naturally or unproblematically from a feminist position. Feminism is not denied by these texts, but what they do expose constantly is the denial by familiar social practices and institutions, including literary institutions (such as realism), of their ideological formation.

Contemporary feminist utopias are not blueprints for a feminist revolution; they are not written to encourage the physical abuse of men or the poisoning of mental hospital staff. They are instead part of an already happening feminist revolution, a revolution pursued not by physical force but by the re-examination of traditional gender roles and the recognition of their appalling injustice, their delimitation and deformation of both women and men. Feminist utopia writers, by constructing a feminist reading position in their texts, show readers the nature of their society from a different (feminist) perspective.

Beliefs, values, institutions traditionally represented as natural or obvious or inevitable are revealed as ideological constructs and the nature of that constructing ideology (patriarchal or heterosexist) is analysed. They also show that social change is not only possible, but constantly in process, and that a feminist perception or understanding constitutes a continual intervention in the dominant patriarchal ideology and its practice; that a feminist consciousness is necessarily activist.

It is not possible to finish this chapter without noting a recent, highly-praised feminist novel, Margaret Atwood's *The Handmaid's Tale*, a dystopia (Atwood, 1986 (D)). Atwood describes a United States society totally dominated by patriarchal ideology. With nuclear and industrial accidents and AIDS taking their toll on the reproductive capability of the Caucasian population a revolution by white, male supremacists has transformed the formerly liberal/conservative society. The conservative ideologies of gender, race and class (favouring white, middle-class men) have been taken to their reactionary extreme and the result is a white supremacist state which oppresses all marginalized minorities and exploits women as surrogate mothers for the powerful, white minority. Like all dystopias it is a representation not of an alternative future, but of the present stripped of its ideological rationalizations. The institutionalized exploitation of women in heterosexual relationships is explored, particularly in the book's displaced interrogation of the nuclear family. Atwood also explores women's interpellation as subjects by patriarchal ideology, which renders them susceptible to, even collusive with, their own exploitation. The description of the dystopian state is followed by a section called 'Historical Notes' in which a group of academics from the year 2195 discuss the manuscript called 'The Handmaid's Tale.' The detachment with which the future historians discuss the story and their joking references to events described constitute a reflexive mechanism designed to obviate the escapist response often associated with the dystopia. Even if readers do finish the tale feeling relieved that they do not live in such a state, the academic rhetoric of this final section of the text demands a response from readers which necessitates a revaluation of the preceding narrative. In a sense Atwood trades on readers' distrust of the academy and its intellectually superior attitude to engage them in a rereading and recognition of the political significance of her text.

The major question this text poses for feminists, however, is not so much what it says about patriarchal gender ideology, which is not particularly innovative, but why a dystopia should be written at this time. Certainly Atwood has a contemporary precedent in Charnas's dystopia, *Walk to the End of the World*, and a dystopian figure has featured in some of the contemporary utopias (including the most influential), yet the twentieth-century experience suggests that dystopias are produced at times of political oppression and (consequent) apathy, arising from the despair of the oppressed about the possibility of intervention in a powerful, authoritarian state. *The Handmaid's Tale*, like the science fiction novel, *Native Tongue* (Elgin, 1984 (B)), seems to express the distress of women facing the renewed strength of the forces of reaction, in contemporary politics, religion, education, the institutions by which ideological discourses are internalized and enforced. The failure of the Equal Rights Amendment (ERA) legislation in the United States was an expression of the power of these reactionary forces articulated via a variety of institutional practices and often with the collusion of women themselves. This is the context within which *The Handmaid's Tale* operates and so it is important to note that Atwood uses a distancing strategy more usual in the utopia to alienate her reader from the dystopian figure and so prevent the empathetic, emotional response which may result in an escapist reading of the text. Perhaps the dystopian figure is more appropriate to contemporary social conditions but the increased political and textual awareness of the writer, a function of the political sophistication of both the Women's Movement and feminist literary theory, places *The Handmaid's Tale* within the context of recent utopian writing as a subversive intervention in the patriarchal discourse which characterizes contemporary gender ideology. The ending of Atwood's novel might be rewritten in the feminist voice of any of these recent texts:

> As all historians know, the [present] is a great darkness, and filled with echoes. Voices may reach us from it; but what they say to us is imbued with the obscurity of the matrix out of which they come; and, try as we may, we cannot always decipher them precisely in the clearer light of our own day.
>
> *Applause.*
>
> Are there any questions? (p. 324)

5

Feminist Detective Fiction

Women don't fit well into a trench coat and a slouch hat ... The hard-boiled private eye is a special figure in American mythology. It's a staple of the myth that he should be a cynical loner, a man at odds with society and its values. That's not something women normally relate to. Women aren't cynical loners – that's not how they like to work. It seems to me that if they want to go into the profession seriously, women writers will have to change the myth itself, instead of trying to fit themselves into it. (Stasio, 1985 (E), p. 1)

Marilyn Stasio quotes Lawrence Block, author of the Matthew Scudder private eye novels, in her article, 'Lady gumshoes: Boiled less hard'. Block is responding to the recent emergence in detective fiction of the hard-boiled female detective, the wisecracking, street-smart private eye familiar to audiences in the male personas of Sam Spade and Philip Marlowe. While Block's generalization about women's work practices may or may not have validity, his point that women writers need to revise or rewrite the detective novel in order to accommodate female detectives is well taken. As noted with the other genre forms already discussed, role-reversal is not a simple process; placing a female character in a male role transforms not only the role itself, but every other element of the plot as well. To make a female detective convincing as a character, to have her operate as more than just an honorary male, reinforcing the masculine identity of the characterization by her aberrant, but temporary, occupation, requires a radical reassessment of the characterization of the detective and the narrative in which she functions. And the same is true of the contemporary amateur female detective. No longer is this the preserve of the dotty spinster. The new amateur female detective is a professional woman of some kind – an academic, nurse, journalist, printer – whose environment is affected in some way by crime and who must find the criminal the police overlook. The economic independence and autonomy of this new breed of amateur also transforms both the detective role and the narrative in which she functions.

Writers of female detective fiction, whether feminist or not, are inevitably involved in changing the myth of the traditional detective. For feminist writers, however, this myth (re)making involves a fundamental reassessment of the genre. While changing the gender of the detective may, for some writers, be primarily a response to changing social conditions, the renegotiation of traditional gender discourses in the face of the 1960s Women's Movement and the higher public and professional profile of women, for feminist writers the appropriation of the detective fiction genre is more than a reflex action. Feminist writers have attempted to use the conventions of traditional detective fiction to construct a feminist reading position in their texts, which may then become the locus for debate on the nature of their society. In this way feminist writers work to challenge the interpellation of the individual within bourgeois patriarchal ideologies, to introduce contradiction and complexity which involves the reader in a renegotiation of her/his own subject position and works toward the production of the feminist subject. Again as with the other genres discussed, this kind of reworking of a popular genre must be accompanied by a thorough reworking of its constitutive conventions which can be achieved only with a detailed understanding of their historical development and ideological significance.

History of the genre

Detective fiction developed as a literary genre in the nineteenth century. Its antecedents include the sensational anthology of crime stories called *The Newgate Calendar* (first published in 1773) as well as the equally sensational, and often more fantastic, Gothic fiction of the eighteenth century. Stephen Knight discusses the politics of the *Calendar* in his study of the detective novel, *Form and Ideology in Crime Fiction*. He notes that the villains of these stories are not inherently evil, but 'are ordinary people who reject the roles society and their families offer them' (Knight, 1980 (E), p. 11). Their crime is their inability or unwillingness to contribute to the common weal, to consolidate the body of society by assuming their appointed place. Society, however, can take care of itself. In these stories it is both the detective and the locus of the crimes. Wrongdoers are detected by other members of the society, 'caught in the act', or are betrayed by their own guilt.

> There is no special agent of detection at all. The stories imply that just as society can sometimes suffer from disorderly elements, so it can deal with them by its own integral means. (p. 11)

So it is not surprising to observe, as Knight does, that organic metaphors for society are used throughout these texts. Society is a kind of organism of which all members are vital parts. Should one cell go bad, the whole body suffers, until the body activates its own self-defence mechanisms – observation, guilt. Knight adds that such methods of detection 'could only develop in a deeply Christian world, with small social units where everybody is known, where hiding is hard and socialisation tends to be public' (p. 13). In the nineteenth century, however, this social formation was no longer viable; mechanization, both in the factories and on the land, had broken up traditional communities and the cities were becoming vast and amorphous conglomerations. As Knight notes, however, 'there is rarely a simple linear progress to be found and one society can sustain quite contradictory views of the world at one time, many of them quite outdated' (p. 18). So nineteenth-century readers were familiar with crime fiction based on a collective view of social organization, individual behaviour and morality, even while the dominant bourgeois ideology of their own time militated directly against this social vision.

Knight adds to the list of influences on, or antecedents of, detective fiction William Godwin's novel, *The Adventures of Caleb Williams* (1794), in which Williams acts as an amateur detective, establishing the facts of a murder. As a result of this activity, he is persecuted by the murderer, his former benefactor, Falkland. The novel ends with the death of Falkland and Williams's guilt because he had not confronted Falkland earlier with the facts. The political interest of the novel lies with Godwin's dramatization of the contradiction at the heart of a society which still clung to the social vision of *The Newgate Calendar* but which operated according to a wholly different ideology: 'His world-view remains a collective, Christian one, though one arrived at by the rational mechanisms that were to destroy such a world-view – and such a world' (p. 27).

This same contradiction is central to Gothic fiction, which deals primarily with the problems engendered for the individual when ideology and experiential reality contradict. Since individual subjectivity is an ideological construct, a negotiation of discursive positionings, the contradiction between the individual's experience of the world and what s/he believes is 'real' (that is, the ideological construction of the world) can lead to a major renegotiation of ideological discourses and so of subject formation, or it may lead to the breakdown of the individual's ability to negotiate and so to total conformity and/or madness (the latter being a dominant motif of Gothic fiction). It is an interesting insight into the detective fiction genre, therefore, that its earliest exponent was a major Gothic writer, Edgar Allan Poe.

As noted in the chapter on fantasy, Gothic very often operates to speak and resolve the contradictions inherent in a society undergoing enormous change, the transformation of the society's economic base, the renegotiation of its dominant ideological formation. By contrast the realist novel, the genre most closely associated with bourgeois ideology, works to contain, rather than expose and resolve, these contradictions. Leo Bersani notes, realism 'gives us an image of social fragmentation contained within the order of significant form – and it thereby suggests that the chaotic fragments are somehow socially viable and morally redeemable' (Bersani, 1978 (A), p. 60). As alternatives strategies for dealing with a problematic reality, both genres can operate, and mostly do operate, to reinforce and preserve the dominant ideological formation. In a study of Gothic fiction, *In the Circles of Fear and Desire*, W.P. Day describes the detective as an ordering agent of similar capacity to the realist novel:

> The detective rearranges the seemingly chaotic and arbitrary events of the mystery story, and in doing so, discovers who is a criminal and who is not, why the crime has been committed, and thus frees the innocent from the terrors of guilt and uncertainty. In a Gothic fantasy, the Gothic world overwhelms the human world, for no character can understand, or stand against, its evils. The detective challenges the encroachment of its terrors, the disorder brought on by crime and the monster in the shape of the criminal, returning the world to order and stability. (Day, 1985 (C), p. 52)

Rereading this description it might be argued that the detective is used to challenge or resolve the terror engendered by social contradictions which include the crime brought on by disorder and the criminal in the shape of a monster, returning the (rationalist, bourgeois) world to order and stability. In a Gothic text terrors may be resolved but often their source remains a mystery (as in, for example, *The Castle of Otranto*) and so remain, to some extent, disturbing. In the detective novel social disorder is criminalized (as theft, murder, etc.) and the perpetrator of the crime is represented not as an aberrant social being, but as a monster, an incarnation of evil who is outside the realm of the social. In Poe's seminal story, 'The Murders in the Rue Morgue', this identification of the criminal is manifest in that the murderer is revealed to be an escaped orang-utan. In detective fiction the resolution of contradiction which is explicit in the Gothic fantasy and implicit to the realist novel constitutes the narrative premise of the text. Detective fiction from Poe onwards is a fiction of explanation and resolution, in both senses of the word; it fictionally resolves social contradictions, and yet those resolutions are themselves ideological constructions – and, to that extent, are fictional.

In 'The Murders in the Rue Morgue' (published in *Tales of Mystery and Imagination* (1852)) Poe's narrator describes the intellectual ability required of the successful detective in categories borrowed from romanticism:

> Between ingenuity and the analytic ability there exists a difference far greater, indeed, than that between the fancy and the imagination, but of a character very strictly analagous. It will be found, in fact, that the ingenious are always fanciful, and the *truly* imaginative never other-wise than analytic. (Poe, 1967 (E), p. 192)

This description recalls Ursula LeGuin's statement of the power of imagination, that its exercise can lead to a perception of truth which evades those constrained by 'commonsense'. Later in the story Poe's detective, Dupin confirms: 'it is by these deviations from the plane of the ordinary, that reason feels its way . . . in its search for the true' (p. 207)[1]. This formulation of the practice of detective fiction places it in the tradition of the fantastic, in which imagination is used to break through the restrictions of rationalism, to reveal the ideological practices constitutive of rationalism and the realist vision it produces – by showing it to be a construct, not commonsense or natural or inevitable. As already seen, however, the subversive fantastic is itself easily subverted. Stephen Knight writes of the resolution of 'The Murders in the Rue Morgue':

> No presentation or analysis of the social causes of disorder is offered, it is merely suggested that strange and terrible things can happen and a clever man will be able to explain them. The crime and the resolution are without history, without recurring roots. This powerful and fright-eningly delusive notion is still with us that desocialised, unhistorical understanding can, by deciphering isolated problems, resolve them. (p. 44)

Dupin may use the tools of the fantastic, but he is presented as a rationalist, a clever man who can reason his way to a resolution of terrible mysteries. And these mysteries are not placed within a social context – how does one socialize an orang-utan? Of course, it would be possible to do so, to investigate further the reasons for the sailor's procurement of the beast, but this is not Dupin's purpose. Dupin demonstrates that the most bizarre events can be explained by an individual who is sufficiently clever and perceptive. In a move similar to the conclusion of *The Mysteries of Udolpho* Dupin reveals that the mystery has a simple, natural explanation; it is a mystery only to those with a less secure grasp of the (bourgeois) real. And this is demonstrated textually when witnesses who heard the murders being committed variously identify the sounds made by the ape as the language of their national foes; so the Englishman hears the ape's gibbering as French, the Spaniard hears it as English, the Italian hears it as Russian. In other words, each observer reproduces her/his ideological beliefs in the interpretation of the mystery. Dupin, however, is represented as a disinterested observer, without prejudice, without ideology. This is the fundamental fiction at the basis of the detective genre, and one which makes it such a useful tool of the dominant ideological formation. The reader is positioned by the detective who demonstrates that correct (that is, bourgeois rationalist) thought is all that is required for success: a kind of theoretical 'Self-Help' lesson.

Knight writes that Arthur Conan Doyle's detective, Sherlock Holmes fulfils a similar role: 'Holmes is his own provider: self-help, that great Victorian virtue, is embodied in his power to succeed with no more than his own abilities' (pp. 77–8). Holmes first appeared in *A Study in Scarlet* (1888), exhibiting many of the traits of Dupin; his rationalism enriched by disciplined imaginative capacity, his eccentricity (Dupin lives in an old house with the windows covered, sleeps during the day and works at night, where Holmes at home wears exotic clothes, plays the violin badly and is an opium addict), and his withdrawal from society (both men shun social interaction and converse only with their faithful offsiders who narrate the stories). Both Dupin and Holmes represent an overdetermined individualism and Knight ascribes Holmes's enormous popularity to this characteristic:

> Great emotional value was found in an individual who seemed to stand against the growing collective forces of mass politics, social determinism and scientific, super-individual explanation of the world, all of which appeared as mechanistic threats to the free individual. A figure like Holmes, who treated all problems individualistically and who founded his power on the very rational systems which had inhumane

implications was a particularly welcome reversal of disturbing currents. (p. 80)

Holmes, like Dupin, is the expression and resolution of a contradiction: rationalism and imagination, commonsense and free imaginative play held in creative tension and serving as an embodiment of bourgeois individualism. Day writes about the fictional detective as the hero Gothic fiction lacks:

> The Gothic fantasy lacks an effective hero, a character who through his own efforts can resolve the mystery and put an end to horror. The figure of the detective develops from the tension created by the lack of a true hero. He is, in effect, the hero the Gothic world needs but cannot sustain. The presence of such a character revises the balance and dynamics of the genre, focussing on the restoration of order and meaning rather than on the steady disintegration of identity and the absolute instability of the world in which the characters live. (Day, 1985 (C), pp. 50–1)

Gothic fiction cannot sustain this kind of hero because he is a denial of the central premise of that fiction which is, ostensibly at least, the dramatization of the 'steady disintegration of identity and the absolute instability of the world' which produced the fiction. At its most critical and/or subversive Gothic reveals the construction of the subject, the interpellation of the subject by ideology, and challenges the naturalization of the individualist bourgeois subject. Gothic may also reveal the instability of the social formation by exposing its ideological construction, showing that it too, like the individual subject, is essentially a negotiation of ideological discourses, not a natural or inevitable state. Detective fiction re-conceals. Paradoxically, the literature of detection operates most commonly as the literature of concealment, of displacement and false resolution. The 'order and meaning' that the detective restores is that of dominant ideological discourses. The narrative of the detective novel, exemplified in the work of Poe and Doyle, operates to naturalize bourgeois discourses.

Conan Doyle frequently alludes to the narrative function of his detective. Towards the end of *The Hound of the Baskervilles* Holmes remarks to Watson: 'I shall soon be in the position of being able to put into a single connected narrative one of the most singular and sensational crimes of modern times' (Doyle, 1981 (E), p. 753). The similarity between the roles of detective and writer have often been noted. Stephen Knight quotes Russell Davies on Philip Marlowe, that he is 'a complete metaphor for the writer's life' (p. 159), while Peter Brooks several times likens the construction of narrative to the work of the detective. Brooks also notes:

we read only those incidents and signs that can be construed as promise and annunciation, enchained toward a construction of significance – those markers that, as in the detective story, appear to be clues to the underlying intentionality of event. (Brooks, 1984 (A), p. 94)

Just as narrative is so often enchained toward the construction of the bourgeois real, so the detective fiction story collaborates in this construction, and is one of its cultural mechanisms. Even so, some writers have attempted to use the genre to express non-bourgeois ideology, to reposition the reader as a non-bourgeois subject.

In the late nineteenth century detective fiction was enormously popular; publication of Doyle's Sherlock Holmes stories in the *Strand* magazine ensured both the success of the genre and of the writer. Detective fiction was also published by non-mainstream papers targeted on the largest possible market, like Keir Hardie's Labour paper, *Labour Leader*. In 1894 Hardie serialized the story, 'The Lone Inn' by detective writer, Fergus Hume (Hume, 1894 (E)) and in 1895 a mystery cum *bildungsroman* called 'By Shadowed Paths' by the enigmatically named Albert T. Marles (Yorick the Younger) (Marles, 1895 (E)). Marles uses elements of the detective novel to describe the political development of his hero, Jack Harper. Jack is influenced by a variety of political opinions embodied in the characters with whom he comes into contact and through whom he learns the nature of those ideologies – Chartist, capitalist, anarchist, and finally socialist. The socialist is Elsie, the girl he marries, so that love and socialism reinforce each other; socialism being the ideology favoured by the author. Jack is also involved in a mystery concerning his brother, lately returned from South Africa as well as a story of corruption which has dispossessed him of his father's farm. He is assisted to untangle these mysteries by the obligingly anti-establishment Inspector Butler, so that Marles manages to have his characters both respectable and anti-bourgeois in the one story. The interesting point about this story is that Marles attempts to use the detection and revelation element of the detective story to a non-bourgeois political end. Specifically he attempts to use the detective format to uncover the truth about different ideological discourses and the social practices they engender. Without going into great detail here[2] it is debatable whether the story succeeds in this purpose; nevertheless, it does show that, as far back as the 1890s when the genre first became enormously popular, writers have attempted to use it to challenge the (conservative, bourgeois) assumptions usually coded unselfconsciously into its conventions.

In the twentieth century detective fiction continued to be a very popular fictional genre. Major twentieth-century proponents of detective fiction include Agatha Christie, Dashiell Hammett and Raymond Chandler. Their detectives, Christie's Hercule Poirot and Miss Marple, Hammett's Sam Spade and Chandler's Philip Marlowe, have all featured in movies of their author's work, reinforcing and perhaps extending their audience. Christie's detectives embody many of the characteristics of their nineteenth-century predecessors. Poirot is as eccentric and as rationalistic as Holmes and Dupin. Like them, he works by making logical deductions from a series of clues and he also, like them, has personal peculiarities which isolate him from other people. He is not English like his author, but Belgian; is fastidious about clothing; favours an outlandish waxed moustache; and is resolutely single, if not asexual. Miss Marple, too, is a charming eccentric – a village spinster who, with the acuity and observational powers of Jane Austen, detects the forces which threaten to fracture the ordered life of county England. She, too, is an eccentric with her sensible clothes and voluminous handbag, her spinsterly curiosity and asexuality. The essential difference between Poirot and Miss Marple is that he is a professional detective, while she is an amateur, if extremely effective, busybody. Both are marginal members of the society in which they work and bring to it values which are non-mainstream and yet representative of the atavistic pre-bourgeois communalist longings of many of Christie's readers. Stephen Knight summarizes Christie's appeal in these terms:

> The persuasive individualism of bourgeois feeling and epistemology is, as has been argued here, crucial to the whole edifice of the clue-puzzle in crime, detection and literary structure. Yet at the same time the style, values and presentation of the material are curiously depersonalised; the upholding of group values, a duty to conform, is very powerful in Christie's work. I believe this confrontation between a basic individualism and a collective value system and style is a crucial meaningful fissure. It reveals the central reason for Christie's success, her almost mesmerising power over readers. She offers a dream of collective security which is based on fully individual systems. The whole construction denies that crime is a natural product of individuality; the threat of anarchy is removed from the pursuit of personal freedom. Through the notion of duty and normalcy, freely chosen not socially imposed, Christie presents as proper a system of living which can promise respectable people the continued enjoyment of the life-style they or their forebears have personally earned by successful conflict with others. (p. 128)

Christie's detectives represent a negotiation of bourgeois discourses which not only caters to the contradictions within the bourgeois social formation, but also performs that other characteristic role of detective fiction – to conceal as it reveals. The detective conceals the nature of crime in bourgeois society even as s/he detects its perpetrator. In fact the mystificatory function of detective fiction is largely a function of this particular form of detection, the identification of a scapegoat. The individual criminal becomes the focus of the social disorder represented in the story as crime, and is resolved – 'put away', 'sent up the river'. So when Sherlock Holmes constructs his 'single connected narrative' to solve a crime, he simultaneously (re)constructs bourgeois individualist ideology with its mystificatory notions of individual guilt and social order. Holmes, like Dupin and later Poirot and Miss Marple, fits the facts of the crime to an ideological description of bourgeois society and so constructs a criminal according to the dictates of that ideology; an aberrant individual is purged, and social order preserved. From another perspective, one might suggest that social fragmentation is embodied in the character of an individual and the myth of social order is preserved by the ritual purging of that individual.

Chandler's Philip Marlowe performs a similar function. Marlowe is a 'hard-boiled' detective, a tough guy who combines the hardy independence of the cowboy with the eccentric isolation of the nineteenth-century detective. Where the cowboy knew the west like the back of his hand, the hard-boiled detective knows the city like his own set of arteries. He is street-wise, smart, cynical, a loner, an individualist who must rely on his own rational powers for survival:

> There is a static, almost meditational quality to a Chandler plot as the hero moves back and forward across his closely charted city and its environs; the affective force of the structure is to retain the action and its interpretation in the hero's consciousness and to make it eventually come clear to him without his cumulative effort but through the actions of characters and his own catalytic presence: his personal value, not his active detection, is the structural focus, the method of detection and the value finally achieved. (Knight, 1980 (E), p. 151)

As Knight goes on to argue, Chandler's Philip Marlowe not only represents a rejection of perceptions of social fragmentation and chaos, like the detectives of Poe, Doyle and Christie, his character is also a bulwark against perceptions of personal fragmentation. Bourgeois individualist discourse is a denial of the complex and contradictory nature of the individual subject; instead it posits a coherent, autonomous subject who stands in romantic opposition to the external, social world.

It was personal spiritual survival, not the desire for property that excited Chandler and his readers. Crime in their world and his novels was merely a symbol for threats to the conscious control of personal life, and the means of detecting and controlling it were no more than sensitive vigilance – to be on watch against hostile forces, to be fully dependent on one's own resources was a sufficient defence of life and mental stability. (p. 166)

Accordingly Marlowe, the archetypal hard-boiled detective, is constructed in terms which reinforce this sense of invulnerability, of personal integration and isolation; he is emotionally self-contained, cool to the point of frigidity, smart, physically hardy, distrustful of others – even, or perhaps especially, of those closest to him. He also has a simple, or simplistic, moral code by which people are judged good or evil and he has no sense of class, gender or race ideology to add subtlety or depth to his range of moral judgements.

Dashiell Hammett's Sam Spade exhibits many of these tough guy qualities. Hammett's detective also finds individuals to take on the burden of social guilt; that is, he also constructs the narrative of bourgeois ideological discourse and constructs characters to fill the roles. However, he does not wholly conceal the nature of the forces that motivate the narrative; for example, the commodity fetishism which is given form in the gold statuette of *The Maltese Falcon*. Like Chandler, Hammett uses the detective form to write about the material determinants of his own society and to expose their social and individual manifestations. Spade also locates the individual criminal, but he shows that this criminal is not an individual aberration, but a social construction. Others also pursue the prize represented by the Falcon statuette; some are simply more likely to be caught than others. The desire it stimulates does not reside in aberrant individuals but is a condition of life in a materialistic, commodity oriented society. This perception of evil residing in society, rather than just specific individuals, is characteristic of twentieth-century detective fiction. Yet this fiction also functions to conceal, rather than reveal. Conventionally (ideologically) evil is not located in the practices which define or describe society; that is, it is not seen as a condition and product of a particular ideology. Rather this evil is located within those who reject social values, such as honour and integrity, in favour of wealth and power. Social roles and institutions are not evil; the individuals who occupy them are. The detective's social analysis has no concept of ideology, of the way individuals are formed within ideology, and so remains an individualist construct.

An analogy may be drawn with realist and modernist writings. The nineteenth-century detective, the scientific (bourgeois) rationalist, was concerned to preserve the coherence and correctness of bourgeois society from subversive and external attack. Therefore s/he was obsessively involved in the (re)construction of its ideological narrative, denying fragmentation and disorder and locating disruption in a single aberrant individual. The twentieth-century detective, the hard-boiled private eye, is more concerned with preserving the coherence and autonomy of the individual in the face of a society which is manifestly fragmented and chaotic. That fragmentation and chaos are not related to fundamental social practices (and their constitutive ideology), but to the moral degeneration of individuals. Fragmentation and chaos are interpreted morally as corruption and decadence and the detective's task is to locate those who embody this evil. Even when the evil is found to be endemic to social institutions, the connection with ideology and the formulation of the individual is concealed by a narrative of individual autonomy and integrity. Individuals, it is implied, can stand outside this corruption, this evil, can be with-out ideology, with-out society, in a contemporary inflection of the romantic ideology of individual subjectivity. The individual who most embodies this ideology is the detective, which accounts for the disappearance of the narrator in much contemporary detective fiction. The nineteenth-century detective's story was often related by a good friend, an off-sider, like Holmes's Dr Watson. This narratorial device emphasized the independence and objectivity of the detective, the dispassionate, scientific observer of his society. Reader identification was with Dr Watson, representative of the average individual, informed and educated but no genius (and no doubt readers had little inclination to be like the wildly eccentric Holmes, who suffered the cost of his genius). The direct narration of the contemporary detective, on the other hand, encourages reader identification with the detective, and so with an illusion of coherent subjectivity, represented as moral integrity, which works equally deftly to preserve the contemporary narrative of late bourgeois capitalism.

This is the background against which feminist writers began to reconstruct the detective fiction genre. Which is not to say that detective fiction is new to women writers. In fact, women have always been well represented as writers of detective fiction, with Agatha Christie, Dorothy L. Sayers, Margery Allingham, P.D. James and Ruth Rendell among the most popular writers of the genre. And there have always been female detectives. In *Crime on Her Mind*

Michele Slung anthologizes 15 stories of female detectives from the nineteenth century to the 1940s (Slung, 1977 (E)), while Betty Rosenberg lists 32 female detectives, from Miss Seaton, British spinster, by Heron Carvic to Patricia Wentworth's Miss Maude Silver, private investigator, in her study of genre fiction, *Genreflecting* (Rosenberg, 1982 (A)). Few of these female detectives have been as popular as their male counterparts, however, with only Miss Marple having an audience approaching the popularity of that of Sherlock Holmes, Lord Peter Wimsey, Sam Spade, Philip Marlowe and Nero Wolfe. The detective fiction genre, like science fiction, fantasy and utopian fiction, has until recently been a male preserve, even if it also had a significant female presence.

The brief history of detective fiction I have outlined above shows the ideological function of the genre, how it developed as a response to the contradictions, uncertainties and frustrations of bourgeois society. Detective fiction operates, ideologically, not to detect, but conceal; to offer false resolution, rather than explanation; to reconstruct continually the ideological narrative of bourgeois society and the unified bourgeois subject. Feminist detective fiction must function differently if it is to be a socially subversive fiction, yet still use the conventions of the genre to remain recognizably of that genre. It is necessary, therefore, to examine those conventions, to understand how they encode the ideological discourses which render detective fiction a predominantly conservative literary genre and how they might be transformed in order to work in a feminist text.

Conventions of the genre

The convention which immediately identifies the text to the reader is the detective, almost always introduced in the first few pages. The most popular nineteenth-century characterization of the detective is embodied in Holmes and Dupin. He is male (though there were some Victorian women detectives), a rationalist who solves crimes by using a version of the scientific method – observation, deduction, hypothesis, verification. His deductions and hypothesis are assisted by his active imagination, the romantic accoutrement of genius. As a romantic hero, he is also alienated from society, an eccentric who imposes exile from human society on himself – by implication because he finds the society of ordinary men tedious and vulgar. Both Dupin and Holmes withdraw almost entirely from the world; Dupin to a decaying mansion, the windows of which are blocked to prevent the entry of light, Holmes to his Baker Street apartment and tobacco haze. The Victorian detective was emotionally detached, to the point of abnormality. He did not become emotionally involved in cases and rarely showed any kind of emotional response. When he did, the result was not reassuring to those around him. In 'The Hound of the Baskervilles' Dr Watson makes the following observation of Sherlock Holmes: 'He burst into one of his rare fits of laughter as he turned away from the picture. I have not heard him laugh often, and it has always boded ill to somebody' (Doyle, 1981 (E), p. 750). Holmes's emotional outbursts have a manic quality which accords with his eccentricity. This overdetermined eccentricity of the nineteenth-century detective signifies not only the individualist ideology which structures the characterization, but also its romantic subjectivity. The nineteenth-century detective is a rationalist, an eccentric, a genius, a man apart from ordinary men – but, essentially, one who upholds the principles of his society by removing from it the individuated sources of disruption which mar its superficial equanimity. The characterization serves a politically conservative end.

In the twentieth century three major characterizations of the detective inherit the mantle of Dupin and Holmes: the eccentric individualist represented by Hercule Poirot, the female amateur represented most popularly by Miss Marple, and the hard-boiled private eye like Sam Spade, Philip Marlowe, Mike Hammer and Nero Wolfe. There are also other popular modern forms of crime fiction, such as the 'Police Procedural' in which the detective is a police officer, or, more often, a pair of police officers. The Police Procedural is particularly popular on television and one of the most innovative series in this format is the American *Cagney and Lacey*, which features a pair of women police officers. The problem of combining the toughness of the detective with a female characterization is apparent in this programme and in its history,[3] the title itself combining the supposedly antithetical signifiers, the tough guy Jimmy *Cagney* and the feminine *Lacey*. In literature the police fiction of the Swedish writers, Maj Sjowahl and Per Wahloo is considered to be among the most interesting and inventive contemporary crime fiction.[4] Yet traditional detective fiction maintains its popular appeal.

Agatha Christie's Hercule Poirot is the neurotic successor to Holmes and Dupin. His characterization is very similar to theirs, though he is rather more emotional and altogether more foreign. Poirot is perhaps too foreign, which suggests that the eccentricity he exhibits is no longer acceptable to readers. Miss Marple is an example of the major form of female detective available until very recently. She is an amateur detective, often a gentlewoman spinster or a married woman with no other career, someone who could be viewed as non-professional. In either case the female detective is represented as sexually unavailable, and it is surely no coincidence that, in her most popular incarnation as Miss Marple, she is a homely spinster. This female detective may be almost as eccentric and as intelligent as her male counterpart but her challenge to male domination is contained by the elimination of her sexuality. In traditional stereotypical terms, a female character may be attractive or intelligent, but certainly not both at the same time. Since female attractiveness signifies sexual availability within this semiotic system, marriage or spinsterhood basically fulfil the same purpose. Like Mina Harker of *Dracula* a female character may be (condescendingly) congratulated for having 'man's brain', but she must be trapped in the feminine body inscribed within patriarchy if she is not to be a threat.

The hard-boiled male detective is the most popular of the twentieth-century investigators and, as with the female amateur, gender issues have a formative influence on his characterization. John Cawelti traces the difference between the classical and hard-boiled detective to the role of women in the more recent texts. Whereas women rarely appear in Victorian detective fiction, in the twentieth-century texts they feature prominently, usually as an evil seductress. Cawelti concludes:

> the intense masculinity of the hard-boiled detective is in part a symbolic denial and protective coloration against complex sexual and status anxieties focussing on women. The function of the woman in the hard-boiled formula then is not simply that of appropriate sexual consort to the dashing hero; she also poses certain basic challenges to the detective's physical and psychological security. (Cawelti, 1976 (E), p. 154)

In other words, the hard-boiled detective represents a fictional resolution of the challenge to patriarchy posed by the twentieth-century Women's Movement. As women became increasingly vocal and visible, as they moved into careers formerly considered male preserves, male fantasies of denial and dominance demanded and found appropriate embodiment – the secret agent, the soldier of fortune, the space adventurer, and the cynical detective. This detective is both sexually active (unlike his Victorian forebears) and emotionally involved, but his sexual activity is a display of power and dominance over women, while his emotional involvement is with the case. His laugh, too, is unpleasant; a scornful dismissal of women and their wicked ways, a helpless grimace of moral superiority over the corrupt individuals infesting all social institutions.

The hard-boiled detective is identified by Cawelti as lower middle class, 'those condemned by their lack of economic mobility to inhabit the decaying center of this urban society' (p. 157). Whereas reader identification in the nineteenth-century detective novel was with the narrator, the ordinary man, in the hard-boiled novel it is with the detective himself, 'a marginal professional with a smattering of culture' but on the whole 'his tastes and attitudes are ordinary' (p. 157). He is a common man figure, but he is also intensely moral. He always occupies the moral high-ground, over bureaucrats and police-men, public servants and politicians, and most especially over women and the rich, whom Cawelti sees as the focus of hostility in the hard-boiled story. Cawelti notes further that this hostility, often expressed in physical violence, is all the more virulent for being compounded with 'attraction and desire'. Women and wealth are represented as the archetypal desires of the common man (in advertising, literature, movies, television, etc.); failure to attain them is attenuated by their fictional rejection as inherently worthless and corrupt. The physical, emotional and intellectual attributes of the hard-boiled detective – his smart talk, brusqueness, physical strength, self-sufficiency, sentimentality – construct a character with an ideolo-gical function as conservative as that of Holmes and Dupin. In the face of a fragmented society, in which the institutions manifestly serve the oppressor rather than the oppressed and where women (evoked terrifyingly as the undifferentiated mass, Woman) threaten to take the lives and livelihood (that is, economic dominance) away from men, the detective operates as a fictional compensation; the corrupt rich are assaulted and arrested, women are seduced, assaulted, arrested or killed. Cawelti writes of this modern detective:

> the hard-boiled hero is potent and courageous. Though he must continually face the fears of loneliness and isolation, of status uncer-tainty and of sexual betrayal, he is the kind of man who can fight his way to the source of the pervasive evil and, meeting violence with violence, destroy it. In the process of his quest, he also lays bare the widespread corruption of the social order, thereby proving and main-taining his own moral integrity. (p. 157)

The problem is, of course, that the detective does not destroy this pervasive evil. Instead, like his Victorian predecessors, he encounters some of those who most embody it, and disembodies them. The evil remains. This persistence of evil is not addressed, not explained, not detected. As noted earlier, engagement with this problem of social evil would involve the detective in an exploration of ideology which would threaten, if not destroy, the individualist discourse which informs his character. This is the conventional form of the detective with which feminist detective writers have to contend, and which they must modify to produce a feminist text. Block's claim that 'women writers will have to change the myth itself, instead of trying to fit themselves into it' is entirely justified.

Another convention, with which I have already dealt at some length, is the narrator, often the detective's own friend/helper. As noted earlier, this convention operated mainly during the nineteenth century where it was both a point of identification for readers and a way of presenting the detective's views without giving them emotional content. It reinforced the detective's detachment and objectivity, as well as his romantic alienation. Twentieth-century detectives usually tell their own tale, which is a narrative of bourgeois individualism and of the coherent and autonomous bourgeois subject.

The criminal of detective fiction is also a conventional construct, as the analysis of the detective's role suggests. In the nineteenth century he was an embodiment of the forces which threatened to disrupt the bourgeois order (the criminal was usually male; women were not considered sufficiently powerful to operate as signifiers of social disruption, except where sexuality was concerned). The criminal was usually motivated by greed, the desire for property and status. His crime was his rejection of the morality which holds those desires in proper check (that is, directs them through the appropriate financial institutions). The detective eradicates a threat to the social order by identifying this criminal. As noted earlier, this criminal can be read as a deconstruction of the prevailing ideological formation. By individuating this criminal, rather than identifying inimical social practices, the detective conceals the true nature of the social order and so eradicates this threat to unmask its ideology. The criminal of Victorian fiction was, therefore, appropriately anonymous, a personification of one or more evil traits. An individualist construct like the detective, he was as morally inferior as the detective was superior. He, too, was outside the social order but unlike the detective, whose (illusory) separation gave him critical power and moral certainty, he was a corrupt and corrupting force threatening an established moral order. A personification of social pathology, he had to be eradicated.

The twentieth-century criminal has several faces. Knight writes that Agatha Christie's great success lay in showing that the criminal could be someone familiar: 'the enemies to life and the property-conscious existence are already within the family or the trusted circle, like the family doctor' (Knight, 1980 (E), p. 128). This domestic villain threatened to expose the contradictions at the heart of bourgeois life, the individualist, competitive ideology which precludes social cohesion and harmony; her/his eradication papers over the cracks in the cosy facade of bourgeois life. This villain is often represented as insane (the crime often revenge for an old injustice, but revenge carried to its obsessive limit), which conveniently explains her/his failure to appreciate the virtues of bourgeois life – that is, why s/he would expose the contradictions of bourgeois ideology to critical scrutiny. Where the domestic villain is mad, the villain of the hard-boiled private investigator is thoroughly bad. This villain is often female and motivated by desires which contradict patriarchal descriptions of femininity. The female villain tries to become as powerful as men by corruptly acquiring wealth and/or influence. Her characterization has no subtlety or nuance; this is not a study in the systematic oppression of women, but an expression of patriarchal concern at the growing influence of feminism. In familiar patriarchal terms her main weapon (her defining characteristic and only value) is her body with which she attempts to seduce and destroy her detective pursuer. He is too clever, too powerful, too potent, and screws her both literally and metaphorically.

When the hard-boiled detective encounters male villains, they are very often in the employ of the rich and powerful, whom he knows from experience to be invariably corrupt, or they are the rich and powerful themselves. If employees, there are characteristically mean, petty and stupid, easily intimidated physically and intellectually. If the main villains, the sources of corruption, they are either brutish, weak men corrupted by power, or sleek, elegant and deadly, wielding power corruptly for their own gain. In either case the villains are not situated ideologically or socially. Again, no subtlety or complexity is evident in their characterization, which is articulated on familiar models – either the loutish usurper or the disdainful aristocrat. The detective succeeds when he exposes the rich and powerful as the corrupt individuals they are; but at the same time he conceals the corrupting nature of the ideology which structures not just these individuals, but the entire social formation.

The individual victim of these criminals is rarely given detailed characterization, which again accords with the tendency of the genre to avoid examination of the nature of the crime. The victim merely indicates that an investigation must occur, not why. That investigation is part of a highly conventionalized plot structure which constructs the characteristic narrative of detective fiction, that of bourgeois individualism. The problem of interpreting a literary text is often likened to the task of the detective, to 'construct a plot that will fill in the gaps of the stories they seek to understand' (Brooks, 1984 (A), pp. 321–2). However, the task of the critic is more than that of ideal reader, the critic must do more than simply locate the reading position of the text. The critic must also analyse that reading position, situating it in terms of its ideological function and practice. Feminist detective writers are engaged in this complex task, their construction of a feminist reading position predicated on their analysis and de/re/construction of the political practice of the contemporary detective novel.

Feminist detective fiction

A distinguishing characteristic of 'hard-boiled' detective fiction is that the heroines, who are always tramps of some utterly enchanting sort, are rescued and forgiven by the hard-boiled one and made pure again, usually by violence and repentance. Violence and repentance: major cultural characteristics of Americans with their Movietone memories, including hers, as she walks through Gate Four struggling with her bags, too confused to find a redcap, and the porters saying, 'Car 129? Straight ahead, ma'am.' (Jiles, 1986 (E), p. 6)

Paulette Jiles begins her postmodern pastiche of detective fiction, *Sitting in the Club Car Drinking Rum and Karma-Kola* by introducing not the detective but the criminal – or is she?

Feminist detective writers must first confront the problem of the detective; how to transform a characterization constituted by ideological discourses inimical to their own. The two most favoured strategies for (re)constructing the detective are: the amateur female detective who also has a profession and the professional female detective, the female equivalent of the hard-boiled investigator. Amateur status places the contemporary female detective in the tradition of Miss Marple, with the important distinction that she is no longer either without a career or asexual. These changes contradict the sexist premises on which the female detective was originally constructed and so completely transform the characterization and the narrative. The female detective now does transgress sexist female stereotypes; she is competent, intelligent and in charge of her own sexuality. Writers have used this transformation in a variety of strategies which have in common the construction of a feminist reading position for their texts.

One of the best-known amateurs is Amanda Cross's American professor, Kate Fansler. Fansler is presented as a role model both inside and outside the text. In *Death in a Tenured Position* Fansler's niece, Leighton tells her: 'mostly you're cool and elegant and intellectual and my absolute one and only role model' (Cross, 1981 (E), p. 32). Cross's major achievement with this character is to create an acceptable female professional who can begin the process of reconstructing the range of narrative roles available to women. It must be noted, however, that Fansler's other characteristics compromise to some extent the innovation represented in this change of gender. She is upper middle class, from a wealthy family who assured her entry and success at university. Her family did not literally buy her degrees, but the educational background, social poise and self-confidence their money bought her virtually guaranteed that with sufficient intelligence and application she would do well. By contrast Valerie Miner's academic detective, Nan Weaver, has to over-achieve in order to reach a position considerably less stable than that of Fansler. In *Murder in the English Department* Weaver is characterized as a working-class woman who, because of her gender, started adult life with no higher ambition than, in her own words, to 'marry "up" and away from Hayward' (Miner, 1982 (E), p. 22). She comes to her academic career after an unsatisfying stint as a schoolteacher, a broken marriage, and years of study as a 'mature student'. Weaver still finds difficulty operating socially and professionally in an institution catering specifically to the middle classes. Where Fansler is, again in Leighton's admiring words, 'tall and slim and soignee' (p. 32), Weaver is intimidated by the sophistication of her own graduate student:

> Nan always felt more like Marjorie's student than her thesis adviser. Statuesque Marjorie with her long, blonde hair as elegantly coifed as any daughter of Augustus Caesar. Marjorie, who looked as if she had been born in a silk blouse and a velvet skirt. Marjorie who always seemed to be wondering – behind her dutiful questions about course requirements and bibliographic techniques – 'Are you sure you're the real Professor Weaver? Are you sure you're in the right place, Shortie?' (p. 4)

Kate Fansler recognizes that her class background was influential in getting her into her chosen university; however, she does not seem to consider its continuing influence. She defends her tenure on the grounds that she is a well-published, well-respected scholar, but does not consider the extent to which self-confidence, the authority of her class, and her ease with institutional practice contributed to her publication and research record. In other words, Fansler is prepared to admit that she had some help with her start in life, but not that her class background is the most significant determinant of her career. If she had chosen a profession which was not so culturally high-coded as the study of literature, she may have encountered more opposition on the grounds of gender; however, she has chosen a field which to all but male academics must seem eminently suitable to one of her social status. Fansler also plays the literary name-dropper to the hilt. On the other hand, Weaver is highly sensitized to class issues. Her unease in the middle-class institution is largely a function of her own unresolved feelings about her working-class background, evident in her explanation of her discomfort:

> Nan sometimes worried that Marjorie and the other students could tell she wasn't smart. Oh, maybe she had a knack for common sense, but she wasn't a genuine intellectual. Nan attributed all her academic success to effort rather than intelligence. Although she was a professor at one of the best American universities, although she had published widely, she still didn't feel like a scholar. She felt like a fraud. (p. 28)

In rejecting its patriarchal ideology she has severed all links with the values, assumptions, principles which were the earliest influences on her and formative of her as a person, her subjectivity. In the course of the novel Weaver is forced to confront her abdication, her self-exile, discovering that sexism permeates middle-class, as well as working-class, families. Near the end of the book she is guest of honour at a party attended by her own family, her university colleagues and Marjorie Adams's mother, Rose, a class mixture which surprises Weaver. The novel ends with her driving into the sunset, future unsettled, but determined to renegotiate her position in relation to the institution in which she works – which means a reassessment of gender and class ideologies. And it is pertinent that she leaves at a time when her tenure is under consideration, refusing to make the compromises which would ensure her security: her colleague, Matt warns her not to leave:

> 'You're crazy, Nan, to go now,' he told her two nights before at the Pogo Cafe. 'The department's sympathy is with you. You could get tenure, just by being inconspicuous for a few months.'
> 'Do I really want to work in a department where half my colleagues fear or despise me?' (p. 167)

The same lack of compromise is evident in Weaver's academic work. Where Kate Fansler name-drops mainstream writers from the Great

Tradition of English literature to validate her own judgements, Nan Weaver has to argue with her own graduate student over the exclusion of women from literary history, their difficulty in being published, and then in being reviewed, the exclusion of women from institutions of knowledge and the number of women writers taught on university courses. Fansler has some power as an alternative role model; however, Cross's apparent obliviousness to the role of ideology in the formation of individual subjectivity substantially reduces Fansler's value in the deconstruction of female narrative roles. On the other hand, Miner's careful placement of Weaver in terms of gender and class enables her to operate as a detective, uncovering the narrative of bourgeois patriarchal culture and subjectivity.

Barbara Wilson's amateur detective, Pam Nilson, functions similarly in her two novels, *Murder in the Collective* and *Sisters of the Road* (Wilson, 1984 (E) and 1987 (E)). Particularly in the first book the characterization of Nilson serves as an investigation of the ideologies of gender, class and race. As part-owner of a left-wing printing press she is constantly involved in debates over issues arising from all three ideologies, during which her own status as a white, middle-class American is repeatedly challenged: what kinds of assumptions, values, beliefs has she inculcated from her own background and training. While involved in her detective work in *Murder in the Collective* Nilson also renegotiates one aspect of her own subjectivity, her sexuality. She has a lesbian affair, which involves and delights her more than any heterosexual relationship in which she has been involved. Nilson has to confront her own interpellation within heterosexism, as Nan Weaver had to renegotiate her class positioning. This investigation of sexuality occurs in a number of recent amateur detective novels, including Val McDermid's *Report for Murder* (McDermid, 1987 (E)) and Mary Wings's *She Came Too Late* (Wings, 1986 (E)), though neither involve their detective in such a fundamental assessment of sexuality. Wings's novel, in fact, reads more like a Chandleresque parody than a feminist novel. Her lesbian social worker cum detective, Emma Victor, evaluates potential female lovers with the same kind of cool detachment as Philip Marlowe. Wings at one stage has her attending a strip show which she describes in titillating, if disapproving, detail. In *Report for Murder* journalist-detective Lindsay Gordon is involved in investigating a murder in which social attitudes to lesbianism are a key factor, their potential virulence contrasting with her own caring and rational lifestyle.

The amateur female detective of the nineteenth and early twentieth century was represented as either asexual or sexually unavailable: she either could not get a man (a spinster) or she already had a man (married). Both representations are structured by a patriarchal discourse which denies women the ability to be both sexually active and autonomous and intelligent. The female amateur of contemporary feminist and women-centred texts may be either married but relatively independent (Kate Fansler), in a committed heterosexual relationship and independent (Gillian Slovo's Kate Baier), single and heterosexual (Nan Weaver), or lesbian (Pam Nilson, Lindsay Gordon, Emma Victor). In other words, she may have a man *and* a career, have a career and not be too bothered about having a man, or she may have a woman and not be at all interested in having a man. In each case the characterization of the detective confronts the exclusions operating in the patriarchal representations. These contemporary amateurs are sexually autonomous, economically independent, intelligent and courageous and on those grounds alone offer a fundamental challenge to the traditional role; that is, they substantially 'change the myth'. And sometimes they simultaneously expose the myth, the patriarchal discourse which so seriously limits the range of activities available to women and which accordingly structures their fictional representations. Books such as *Murder in the English Department* and *Murder in the Collective* do not rest on the implicit challenge of the revised characterization of the detective, but also engage textually in a debate about the operation and power of patriarchal ideology – as observed in sexist social practices or in assumptions about (hetero)sexuality in the constitution of the individual subject.

> A small sign stands up beside the track; it says CHINA BAR. She sees a man in a fedora and a big long dirty coat swing aboard the train two cars ahead, carrying a grip.
> *Why has the train stopped for this man?*
> For the plot, of course.
> For the plot and for the polarity, for his battered case and his face and his way of occupying space; that's why the train stopped. Hiatus. Pause. Pause steam, pause wheels, pause *whistle!* . . . Like the man in the Camel advertisements; like photographs of photographers taking photographs surrounded by admiring Pathans; like lies, prevarications, inventions, illusions, stories, pacifiers, anything you can think of that causes human beings to act like idiots; a *romantic presence.* (Jiles, 1986 (E), pp. 16–17)

Into Paulette Jiles's train of thought steps the ultimate trickster, the grand illusionist, the bogus Bogey in mac and fedora, the Camel man, the Depardieu of dreams, the bourgeois patriarchal male subject, the detective – or is he?

Into the pages of contemporary detective fiction steps a new kind of hard-boiled private investigator, a woman. Sara Paretsky's V.I. Warshawski, Marcia Muller's Sharon McCone, P.D. James's Cordelia Grey, Sue Grafton's Kinsey Millhone and Marele Day's Claudia Valentine are all detectives by occupation, work in the tough world of big city corruption, face the same kind of violence as their male counterparts, and take care of themselves. Sara Paretsky says of her decision to write a professional female sleuth:

> As a reader of mysteries, I always had trouble with the way women are treated, as either tramps or helpless victims who stand around weeping. I wanted to read about a woman who could solve her own problems ... I was determined to write a hard-boiled sleuth who was both a woman and a complete professional, someone who could operate in a tough milieu and not lose her femininity. (Stasio, 1985 (E), p. 38)

Marilyn Stasio records that Paretsky and her contemporaries agree on a number of issues which must be negotiated in constructing a female detective. Firstly, the detective should compromise neither her femininity nor the conventions of the genre. That is, she should not operate as a male detective in drag, but should bring female characteristics to the role which transform it. Yet that transformation should not obscure the nature of the work; it should remain recognizably detective fiction. For the feminist writer the relevance of these conditions is apparent. If the female detective should lose her femininity, should not be somehow specifically female, then the difficult exercise of creating a female hero loses all value. And if the revised work is not recognizably of the detective genre, and so loses its audience, once again the value of the exercise must be questioned. It may be that the reworked text operates primarily as an interrogation of the genre, rather than as a new formulation of it, but again, if the writer ignores genre convention, this interrogative mode will be difficult to maintain.

> The man who got on at China Bar walks into the club car; he walks down the aisle, puts his grip into Compartment D (remember that) and looks down to the bar beyond the frosted glass. And there she is:
> *Sitting in the Club Car Drinking Rum*
> *and Karma-Kola,*
> like a book title.
> Is this a detective novel or what?
> His effortless story falls into place, a series of delayed images.

> She continues to make hers up, spending her imaginative
> energy like a gambler.
>
> Paulette Jiles, *Sitting in the Club Car*

The writers all agree that the female detective must involve herself as energetically as any male character in the action of the story. She must not sit on the sidelines and narrate or work in a purely cerebral manner, as this would destroy the impact of the role revision and is fundamentally out of character for the modern detective, who tends to be far more involved in the action than his nineteenth-century predecessors. For feminist writers the same reasoning applies, with the added incentive that the characterization of an active female role is an implicit interrogation of the passivity conventionally associated with female narrative roles; or at least, good female roles (evil women only may be active).

> And he asked her,
>   'Who are you?
> and she said,
>   'I'm a railroad dick.
>
> Paulette Jiles, *Sitting in the Club Car*

The new female detective should also be able to look after herself physically, to practice some form of self-defence. Violence is regarded as an area of major difference between male and female detectives. Marcia Muller notes:

> My detective definitely gets scared when the bad guys start coming after her. Sharon isn't one of those super-assured people who think they know it all. Those supermacho types in male private-eye novels set themselves above the law and take it into their own hands. It's that superior attitude that leads to their patronizing treatment of women, as well as their lack of human sympathy for all the people they deal with. (Stasio, 1985 (E), p. 38)

Sue Grafton agrees that this blasé attitude to violence is careless of the real emotional impact of violence on the individual:

> Most of the hard-boiled detectives go through murder and mayhem, and it has absolutely no impact on their personalities. I find it more interesting to see what the constant exposure to violence and death really does to a human being, how an individual incorporates that into their psyche. (p. 38)

It might be objected that Grafton is pursuing a realist reading here. That the point is that the 'personality' of the detective is formed precisely in terms of this violence and that this is concealed by his failure to register its effects. As Claudia Valentine muses in Marele Day's *The Life and Crimes of Harry Lavender*: 'I could never understand how Philip Marlowe and those guys, from one end of the story to another, got shot, beaten up, and sometimes laid, without ever going to bed' (Day, 1988 (E)). In feminist texts violence must be carefully negotiated. As analysis of the hard-boiled male detective confirmed, the violence endemic to this characterization is largely an expression of misogyny, a fictional recompense to the conservative male reader for the growing autonomy of women in the real world. Its other component is helplessness, the impotence of the individual in the face of institutionalized corruption given fictional expression and resolution in the vigilante violence of the male detective. Since feminist texts specifically eschew this misogynistic response to women, and since they also sometimes locate this institutional corruption in dominant ideological discourses, rather than in corrupt individuals, the rationale for individual violence must be carefully considered. While it is a convention of the genre particularly associated with the hard-boiled detective and so must be addressed in some manner, feminist and woman-centred writers usually resolve the dilemma by associating violence with evil, with anti-social forces in the text. The female detective can rarely outmatch a male opponent on the grounds of brute strength, so she must rely on more sophisticated means of self-defence such as karate and, where possible, running away. She also tends to avoid using a gun, on the grounds that it might be taken from her and used against her. Not only does this have a rational basis, it also means that female detectives are not doomed to spend their lives furtively fingering the smooth metal shaft in their pockets, an omission which surely emphasizes the phallic significance of the weapon used by so many male detectives.

Another common characteristic of professional female detectives is that they work alone, contradicting Block's analysis quoted at the beginning of this chapter. If the female professional employs a male off-sider, then the impact of traditional semiosis is not difficult to predict. Whether or not the male character protected her from violence, he would be seen to do so, even where that totally violated observable fact. And the power of traditional semiosis also makes a female off-sider an unwise choice: she would be read as proof that it takes two women to do a man's job. The female detective therefore must work solo if she is to have the same textual authority as a male character.

Similarly she must not use her sexuality to manipulate her opponents or clients. Since women are traditionally characterized as having value only in terms of sexuality, and since active female sexuality is characterized as evil, such a move would be self-defeating and the detective would lose all professional credibility. On the other hand, this new breed of professional detectives do express their sexuality. Their professionalism is not bought at the cost of asexuality, as intelligence was by Miss Marple and her colleagues. Professional female detectives do have lovers, with whom they may become emotionally involved. Marilyn Stasio notes:

> Attitudes towards love and sex range from casual to very intense, but that emotional element is always around and is often crucial to the plot. These women will not sleep with clients, but they will kill for someone they love. (p. 39)

The female detective writers reject also the exploitative casual sex of their male counterparts. Their detectives may have casual sex, but it is rarely exploitative, and they specifically avoid the misandry which would be the female equivalent of the attitude to heterosexual partners expressed in so much hard-boiled fiction.

Professional female detectives use and transform many of the conventions of traditional hard-boiled detective fiction. As this analysis shows, those transformations are necessitated by the gender identity of the detective. If she is not to become a counterfeit male, she must operate differently, yet operate within the rules of the genre. In doing so, and changing the genre, the myth, in the process, the female detective reveals the discursive basis of many of the conventions used in the construction of the hard-boiled private investigator. Most importantly, for this study, she reveals his character to be constituted in sexist terms, his violence and his sexual power an expression of the fear of (patriarchal) readers, the patriarchal subject, of female autonomy, of female economic and sexual independence and assertiveness.

> The Man held up all the face cards he had: a queen of spades, a king of diamonds, a jack of hearts. He held them up with their faces toward her.
> 'You know, sweetheart, someday you're going to have to tell these nice people the truth.'
> Paulette Jiles, *Sitting in the Club Car*

Another convention of the genre which is sometimes transformed significantly in the feminist detective novel is the characterization of the criminal and/or victim. In many of the hard-boiled texts the victim is familiar from the work of male colleagues; big business and corrupt businessmen rub shoulders with petty criminals and small people who murder out of fear or for revenge. In some of the feminist hard-boiled novels, however, political issues become the focus of the detection and the criminal embodies the social disruption caused by invidious social practices. In two recent Kate Baier mysteries, for example, South African political operations in the United Kingdom (*Morbid Symptoms*) and incest (*Death Comes Staccato*) are major plot elements; the politics of race and gender an essential part of the detection (Slovo, 1984 (E) and 1987 (E)). In both cases tracing the social and institutional consequences of injustice – institutional corruption, personal trauma – is as crucial to the development of the narrative as is the identification of the criminal. In fact, the crime itself, though serious, is diminished in impact by its contextualization within a society which tolerates such injustice. In other words, investigation of a single crime becomes the means by which the author constructs a critique of particular aspects of her own society. In *Death Comes Staccato*, for example, the incest theme pursued in the story is not literally the cause of the murder which occurs, but the murder happens because the characters live in a society which tolerates and conceals, and to that extent colludes in, the exploitation of the vulnerable.

The amateur female detective writers are even more inventive in their treatment of criminals and victims. Two of the most interesting examples of the revision of the conventional criminal/victim roles are Miner's *Murder in the English Department* and Wilson's *Murder in the Collective*. Miner produces a situation in which the victim is also the criminal and the criminal also the victim. Her story tells of the murder of a professor, Angus Murchie, by the graduate student Marjorie Adams he is attempting to rape. Miner's characterization of the student as upper middle-class, wealthy, beautiful, fashionable and intelligent is a master-stroke, preventing the displacement of the crime in class terms. It cannot be interpreted as the revenge of a woman against the male establishment or working-class jealousy of middle-class power; it has to be read as an act of violence by someone who has no need to use violence to achieve her personal and professional objectives. Furthermore Adams does not even perceive the sexism which has placed her in the position to kill; Nan Weaver, her supervisor tries vainly to explain to her how sexism permeates every aspect of life. The reason Adams cannot see or understand this sexism is that she is sheltered by her class position, which makes her inaccessible to the more palpable levels of sexual abuse. Only with the attempted rape does Adams understand that she can be positioned as a victim simply because she is a woman. By then, of course, it is too late and her only possible response is one of equal violence. She defends herself and accidentally kills her attacker. Is she, therefore, the criminal or the victim?

Miner treats the murder victim to a similar analysis: is Murchie victim or criminal? He is characterized in some detail as an exploitative, condescending, sexist man, but he is not diabolic or fiendish. Murchie, too, is a product of a sexist society and a sexist institution. While this does not excuse his behaviour, it does show that at its basis is not individual psychology but social pathology. Murchie is not the scapegoat for his crime of violence any more than Adams is for hers; both are motivated by the sexist discourse which structures the institution in which they work, the society in which they live, and their individual selves.

Barbara Wilson uses a similar role reversal in *Murder in the Collective*. The murdered man, Jeremy, turns out to be a CIA informant who has been blackmailing Filipinos exiled under the Marcos regime with threats of exposure, deportation and certain death at the hands of Marcos death squads. He also threatens to blackmail a lesbian worker at the printery around which the story is set into having sex with him. As a result his ex-wife, Zenaida, herself a Filipina, shoots him with his own gun. Wilson clearly indicates that the reason for Jeremy's death is the ruthless exploitation, of other countries (the Philippines by the US government) and of women, which Jeremy embodies. Jeremy himself is more of an idiosyncratic construct than Murchie and the description of his motivation by the detective's sometime off-sider/lover is scarcely adequate, given the complex significance of the characterization: 'He was a weak man who needed a sense of power. the more he got the more he used it' (Wilson, 1984 (E), p. 179). Nevertheless, Wilson's text does work more effectively as detective fiction than Miner's, building suspense around both the identification of the murderer and the reason for the crime. And Wilson's use of him as an embodiment of exploitation is effective.

The characterization of the murderer works in a similar way, with Zenaida combining the attributes of the oppressed, a Filipina woman. Zee explains her position to Pam when she is in hiding from the police, telling her of the exploitation of the Philippines by the American military, and especially of the abuse of her countrywomen in the brothels around the Subic Bay base. When Zee shoots Jeremy, she acts very like the hard-boiled detective who knows that justice will not be done by the judicial institutions and so takes it into her own hands. The position is problematic, whether in a feminist or non-feminist text. The question raised by the conclusion is again whether the murderer is as much a product of the system as the victim, who is himself a murderer, through his betrayals of Filipinos.

The narratives of the female detective texts are as conservative or as radical as their characterizations of detective, criminal and victim. The narrative of the professional female detective is often relatively unaffected by the change in gender of the detective. She constructs the narrative of the crime as Holmes before her, succeeding when she has formulated the character of the criminal. The novel concludes with the arrest or disposal of the criminal and the detective's explanation of the reasoning which resulted in her/his identification. Hard-boiled female private investigators operate similarly, identifying the criminal who has violated social laws, most commonly by committing murder. As noted earlier, however, professional female detective writers sometimes incorporate as plot elements incidents which challenge the beneficence of the social system within which the detective operates, not just of the individuals in positions of power (though that also occurs), but more fundamentally of the discourses of gender, race and class which operate in that society producing the situations in which crime occurs. In other words, their plotting of a crime may include the patriarchal bourgeois narrative of contemporary Western society as a plot element, and sometimes it is found to be as guilty as the individuated criminal, as in the Kate Baier stories mentioned earlier. In *The Life and Crimes of Harry Lavender* Marele Day reaches a similar conclusion, which she reinforces by the use of interacting narratives, the narrative of detective Claudia Valentine fragmented by that of crime boss, Harry Lavender, who describes his background and rise to power. Lavender cannot be dismissed as an aberrant individual when the circumstances of his life are known; instead the social formation which offered crime as a legitimizing activity to a penniless migrant is called to account.

The narratives of the professional female detectives may be fundamentally conservative, the only feminist element of the novels being the gender of the detective. Or the narrative may be disrupted by references to contemporary social debates or by the narrative of the criminal, preventing the glib representation of social injustice in a single aberrant individual. When the criminals of these texts are dispatched, the reader is left in no doubt that the injustice will continue – and not simply because there are so many aberrant individuals, but because the patriarchal bourgeois discourse of her/

his society constructs injustice and the individuals who are its agents.

'Who the hell do you think you are?' she says, and doesn't wait
for an answer. 'Now I won't even be able to get a job!'

'Ah darling, do not fall further into the ranks of crime,' he
advises her. 'It pays too well.'

Every dream is an adventure story, detective fiction, a mass
paperpack with You as the protagonist but not quite; the trick is,
which one of you? And in every detective story there is the point
where you finally see the person pursuing you, and everything
is clear to both of you, and you have to run.

Paulette Jiles, Sitting in the Club Car

The narratives of the amateur female detectives are often experimental, avoiding the traditional pattern of detection (which is not
detection) and revelation (which is concealment). As the discussion of
the role of the criminal indicated, these narratives may end with the
reversal of the roles of criminal and victim or with the criminal being
shielded from prosecution. While criminals were sometimes protected in traditional detective fiction, because their motives were
good, they were invariably dispatched by the end of the story – dying
of cancer, suicide, disappearing to parts unknown. They were not left
to serve as a continual challenge to their own society. In some of the
more radical texts, however, the criminal gets away with murder. This
conclusion is disturbing for readers, and only acceptable if they
accept the social criticism of the writer; that is, if they accept that the
social order with which they are familiar is not as just and harmonious as they have been taught to believe. These radical texts rely for
effectiveness, therefore, on their ability to produce a reading position
which incorporates a subversive social critique. In *Murder in the
Collective*, for example, Pam decides not to reveal to the police her
discovery that Zee is Jeremy's murderer, because she believes that
Jeremy's own actions justify Zee's action. As a covert government
employee Jeremy had both the power to blackmail and the implicit
endorsement of the system. Wilson's conclusion thus constitutes a
subversive critique of notions of social harmony and justice, and of
the fiction which operates to reinforce conservative social attitudes.
This interrogation of the role of detective fiction as an agent of the
dominant ideological formation is reinforced in the final pages of the
book where Wilson gives a list of sources 'For Further Information On
the Philippines, On Filipinos in America, And On the Role of Women
in Developing Countries' (Wilson, 1984 (E), p. 182). So her 'fictional'
narrative concludes with a list of 'real' resources, which immediately

challenges the status of the detective novel. What else about the novel is 'real'? If it is entirely fictional, what purpose does such an appendix serve?

Valerie Miner's *Murder in the English Department* also ends with the release of the criminal, but this time via the judicial system. Marjorie Adams is found to be operating in self-defence and freed of Angus Murchie's murder. Of course, a cynical reader might question whether a society so permeated with sexist attitudes would reach such a conclusion – or, at the least, how much Adams's social status contributed to her acquittal. Nevertheless, the point is made that the murder committed in the story is a result of invidious social practices perpetrated not by a particularly nasty individual, but by a weak man who practises too literally the sexist discourse of his institution. Miner's novel, perhaps more than any other discussed so far, is a story of detection and revelation. Little attempt is made to hide the identity of the murderer; instead, Miner concentrates on discovering the events which led to the murder. The culprit Miner detects is the sexist discourse which motivated both Murchie's attempted rape of Adams and his murder by her. Interestingly Miner's novel does not maintain the level of suspense conventional with the detective novel, and has been criticized on those grounds. This response itself recalls the individualist ideology of bourgeois society, showing it to be complicit in the concealment of the inequalities fundamental to dominant ideological discourses.

> It has become his story without any effort on his part; it was preconstructed. He feels suddenly overwhelmed with loss, and so tries to light a cigarette and takes on water. He feels he has lost something (a story) forever, that was of immense value, that would have made all the difference. He remembers what he thought he wanted was not what he really wanted, but who does? You know. He wanted the end of her story.
>
> Paulette Jiles, *Sitting in the Club Car*

Miner's 'failure' to construct conventional detective fiction, complete with suspense and an appropriate scapegoat, is indicative of the problems for feminist writers in using this genre. The characteristic narrative of the detective novel is that of patriarchal bourgeois ideology; to challenge any aspect of that narrative seriously compromises the writer's ability to produce an otherwise conventional text. In that respect, detective fiction, perhaps more than any other genre discussed so far, reveals the extent to which genre conventions are encoded with ideological discourses.

So why the feminist incursion into the detective fiction genre? Why have feminist writers, that is, writers working within a feminist framework, with a feminist ideology, textually constructing a feminist reading position for their readers, chosen to write detective fiction? The answer to this question is partly answered at the conclusion of Marcia Muller's story 'The Broken Men'. Her detective, Sharon McCone has solved the mystery surrounding the death of a clown and the story ends with her musing on the social function of clowning:

> What was it, I thought, that John had said to me about clowns when we were playing gin in the dressing room at the pavilion? Something to the effect that they were all funny but, more important, that they all made people take a look at their own foibles. John Tilby and Elliot Larson – in a sense both broken men like Gary Fitzgerald had been – knew more about those foibles than most people. Maybe there was a way they could continue to turn that sad knowledge into laughter. (Muller, 1985 (E), p. 221)

Muller concludes her text with the self-referentiality characteristic of the feminist generic texts analysed in previous chapters. Like them, detective fiction can be a means of examining contemporary social issues, including the nature of contemporary gender ideologies. Detective fiction may make a society look at its own foibles, at the ideological discourses which structure social practices and individual interactions, the constructions of social institutions and individual subjectivity. If detective fiction truly detects, it might offer social criticism and self-knowledge along with its entertainment – just like the carnivalesque clowns of Muller's story.

For feminist writers this self-knowledge must include an awareness of the way that the individual subject is constructed through the negotiation of a number of ideologies, including race and class as well as gender. If the detective novel is to do more than extend the idealist construction of women as Woman, it must engage with women's negotiation of a matrix of ideological discourses and so reveal the differences between women, as well as their similarities. Both *Murder in the English Department* and *Murder in the Collective* address this complex task. In Miner's novel the influence of class background on the individual is considered in some depth. The detective, Nan Weaver renegotiates her relationship with her own working-class background in the course of the novel. It is also interesting that this book has been criticized for its representation of class in that it does not adopt an unequivocal pro-working-class line. In fact, Miner achieves a more complex and interesting, and realistic, end; to have a woman who has fled her working-class background reconsider that decision, not because of her own actions, but because she recognizes the dignity and autonomy of a working-class woman (her sister) who has successfully negotiated the compromises attendant on her accept- ance of that class status. At the party to celebrate Adams's release she is the most uncomfortable participant, the working-class emigre who watches from the outside as working-class and middle-class indi- viduals interact on the basis of mutual respect. When Weaver drives off into the sunset at the conclusion of the novel, unsure of her future, Miner signifies that her narrative is not resolved; the negotiation continues. The resolution of this novel cannot be constructed in terms of a simple acceptance of bourgeois individualism, nor of an essential- ly bourgeois representation of working-class life (itself the construc- tion of working-class emigres). The reading position of Miner's novel produces a complex understanding of both the similarities between women, the product of their construction by (patriarchal) gender ideology, and of their differences which are a function of their individual negotiation of (bourgeois) class ideology. In *Murder in the Collective* Wilson achieves a similar complexity, with the negotiation of (white supremacist) race ideology seen as a crucial difference between the women represented in the novel.

Many of the female detective novels written in the hard-boiled format do not address issues of difference. Their achievement is to develop a radical female characterization, the competent, caring, professional woman, one who breaks the virgin/whore dichotomy of traditional female characterization. The narrative of bourgeois indi- vidualism is left entirely unchallenged in the text, along with its assumptions about race. Certainly the traditional male-oriented de- tective narrative stands as a discursive referent for these texts, but it inflects similarly the ideologies of race and class. In other words, it does seem that a distinction must be made between those texts which address only gender ideology and so may be termed critical and provisionally radical, and those which cross-reference the negotiation of gender ideology with the ideologies of race and class and so challenge the idealist conceptualization of women (as Woman, with- out race, without class) and so may be termed radical or subversive. The hard-boiled revisions tend to fall into the first category; the amateur detective revisions into the second. So perhaps it is not so surprising to find that books in the first category are published by a variety of mainstream publishers, whilst those in the second category line up on the bookshelf in the familiar striped livery of the Women's Press.

6

Feminist Romance

Lia, about to be swayed, remembered her father. She gave Flint a chaste kiss. 'Flint, I can't do it darling,' she said. 'We've got to have a wedding . . . Don't look so stunned. Just my parents and the Burneys and half a dozen friends to see my dad do what he's been waiting for since the day I was born. I couldn't deprive my father of the satisfaction of giving his daughter away to the right man.'

She could see by Flint's eyes that he was pleased.

Jenny Loring, *The Right Woman*

Sweet tears filled her eyes, tears of incredible joy. It was as though she was too full of happiness, satiated with satisfaction, and her body overflowed with the wonder of it all. Smiling down at her with a tender warmth, Scott lovingly kissed the tears away.

After her breathing neared normal she whispered softly, 'Oh, how I love you.'

He took her hand and brought it to his lips. 'You're all the woman I'll ever need,' he promised her throatily.

Sarah James, *Public Affair*

Women are, in the sense that Hoggart and Seabrook present in their pictures of transition, without class, because the cut and fall of a skirt and good leather shoes can take you across the river and to the other side: the fairy-tales tell you that goose-girls can marry kings.

Carolyn Steedman, *Landscape for a Good Woman*

In 1979 the distribution figure for Harlequin books, a leading publisher of popular romances, stood at 168,000,000 copies, spread through 98 countries of the world. Given the popularity of this genre and its predominantly female audience it is mandatory to include some analysis of the romance in this study, even though, perhaps surprisingly, feminist rewritings of the romance are not easy to find. This scarcity also characterizes several other genres I do not have space to consider here, but which also promise interesting insights into the formation of subjectivity and the ideological significance of generic conventions: westerns, the spy/thriller subgenre of detective fiction, occult fiction.[1] However, it is romantic fiction which foregrounds the central problematic of many feminist generic texts, the nature of female/male relationships in a patriarchal society and the constitution of the gendered subject.

The romantic novel is structured by two central ideas or aims: the characterization of a strong, male figure, the hero, and the romance and marriage between him and the heroine. This is not an innovative plot, having been used in many texts as the focus for a discussion of such issues as social propriety, marriage arrangements, and the nature of fidelity. What is new is the fetishisation of the romance plot; in these contemporary romances the romantic plot itself is the focus of the text.

History of romantic fiction

A novelistic antecedent of the contemporary romance is Samuel Richardson's epistolary novel, *Pamela: or Virtue Rewarded* (1740) which deals with the constant battle of the servant girl heroine, Pamela Andrews, to protect her virginity from assault by her 'master'. Her success results in her marriage to this same man; that is, he does eventually deflower Pamela, but at a price. The tension in the novel arises from the fact that Pamela is constantly under threat of rape from the man who will become her husband and this rape fantasy remains a motivating force in romantic fiction. It also features in one of the two novels which seem to be the foundation of virtually all contemporary romance, *Wuthering Heights* and *Jane Eyre*.[2]

In *Wuthering Heights* (1847) Emily Brontë constructs the archetypal romantic hero, Heathcliff, while in *Jane Eyre* (1847) Charlotte Brontë constructs the typical romantic plot, the romance and marriage of Jane Eyre and her wealthy suitor, Edward Rochester. The books feature two great loves, that of Heathcliff and Cathy, and of Jane Eyre and Edward Rochester, but the outcomes of these loves are very different. Heathcliff and Cathy do not marry, though their love continues undiminished. Jane and Rochester do marry, but only after he has been blinded and maimed, symbolically castrated. These different outcomes are a function of the representation of power in these texts and the way that this structures characterization.

Heathcliff is originally presented as *déclassé*, brought home from the Liverpool slums by Mr Earnshaw. Heathcliff may be Earnshaw's bastard, or a gipsy, or a member of some other marginalized group, but his origins are never explained. At the Heights he is raised as a member of the yeoman-farmer class of the Earnshaws, though Heathcliff will not inherit the land on which he works. This class of working farmers is dying out, superceded by the new class of capitalist farmers, who may live on their land but pay others to work it. Heathcliff goes on to learn and use the practices of the bourgeois class (when he returns to the Heights as a gentleman) against both his own adopted class (when he takes the Heights from Hindley) and later against the capitalist farmer (as he destroys the Linton family). In betraying his own class, constitutive of his own subjectivity, he too is destroyed. In a novel which describes in detail the changing social formation of rural England Heathcliff represents a transitional phase, from yeoman farmer to capitalist landholder; his violence is the violence of revolutionary social change.

In terms of race, also, Heathcliff is the outsider. He is tall, dark, passionate, violent, uncivilized, the stereotypical Celt who stands in marked contrast to the fair, rationalist, physically untried, 'civilised' Englishman. Heathcliff is a member of a marginalized race and culture in nineteenth-century Britain, one being driven to extinction by the 'civilising' British.[3]

The love of Heathcliff and Cathy is represented in the text as an elemental force, as basic and powerful as the windswept moors on which they live. Their love seems outside social law, non-ideological, because it is not dependent on economic circumstances. This is also the reason for its non-consummation in social terms, as marriage. Cathy and Heathcliff do not marry, because they would not be able to survive in their society. So Cathy explains to Nelly Dean her decision to marry Edgar Linton:

> 'Nelly, I see now that you think me a selfish wretch; but did it never strike you that if Heathcliff and I married, we should be beggars? whereas, if I marry Linton I can aid Heathcliff to rise, and place him out of my brother's power.' (Brontë, 1966 (F), pp. 83–4)

Cathy deserts her own class to join Linton as a capitalist farmer, but, in so doing, she too is destroyed. By this means Emily Brontë signifies that love *without economic motive* cannot exist in a bourgeois society. It is a disruptive force which will inevitably be destroyed, or at least be denied any material reality. Accordingly, in representing this transgressive love, Brontë employs non-realist, fantastic elements (the ghostly apparition of Cathy, Heathcliff's increasingly bizarre appearance) which disrupt the (bourgeois) realist surface of her text.

In *Wuthering Heights* both Heathcliff and Cathy are strong characters, in the sense that they are both independent, autonomous, self-willed. This strong, female characterization is also transgressive, violating conventional representations of women. If the text is not to become totally fantastic or utopian, Cathy must be destroyed. It is, therefore, highly significant that she dies in childbirth; that is, that her defining (under patriarchy) gender identity, which she disrupts by her refusal of femininity, destroys her. Cathy is sacrificed to her biological deteminants, and hence to her ideological definition.

In *Jane Eyre* both characterization and plot structure are very different, the relationship between Jane and Rochester hearkening back to that of Pamela and her 'master'. Rochester is established as a powerful figure within the text, not seemingly outside ideology like Heathcliff, but in terms of the dominant ideological positioning of his society. Rochester's power is a construct of class and race ideologies. His first wife, Bertha Mason, is of mixed blood which, given the white bias of his society, establishes him as the dominant partner even though she is very wealthy (the reason for their marriage). When Bertha Mason refuses to accept her subjugation, remaining an assertive, powerful woman, she suffers the fate of many Victorian women, fictional and real; she is declared mad. Jane Eyre, his second wife, is of a lower social status than he, from the respectable but impoverished lower middle-class. Rochester has great economic power over Jane which he uses constantly to test her, much as Mr B. tested Pamela. Rochester's ugliness, which is almost fetishised in the text, cannot detract from his power and consequent attractiveness. In fact, this fetishisation of Rochester's homely appearance is used by Charlotte Brontë to show that male attractiveness is not a physical attribute, but a social (ideological) construction; a function of power, which is in turn a construct of the ideologies of class and race.

Jane and Rochester are able to marry because, in a patriarchal bourgeois society, a woman from a lower class position who assents to her own construction as a patriarchal subject – that is, who preserves her femininity at the cost of her own desires – can, supposedly, marry into a higher class. This is so because, in this (sexist) discourse, a woman's social status is identified with that of her father and then of her husband. She is essentially class-less, an object, a commodity, without any class positioning of her own. Rochester's blinding and maiming, his symbolic castration, is subsequently used by Brontë to demonstrate the consequences of this ideology for women, the denial of their desire. Jane's last minute inheritance of a fortune which makes her no longer dependent economically on Rochester signifies, by its very absurdity, the true nature of these fictional unions – not *grande passion*, but a socially-sanctioned, economically viable marriage. In other words, Charlotte Brontë's text not only foregrounds the romance plot and the female fantasy of marrying an attractive (that is, powerful) man, but it also demonstrates both the consequences of this fantasy for women and its ideological – economic – determinants.

Contemporary romantic fiction combines the construction of a strong, male character, a combination of Rochester and Heathcliff, with the development of a romance between him and the heroine. The conventions used in the characterizations and the plot structure of the modern romance reveal its ideological function as did those of their nineteenth-century predecessors. In the modern romance the male hero is usually an established professional man, often from a wealthy family, and occasionally from an aristocratic background. He is often some ten to 15 years older than the heroine, with the added experience – personal and professional – this entails. The assumptions are that he is white, middle- or upper-class and heterosexual. The heroine is correspondingly younger, less experienced, less established, less wealthy, and often from a poorer and less socially elevated background. The plot usually traces the subjugation of the heroine to the hero whom she initially dislikes because of his arrogance. In recent books this arrogance is often characterized as male chauvinist behaviour, which it usually is, but which the heroine eventually learns is the result of his true sensitivity. Accordingly the heroine learns that feminism is rather limited and immature, masking a fear of men. In the Harlequin romance, *Public Affair*, for example, the heroine is a university secretary who rejects the advances of a presumptuous male academic. She belongs to a women's group and rejects his overt sexism. However, the main arguments for feminism in the book are presented not by other women, or by the heroine herself, but by another *male* academic, Jeffrey, a truly loathsome piece of work. Jeffrey's 'feminism' is clearly a strategy to deny women even the superficial courtesy of patriarchy.

> Jeffrey had never ever opened a door for her or held her chair. Instead he gave her high-sounding intellectual arguments on how such behaviour was demeaning.

> 'When I do something for a woman that she could perfectly well do
> for herself, I'm transmitting un unspoken message to her. The message
> is, "You are incapable. Weaker. You must depend on me." It is an
> integral part of the reason women have never achieved equal status
> with their male counterparts. They unwittingly permit themselves to be
> demeaned by a cultural norm that, on the surface, is designed to
> display favoritism,' he told her in his typically wordy, arrogant manner.
> 'Never let a man do that to you,' he warned.
> After her own bad experience Liza had taken his warning quite
> seriously.
> Jeffrey had established another rule. (James, 1984 (F), p. 28)

Jeffrey is a bore and an exploiter, so it is highly significant that the
'feminist' discourse should be identified with this character. Of
course, Jeffrey's feminism is as superficial and absurd as his character, but represents fairly accurately the reductionist view of feminism
commonly propagated by its detractors. In other words, the reader is
positioned by the text to identify feminism with an exploitative and
dismissive attitude to women and, quite appropriately, to dismiss it.
The fear of men to which this feminism is often attributed is also
shown to be misguided, particularly by the association of feminism
with a pathetic male character like Jeffrey. And yet this fear is
constantly evoked by the text, by descriptions of the strength of the
hero and by allusions to the barely suppressed violence suggested by
his physique and often by his look, his 'penetrating' male gaze.
Violence is associated so regularly with the hero that it is a major
preoccupation of critics of the romance who, like Tania Modleski,
consider that these novels 'perpetuate ideological confusion about
male sexuality and male violence, while insisting that there is no
problem (they are "very different")' (Modleski, 1982 (F), pp. 42–3)

The powerful (brutal, violent) masculinity of the hero is fetishised
in these texts; that is, he is fetishised in gender terms, his class and
race characteristics apparently marginalized. The resolution of these
narratives devolves upon a rape fantasy, with the hero's dangerous
masculinity the source of the heroine's fear and admiration. The
discursive practice she acts out in the text is that, so long as she is
very feminine (like Pamela, like Jane Eyre), she will not be attacked, a
common ideological (mis)conception. She and the hero are united
when Heathcliff becomes Rochester, not through physical disability,
but through revealing his disabling and endearing sensitivity. (In
Wuthering Heights Cathy disabuses her sister-in-law, Isabella of any
such interpretation of Healthcliff: 'Pray, don't imagine that he conceals depths of benevolence and affection beneath a stern exterior!

He's not a rough diamond – a pearl-containing oyster of a rustic: he's a fierce, pitiless, wolfish man' (Brontë, 1966 (F), pp. 105–6). The resolution of the narrative comes with the heroine's marriage to a man of elevated social status and wealth; his violence is revealed as healthy male sexuality and the rape fantasy vanquished by the legalization of their intimate relations. In these texts rape and marriage are antithetical concepts, precisely because marriage, the end-point of the romance, is primarily a legal and economic relationship, not an intimate or personal one. This interpretation of the patriarchal marriage is not new; Richardson wrote about marriage in these terms in 1740. Modern romances, however, do not deconstruct the patriarchal marriage or the erotic relationship which is its initial phase. Instead they fetishise it; the relationship itself is the focus of the narrative, displacing from reader attention its economic determinants. The erotic desire which motivates the narrative enacts, in displaced form, not only the erotic desires of the reader, but her or his economic desires – for wealth, security, status – from which the erotic is inseparable. Simultaneously these texts conceal or mystify the threat of violence, of rape, which sustains male dominance under patriarchy, and the essentialist patriarchal characterization of masculinity.

As noted earlier, a rape fantasy is also the basis of many traditional fairy-tales, such as *Sleeping Beauty*, *Beauty and the Beast* and *Red Riding Hood*.[4] These tales also teach patriarchal gender roles to women; that is, that women must deny their own sexuality in order to achieve a satisfactory marriage. They must not wander off the narrow path of patriarchy into the wild woods peopled by wolfish men with uncontrollable sexual appetites. Romantic novels operate, in this respect, as patriarchal fairy-tales for grown-ups in continuing this fantasy. However, they also foreground the central problem of representing attractive male characters and female/male relationships in a way which does *not* depend on either a rape threat or on offensive portrayals of women and men. That is, their continuing use of a power differential substantiated by threat of physical violence to characterize both individuals and interpersonal relations suggests an overdetermined inflection of gender ideology. Since, as in *Wuthering Heights* and *Jane Eyre*, the resolution of the love story is predicated not on the physical, emotional and spiritual compatibility of the lovers, but on their economic circumstances, it must be suggested that these romances construct a representation not of patriarchal gender ideology, but of bourgeois, patriarchal ideology; that these are not love stories so much as economic stories displaced into love story terms.

The difficulty in rewriting these love stories in feminist terms, with a feminist reading position, may be related to the failure of producers and consumers to recognize the extent to which the stories are concerned with economic, rather than gender, issues – with the (re)construction not of patriarchal, but of bourgeois, ideology.

Some of the generic texts already discussed do represent women and men in fulfilling egalitarian relationships, with strong female characters who are not forced to accept either subjugation or a castrated partner as a result of their independence, and strong male characters whose power is not a function of their ability to subjugate others. However, these relationships usually appear in utopian and science fiction, in which non-realist conventions are used to displace the setting to another time and/or place. Strong female characters exist and are happy *because* they are represented in an entirely different social formation, non-patriarchal and non-bourgeois. Similarly strong male characters can be formulated without the threat of rape to sustain them *because* they no longer represent the dominance of a particular class and race. The nature of the social formation has been changed and so accordingly has the ideological significance of textual conventions. But do the egalitarian relationships represented in these texts constitute a romance? Or is the romance actually defined by an unequal power relationship and a dominant male?

Feminist analysis of romantic fiction

In her novel, *Lady Oracle* Margaret Atwood deals with the romance relationship in yet another way, by writing about the content of romantic fiction and the concept of reader position within her fictional text (Atwood, 1982 (F)). Her main character, Joan Foster, is the writer of a best seller called *Lady Oracle* which critics describe as an interrogation of the problems and frustrations of contemporary relationships from a woman's point of view. Foster actually wrote the book during experiments in automatic writing, when she hypnotized herself and then allowed her subconscious to dictate her writing. She does not even understand the resultant manuscript which the publishers agree is a montage of contemporary popular writing. Foster also writes romantic fiction under the pen-name Louisa K. Delacourt and the implicit suggestion Atwood makes is that the same critical opinion might be applied to all of the same author's writing, so that her Regency romances are also an interrogation of contemporary relationships from a woman's point of view. Throughout the book

Atwood has Foster experiment with the development of her latest novel, *Stalked by Love*. Tiring of her traditionally virtuous heroine, Charlotte, Foster decides to favour her tempestuous villainess, Felicia, who, like herself, has long red hair. But Foster's own life begins to intrude into the text and Felicia feels herself abandoned not by Redmond, her fictional rake/husband, but by Foster's own husband, Arthur. Then Foster has Felicia attempt to murder the nauseating Charlotte, only to have her saved by Redmond in typical male hero fashion. Finally Foster arrives at the most radical conclusion of all:

> [Felicia] took hold of the doorknob and turned it. The door unlocked and swung outward ... There, standing on the threshold, waiting for her, was Redmond. She was about to throw herself into his arms, weeping with relief, when she noticed an odd expression in his eyes. Then she knew. Redmond was the killer. He was a killer in disguise, he wanted to murder her as he had murdered his other wives ...
>
> 'Don't touch me,' she said, taking a step backward. She refused to be doomed. As long as she stayed on her side of the door she would be safe. Cunningly, he began his transformations, trying to lure her into his reach. His face grew a white gauze mask, then a pair of mauve-tinted spectacles, then a red beard and moustache, which faded giving way to burning eyes and icicle teeth. Then his cloak vanished and he stood looking at her sadly; he was wearing a turtle-neck sweater.
>
> 'Arthur?' she said. Could he ever forgive her?
>
> Redmond resumed his opera cloak. His mouth was hard and rapacious, his eyes smouldered. 'Let me take you away,' he whispered. 'Let me rescue you. We will dance together forever, always.'
>
> 'Always,' she said, almost yielding. 'Forever.' Once she had wanted these words, she had waited all her life for someone to say them ... She pictured herself whirling slowly across a ballroom floor, a strong arm around her waist ...
>
> 'No,' she said. 'I know who you are.'
>
> The flesh fell away from his face, revealing the skull behind it; he stepped towards her, reaching for her throat. (pp. 342–3)

Redmond is revealed as a composite of all the men in Foster's life, her husband, her lover and the fictional men who sustain the behaviour of the real ones. In deconstructing Redmond Atwood reveals the true nature of this character, the patriarchal male who appears in one guise as a fictional hero, in another as an eccentric artist, in yet another as an academic and husband. All are deadly to women in wanting to annihilate their individual subjectivity, to make the women the passive objects of their affection and abuse. In this way Atwood demonstrates to the reader the relationship between fictional representation and social practice, that these fictional heroes do not compensate for the inadequacies of reality but are constitutive of that reality. Which is perhaps the reason for the equivocal ending of the novel which has Joan Foster paying hospital visits to the reporter she mistakenly hit over the head with a bottle, a Jane Eyre ending for Joan Foster.

In *Stalked by Love* class inequality is an essential part of this characterization; the virtuous Charlotte is a poor but respectable servant in an aristocratic household. When Felicia confronts Redmond with his infidelity, she demands: *'If you must behave this way, you might have a little more taste. Next time have the goodness to select someone from your own class'* (p. 193). If he did, the readers would not have a Regency romance; the elevation from serving-girl to mistress of the household is the defining characteristic of the genre. As Carolyn Steedman observed in *Landscape for a Good Woman*, one of the principal fairy-tales of our society is that 'goose-girls can marry kings'. And the most disturbing feature of this fairy-tale is that it has infiltrated critical analysis of the role and status of women; or rather, that critical analysis of the role and status of women reproduces this fairy-tale narrative.

Inequality of class is as much a mechanism of the romance as the gender relationships and this may be both an essential feature of the romance and a key to its operation. The desire these texts encode is not sexual, but economic; the desire for solid middle- or upper-class status, for money and power. Since we live in a society in which men hold economic power and in which a woman's status is identified with that of her husband, then finding an appropriate husband is the problem. To make this search more palatable, less seemingly acquisitive, it is displaced into gender terms. The woman's search becomes a sexual and emotional one, a matter of fulfilling her natural, heterosexual needs for sexual and emotional fulfilment – and eventually for children. This displacement accords with the ideological representation of women; the economic imperative is validated in natural, biological terms, the commodity-fetish displaced into a fetishistic desire for love, with the *right man* . . . and *right* means. . . . Again one might refer back to the different resolutions of *Wuthering Heights* and *Jane Eyre*. Both Brontës give a realistic ending to their stories, this realism being a function not of the spiritual or emotional compatibility of the lovers, but their economic viability.

Issues of gender and of class are not, therefore, mutually exclusive, as romantic novels with their fetishistic focus on love try, too hard, to suggest. Rather the two are intimately related, as descriptions of the romance formula confirm: 'a young, inexperienced, poor to moderately well-to-do woman encounters and becomes involved with a handsome, strong, experienced, wealthy man, older than herself by ten to fifteen years' (Modleski, 1984 (F), p. 36). Representations of gender and class are related via their disposition of power. The male character is powerful, not integrally (like Heathcliff), but as a function of his economic status. He may also be physically attractive, although this is not really necessary. In romantic fiction, however, his physical appearance is often fetishised, objectified, as female appearance conventionally is in the (male-centred, male-focused) texts of our society. This objectification of the male is often read as an articulation of female desire, and it probably is, but the questions that then arise are: to what extent is this female desire constructed by patriarchal ideology, and, even if that question is considered irrelevant, how much is the articulation of that desire used to coerce readers into an acceptance of patriarchal ideology? This acceptance need not be passive, but an active, bitter resignation to a system which seems unchangeable. It might then be argued that, even if romantic fiction does have this role, it nevertheless continues to challenge patriarchal assumptions, by stating female sexual desire as a reality, reconstituting women as sexual beings. Romantic fiction might then be read as part of the process of negotiating new social meanings, a new understanding of female social roles. Romantic fiction might be a part of the process of renegotiating female subjectivity, even if it also, at the same time, constructs and reinforces patriarchal discourse and a bourgeois discourse of class, which may after all be its main function.

These texts also assume an Anglo-Saxon background for the main characters, with only the occasional European aristocrat extending the stereotype. This does not mean that race is not an issue, but that it is such a powerful assumption that it does not require specification. The question this raises is, what is the effect of this racial stereotyping on a non-white member of Western society (the society in which the novels are set and to which they refer)? Again the disposition of power is the issue, with the white middle-class male established as the position of power and non-white readers confirmed as marginalized and powerless. And again it confirms the white middle-class male as the key to power, the means of access for non-white women. Non-white goose-girls can marry kings; the problem is that, like working-class women, they are often simply exploited and then rejected. Still, the fantasy remains a key factor in these texts which can then be seen as mystifying or concealing another major discursive component of contemporary society, its white supremacist ideology.

Romantic fiction, and the fairy-tale it encodes, might be seen as one of the foremost propaganda tools of bourgeois ideology, mystifying the nature of both interpersonal relations and individual subject formation. Their fairy-tale of female access to the privileged classes may also be a major source of class antagonism. After all, kings are in no danger from goose-girls; they may choose to marry them or they may not. But goose-boys are in an extremely precarious situation. Not only do kings appropriate their labour; they also appropriate their women. Women, therefore, may be read as class traitors, all too ready to abandon their own class for another which is more socially and economically advantageous. Of course, the Brontës showed the dangers for women in this transaction, the entire loss of their own subjectivity (the death of Cathy) or the acquisition of damaged goods and a lifetime of servility and feminine nurturing (Jane), but the fairy-tale is not concerned with reality. In other words, what the fairy-tale may encode as well as the ideologically-sanctioned desire for class elevation, and the corresponding reinforcement of bourgeois ideology, is the resentment and jealousy of men towards women who are, supposedly, more socially mobile than themselves (hence Henry Fielding's response to *Pamela, Shamela* (1741), in which Pamela is depicted as a gold-digger who traps her employer into marrying her by flaunting her sexuality). Women, so the fairy-tale promises, are able to make these inter-class transitions solely on the basis of gender – because, under patriarchy, women are defined solely on the basis of gender.

Racial identity is a more complex issue, simply because it is often more visible. Non-white women may be visibly non-white, whereas a working-class woman may not be identifiably working-class purely on the basis of appearance (though even that is arguable). Romantic fiction is not so concerned with marrying non-white women to white men, as it is with marrying working-class women to bourgeois men. Its racist ideology is a matter of omission, of silencing, of marginalization. However, given that these romantic fictions are produced within a society which is multi-cultural, its white bias must be recognized and the effect of this on a multi-cultural audience questioned.

The fairy-tale which continues to structure romantic fiction, that goose-girls can marry kings, not only reinforces the patriarchal construction of women solely in terms of gender (as Woman), whose desires, therefore, are fetishised in gender terms as men, sex, love, marriage, babies, but also simultaneously constructs women as class-less and (by implication) as race-less, as traitors to their own class and race and so as appropriate scapegoats for male frustration and anger.

It does not seem surprising given this analysis of romantic fiction that feminist romantic fiction is difficult to find. Certainly some texts use elements of the romance to discuss the realities of women's lives – the utopian and science fiction discussed earlier, Fay Weldon's novel about a woman who loses her husband to a romance writer and then gets him back again, *The Life and Loves of a She-Devil*, lesbian romances like *Desert of the Heart* and *Pembroke Park* – but it is questionable that any of these texts operate purely as romantic fiction, whether the Mills & Boon/Harlequin readers would find them satisfying reading. The Weldon text is the most likely contender, with its heroine achieving both economic independence and the man; however, the cost of this achievement is high – by implication, too high. The heroine, Ruth, begins the novel as a very plain woman – tall, awkward, unprepossessing. She has two spoilt children, an accountant husband, a middle-class home, and a massive inferiority complex. Her husband, Bobbo, married her because she was the boss's daughter (that is, for his own economic gain) and now despises her for her lack of femininity. When she questions his emotional cruelty, he continues it by describing her as a she-devil: 'In fact I don't think you are a woman at all. I think that what you are is a she-devil' (Weldon, 1983 (F), p. 42). This accusation has the opposite effect to that intended by Bobbo. Instead of reinforcing Ruth's passivity it alerts her to the only kind of power she has – as the transgressive woman, a she-devil, who takes her destiny into her own hands and becomes an active, oppositional subject. After much plotting and some clever action Ruth succeeds in compromising Bobbo professionally and financially ruining the romance novelist, Mary Fisher, for whom he worked and to whom he fled after Ruth's disappearance. Ruth destroys the romantic idyll of Bobbo and Mary Fisher, with not a little (unwitting) help from her awful children. However, the final step of her revenge is very strange. She undergoes months of excruciatingly painful plastic surgery in order to transform herself physically into Mary Fisher – the female patriarchal subject, the feminine woman. This ending can be read equivocally as either the wish-fulfilment fantasy of women who accept the feminine subject position of patriarchy or a radical critique of this position, with Ruth's physical pain a displaced representation of the pain that positioning causes women in almost every sphere of activity. Ruth's own description of her revenge functions as a commentary on this gender ideology:

> I cause Bobbo as much misery as he ever caused me, and more. I try not
> to, but somehow it is not a matter of male and female, after all; it never

was, merely of power, I have all, and he has none. As I was, so he is now. (p. 240)

It may be that some readers will refuse the reading position Weldon constructs and read the ending merely as wish-fulfilment, which is the problem in dealing with such a highly fetishised genre. However, Weldon contextualizes her narrative repeatedly for readers, constructing the romantic novels of Mary Fisher as a gloss on her narrative of Ruth and Bobbo and Mary; the book begins: 'Mary Fisher lives in a High Tower, on the edge of the sea: she writes a great deal about the nature of love. She tells lies' (p. 5).

Feminist attention to the romance genre has focused mostly on a re-evaluation of conventional texts and their criticism, rather than on rewriting romantic fiction in feminist terms. This lack of feminist revisions indicates that the difficulties in reworking this genre are more severe than those encountered with any of the other genres already discussed. The reason for this lies with its elision of the ideologies of gender, race and class, its representation of a particular negotiation of these ideologies purely in terms of gender, which obscures or mystifies the formation of subjectivity in a patriarchal, bourgeois society. Other genres also intervene in this process of subject formation, but the romantic novel alone fetishises it purely in terms of gender; in these novels, more than in any other genre text, a woman's achievement of individuality is represented as a specific negotiation of the patriarchal gender discourse, that is, as femininity. The fact that subjectivity is a negotiation of the ideologies of class and race, as well as gender, is obfuscated, and this obfuscation is one of the key mythologies, fairy-tales, perhaps even the 'grand narrative' of capitalism.

As noted earlier, romance is often written into texts dominated by other genres, such as SF, utopian or detective fiction, where it may operate as one of the conventions of those genres. Feminist revisions of these genres also use romance and, in dialogue with other generic conventions, it has been used successfully to interrogate the construction of masculinity and femininity and of interpersonal relationships. But this success is predicated on dialogue, on the romance narrative operating in a context where other narratives and other conventions are working to construct gender, race and class discourses, which thereby prevents the fetishisation of gender characteristic of the romance text.

Feminist critics have concentrated instead on re-evaluating the obsessive consumption of romantic fiction by women from all cultural backgrounds. This critical work has been particularly innovatory in relation to notions of audience. The traditional critical response was to reject the readers of romantic fiction as fools, typical of their weak-minded gender (patriarchal critics), complicit in their own subjugation (feminist critics). The latter response does have conditional validity; however, these texts are more complex than that response allows. The revised feminist criticism refuses the patronizing attitude to the readership assumed in the traditional work and instead questions what an audience of millions of intelligent, capable women can find valuable in romantic fiction. Certainly this attitude, too, can become a problem, if the audience is romanticized (as working-class audiences sometimes are); it must be remembered that these intelligent and capable women are fighting to subsist in an essentially hostile environment. Nevertheless, this criticism has been enormously productive, resulting in a number of interesting and provocative propositions: for example,

1 that romantic fiction objectifies male characters and, since this objectification is an erotic mode in Western society, can be read as an expression of female desire;
2 that it is an expression of female unrest and dissatisfaction with contemporary society, particularly female/male relationships and gender roles;
3 that women who are involved mostly in domestic work use their reading time to resist the demands constantly put on them in their patriarchally-defined role;
4 that romantic fiction asserts the 'female values of love and personal interaction to the male values of competition and public achievement';
5 that the reader's familiarity with the plot gives her an assurance of her own ability to understand both texts and human behaviour;
6 that the violence coded into these texts as sexual desire 'innoculates' readers against violence they encounter in their own lives;
7 that the ending of the romance is a utopian projection which expresses a critical evaluation of the contemporary patriarchal order.

These ideas and others are contained in such recent studies as Tania Modleski's *Loving with a Vengeance*, Carol Thurston's *The Romance Revolution*, Janice Radway's *Reading the Romance* and Barbara Creed's article, 'The women's romance as sexual fantasy: "Mills & Boon".' All demand detailed analysis, but need to be placed within the context of the romantic novel as a purveyor of not only patriarchy, but also bourgeois ideology.

In this study feminist science fiction, fantasy, utopian fiction and detective fiction have all been analysed and evaluated for their exploration of the role of fiction in the construction of individual subjectivity and interpersonal relationships. In feminist generic fiction the writer constructs a feminist reading position which involves a particular negotiation of the discourses inflected by the traditional text and those discursively indicated by the revision of traditional conventions. This (re)negotiation and (re)construction of an alternative, non-patriarchal and non-bourgeois reading position can operate as the basis for a renegotiated subject position; it is a negotiation which fundamentally challenges the discursive negotiation constitutive of the patriarchal, bourgeois subject. Feminist generic fiction constructs a reading position which (1) deconstructs femininity, revealing it as an ideological construct, (2) deconstructs the patriarchal narrative, showing it as a mechanism by which women are constructed in purely gender terms, and as subject to men who are constructed in terms of gender, class and race, (3) deconstructs the bourgeois narrative, showing it to be a mechanism by which the white, middle-class male is defined as the value position in relation to which those negotiating differently the discourses of gender, race and class are ranked.

Romantic fiction is the most difficult genre to subvert because it encodes the most coherent inflection of the discourses of gender, class and race constitutive of the contemporary social order; it encodes the bourgeois fairy-tale. It also encodes the anger and frustration of all those whose lives are devalued by that negotiation – goose-girls and goose-boys – and it sets them at each other's throats; the kings stand by to appropriate the spoils. But at least the goose-girls and goose-boys have a voice, and that voice is increasingly vocal; even Mills & Boon/Harlequin heroines now have decent jobs. As Tania Modleski notes: 'An understanding of Harlequin Romances should lead one less to condemn the novels than the conditions which have made them necessary.' It is crucial to recognize that this condemnation must be directed not only at patriarchal, but also at bourgeois, white supremacist ideology.

7

Conclusion: Gender and Genre

Each chapter in this book deals with one particular genre of fiction and in each I have attempted to evaluate the possibility of subversion of that genre by feminist writers. In some chapters this involved dealing with a body of work now clearly identifiable as feminist fiction, including feminist science fiction, feminist fantasy and feminist utopian fiction. In other chapters the position was not so clear. Detective fiction is problematic for feminist writers because of its encoding of a bourgeois narrative of mystification which foils attempts to use it as a narrative of detection. Romance is even less accessible for feminists, premised, as it is, on an unequal relationship between women and men which is readable as a displaced narrative of class interaction, a bourgeois fairy-tale.

Feminist writers work extensively with science fiction and the work of James Tiptree Jr. is perhaps the best example of the use of science fiction as feminist practice. We have seen that several of the conventions of science fiction are particularly useful in constructing a feminist reading position in the text. The convention of estrangement, for example, enables writers to displace the story setting to another time and/or place, immediately denaturalizing the society portrayed in the text and the events and characters set there. So readers and writers are freed from the restrictions of a realist reading which tends to restrict representation to an imitation of contemporary social practices. As Pamela Sargent noted in her book, *Women of Wonder*, in SF writers are able to portray conditions and characters defined as impossible by the contemporary (patriarchal, bourgeois) discursive formation, such as equal female/male relationships and strong female characters. This use of estrangement is familiar from the work of the earliest SF writers, from Mary Shelley to H.G. Wells. Socially committed writers have always used science fiction to write about their own society in a way precluded by realist fiction, to construct a textual representation of a world in which the causal relationships of their own society (bourgeois, patriarchal, white supremacist) operate but in which that operation is not mystified or concealed by the 'naturalization' of particular power relations, subject positions or events (for example men are naturally more powerful than women, women are naturally passive, women naturally want to be dominated by men). Instead these texts show patriarchal, bourgeois, white supremacist social practices in practice, denying a voice to those who are marginalized by those discourses (like Frankenstein's creature or Tiptree's women men don't see), illustrating the kind of class relations they describe as 'natural' (like H.G. Wells's Eloi and Morlocks in *The Time Machine*), the gender relations and gendered subject positions they define (as in LeGuin's *The Left Hand of Darkness* and Tiptree's 'Houston, Houston, Do You Read?') and white supremacist practice as colonialism (in LeGuin's *The Word for World is Forest* and Tiptree's 'We Who Stole the *Dream*').

The alien is another convention useful to the feminist writer and it is often used to describe the situation of those who are either powerless within or totally outside the dominant discursive formation – marginalized and oppositional voices. Frankenstein's creature was perhaps the first alien of science fiction. Excluded from human society because of his monstrous appearance, the creature is able to observe dispassionately the institutional practices of that society which outlawed him and to find them singularly lacking in honesty and goodness. Instead he sees a bourgeois world in which to be rich is to be good, to be ruthless is to be clever. So Mary Shelley uses her creature character to comment on the society of her own time. In recent feminist science fiction the alien is used to comment on the position of women in contemporary Western society; after all, women *are* aliens in a world in which humanity is described as masculinity.

In both these cases the convention is inflected in the terms in which it was originally constructed; that is, feminist writers do not substantially alter the convention in using it. However, a convention which feminist writers do enact and change is the characteristic narrative of genre fiction, which encodes a patriarchal gender discourse; in this narrative women can be only object, not subject; passive, never active. One technique employed by feminists is the use of more than one narrative in a text. This means that no one narrative can be read as the definitive causal sequence, the site of knowledge. Instead the reading position of the text is constructed as a dialogue of narratives and other semiotic practices (such as other generic conventions): Tiptree's 'The Women Men Don't See' employs this strategy to construct a text which both uses or inflects a masculinist discourse about women and the power relations characteristic of patriarchy and then deconstructs that discourse, by placing the masculinist narrative of the male narrator in dialogue with the feminist narrative of one of the female characters as well as a feminist narrative of the interaction between these two characters. This attention to narrative is essential because of the danger of co-option, because the feminist text may be recovered for patriarchy by a narrative which contradicts discursively the story told by the narrative (for example as Menolly's story in *Dragonsong* and *Dragonsinger* reconstructs the patriarchal discourse about gender roles which Menolly's own experience would seem to contradict).

This danger of co-option is present with the use of many generic conventions. Where it seems most apparent is in the work of writers who seem concerned only with the representational or story aspect of their text. So the writer might tell a story about the oppression of women, yet find that the conventions of the text in which this story is told rely for intelligibility on the reader's adoption of a patriarchal reading position – again McCaffrey's Menolly books provide a good example. This does not mean that oppositional voices are not heard within these texts, but that the reader is nevertheless positioned to discount them. Thus the reader of the Menolly stories is positioned not to read them as a story of female oppression, but as the story of a remarkable girl who is able to act in a traditionally male role – a measure of her power. The story of oppression is there, but the individualist ideology of the text directs the reader away from that story to one of individual effort, premised on an acceptance of masculinity as the site of power.

The other side of the co-option argument, however, concerns intervention. In using and revising the conventions of particular genres, feminist writers are changing those genres. If a genre is a collection of texts which all use a particular set of conventions to construct meaning, then changes to those conventions change the kinds of meanings those texts can make. And if genres are, as Bakhtin demonstrates (Bakhtin, 1981 (A)), a socio-historical construct, then those changes are the result of and contribution to changes in the social formation in which the texts are produced. The modifications of the science fiction genre by feminist writers, like the modifications introduced by writers from other discursive positions, renegotiate not only the genre and the meanings it constructs, but also the social/ ideological formation of which they are constructions or realizations. So feminist science fiction renegotiates the contemporary social/ ideological formation – bourgeois, patriarchal, white supremacist society – by constructing for readers a reading position which is discursively at odds with that constructed by texts which simply (re)construct the dominant formation; that is, whose reading position assumes the reader is a bourgeois, patriarchal, white supremacist subject.

Since readers consume these texts from a variety of different subject positions (they may, for example, be feminist or anti-feminist), then feminist science fiction may perform a number of different roles. It may reinforce the reading and subject position taken by feminist readers, which is not in itself a small achievement in a society dominated by patriarchal texts. It may also serve to disrupt or disturb the position taken by non-feminist readers. This interaction is evident in the total rejection of feminist SF by those readers either as not 'real' science fiction or as propaganda, the latter suggesting that the grounds on which these readers are disturbed is political or ideologic- al. For yet another group of readers one can theorize a compromise position in which the text's articulation of an oppositional ideology, in the construction of a feminist reading position, is negotiated by the reader as a (re)construction of her/his own subject position; that is, the individual subject is somehow changed by this negotiation. S/he may adopt a subject position which involves a greater understanding of her/his own patriarchal positioning, a demystification of the process of subject formation which irrevocably alters her/his suscepti- bility to that positioning. So feminist science fiction may operate as feminist practice.

Feminist fantasy is a more complex genre to analyse since it involves at least three different kinds of non-realist text: secondary world fantasy, fairy-tale and horror. Secondary world fantasy is another genre of which estrangement is a major convention. It operates in a similar way to science fiction, using a setting displaced in time and/or space to denaturalize events on the representational or story level of the text. Like feminist science fiction, however, feminist secondary world fantasy risks being subverted by the ideological content sedimented into the socio-historically constructed conven- tions of the genre, particularly its use of narrative.

As noted earlier, this narrative tends to encode both patriarchal subject positions and a normative causal sequence antithetical to feminism. Again the strategy employed by many feminist fantasists is the use of several interrelated narratives, each situating or contextualizing the others. In this way the reader is positioned to see no one narrative as the site of 'truth', but rather that meaning is a negotiation of several narratives which may be in contradiction or harmony or both. Of course, feminist fantasy resolves the contradictions to some extent by constructing a feminist reading position from which the presence of these contradictions is explained. The contradictory narratives and their discursive premises are contextualized for the reader from a feminist position, so that the reader adopting this feminist position understands the operation of the text. This positioning is clearly coercive, as all texts are, but it does not deny or gloss over or mystify the presence of contradictions, as do texts arguing from a politically or ideologically conservative position. These texts, in so doing, constitute the political practice of the dominant discursive formation denying a voice to those rendered marginal or oppositional by that particular negotiation of discourses (bourgeois, patriarchal, white supremacist).

Even feminist secondary world fantasy which is not dialogic in this sense, foregrounding an interplay of narratives, is nevertheless in dialogue with other texts of the genre (as are all generic texts). The radical difference between the feminist and conservative secondary world fantasy texts itself constructs the feminist text as a metanarrative which, by implication if not overt reference, questions the ideological function of the conservative fantasy narrative.

This metafunction is perhaps the principal strategy of the other feminist fantasy studied here: fairy-tale and horror. Feminist work in both of these genres is primarily a construction of metatexts; that is, oppositional or critical texts which comment directly on the major texts of the genre by reworking or revising them in ways which reveal the mechanisms by which they operate, by which they make meaning in our society. In other words, feminist fairy-tale and feminist horror works primarily to denaturalize those genres, both of which are so heavily involved in the construction of children and young adults as patriarchal, bourgeois subjects.

Feminist fairy-tale writing concentrates on revising traditional fairy-tales to reveal the ideological content they encode, particularly their construction of a patriarchal reading position. This uncovering of ideological content reveals the 'innocent' fairy-tale as an ideological practice. 'Red Riding Hood' and 'Cinderella', for example, are repeatedly revealed as patriarchal morality plays, instructing female readers in the proper role – that is, subject position – for women under patriarchy: women are passive, powerless, subordinate to men

(Red Riding Hood's hunter/father who rescues her from the wolf, Cinderella's prince) and valued for their bodies (fertile like the newly menarchal Red Riding Hood, beautiful like the helpless Cinderella). This ideological function of fantasy can be traced in the historical development of fairy-tale, particularly its institutionalization as children's literature in the nineteenth-century when the older folktales collected by Perrault and the Brothers Grimm were glossed with the bourgeois, patriarchal, colonialist ideology of the Victorian middle classes for whose children they were to provide moral guidance. Feminist fairy-tales reveal both the presence of this ideological material and its nature. Further they show one of the means by which both women and men are coerced from an early age into acceptance of subject positions which define and delimit many of the choices they make about themselves and their lives; fairy-tale is revealed as a propaganda tool of patriarchy.

Feminist horror fiction also functions in dialogue with conservative horror texts. It was noted that one of the earliest horror novels was by a woman writer, Ann Radcliffe's *The Mysteries of Udolpho*, and that this text voiced female fears of patriarchal domination. However, in the narrative the fears she described are resolved as the misapprehensions of the hysterical female character. In other words, her narrative of events is proved wrong; it makes no sense. She does not participate in the bourgeois narrative which constructs the narrative; she does not recognize her 'natural' role in that 'natural' narrative. But once she accepts the (bourgeois, patriarchal) narrative of the text she, and the reader positioned with her, is shown that fears (of male domination) are groundless; acceptance of domination dispels fear of domination. The horror text, too, operates as moral (i.e. ideological) training.

Recent feminist horror, such as the revisions of the vampire story, concentrate on reconstructing the heroes of patriarchal horror. Suzy McKee Charnas's retelling, *The Vampire Tapestry*, employs the technique of multiple narratives to deconstruct the vampire as a powerful characterization of masculinist discourse (the male-centred, *machismo* discourse of patriarchy). As her vampire, Edward Weyland, begins to reject his patriarchal subject position, his character begins to disintegrate. He cannot find any non-patriarchal subject position to occupy because his whole existence is based on objectification and predation. Rather than live that life, now repugnant to him, Weyland chooses hibernation and another life. Charnas's text uses the semiotic practices of vampire fiction, conventions such as the use of blood-sucking to signify sexual intercourse, to reveal the practice of vampire fiction as an encoder of patriarchal ideology; that is, as a fictional genre which positions the reader as a patriarchal subject. Like feminist writers in other genres she constructs her text as a collection of interrelated narratives (as does Bram Stoker in his germinal novel, *Dracula*), the dialogue of which constructs the feminist reading position of the text.

Feminist horror is not common, perhaps because of the difficulty in reworking a genre so often devoted to the delineation of the masculine patriarchal subject and the establishment of patriarchal reading positions for female and male readers. It was noted that a rape threat/fantasy is central to many horror fictions, from *The Mysteries of Udolpho* to contemporary vampire stories, and this must contribute to the problems for feminists in dealing with this genre. Charnas's achievement is to have constructed and then deconstructed this masculinist character and his narrative, and in so doing to have revealed the sexist basis of this fiction.

Feminist utopian fiction is different again. Another estranged genre, like science fiction, it too has been widely used by political writers as part of their own ideological practice. Utopian fiction is highly conventionalized and feminist writers use the generic conventions in a displaced (time and/or space) setting to tell stories that reveal the ways in which patriarchal practices are naturalized in their own society. This demystification practice is reinforced by a convention of the genre which often renders the text obscure or tedious to non-contemporary readers, and this is its continual references or footnotes to the 'real' world of the writer and contemporary reader. By means of this convention readers are constantly referred from the utopian society described in the narrative to their own society, which is inevitably found to be inferior. In addition, it is part of the practice of the text to reveal why the contemporary 'real' world is so inferior: to trace its comparative injustice and oppression by means of an interrogation of the ideological practices of contemporary society conducted as a comparison with those of the utopian society (which may be socialist, feminist, anarchist, bourgeois individualist, etc.).

We saw that utopian fiction had two periods of great popularity, the late nineteenth century and the 1970s. In the late nineteenth century utopian fiction became a focus of debate about the nature of the most just and equitable social formation. Characteristically the antagonists were socialism and bourgeois capitalism. William Morris's *News from Nowhere* was a major contribution to the debate, not least because it released utopian fiction from naïve realist readings of the utopian society (or utopian figure) as a blueprint for the future.

Morris instead used the utopian figure as a polemical strategy to present theoretical arguments in an accessible form, at the same time speculating reflexively on the role of fiction as political practice.

Recent feminist utopias follow Morris's lead. Their utopian societies are not blueprints for the future, but elements in a debate about the nature of their own society – about its patriarchal ideology and the social or institutional practices through which that ideology operates. One way in which that debate is conducted is through an interweave of narratives, now familiar in feminist generic fiction. So in Marge Piercy's *Woman on the Edge of Time* Connie Ramos's realist narrative of life as a marginalized 'ethnic' woman in contemporary US society functions in dialogue with a fantastic narrative of Connie's visit to a utopian future state characterized by, among other things, sexual equality and with another fantastic narrative of a dystopian future characterized by extreme sexism. No single one of these narratives constructs the text as utopian; it is the dialogue between them which makes *Woman on the Edge of Time* a feminist utopian text. And it is the dialogue between them which deconstructs contemporary US society and its institutions. Similarly in *The Female Man* Joanna Russ uses four different characters and their narratives to construct a composite female subject, only one of which is the patriarchal feminine subject. As in *Woman on the Edge of Time* the meaning of the text is constructed as a dialogue of narratives, no single one of which is the site of knowledge or truth but each of which contextualizes the others. Russ's feminist reading position in this text is the place at which the construction of the feminine subject is visible, as is the rage of the oppressed and marginalized female subject of patriarchy and the alienness of the active female subject who refuses to comply with the feminine subject position.

Feminist utopias also use the other conventions of the genre – the utopian society or utopian figure, the traveller, the guide, the continual reference back to the writer's contemporary reader's own society, the love story – as part of the meaning-making, semiotic practice of their texts. Again they have to be careful to avoid co-option by sedimented ideological content. An obvious place for such co-option would be the love story or romance, a convention popularized by Edward Bellamy in the late nineteenth century. His utopian traveller, Julian West, falls in love with Edith Leete, one of the utopians and so, to fulfil the happy ending convention of romance, West stays in the utopian society with his love. In the contemporaneous *News from Nowhere*, on the other hand, Morris's traveller, William Guest, is separated from his utopian love, whom he watches gradually lose any consciousness of his existence. The text ends with the traveller back in his own time, with only a vision of the utopia left to sustain him. Bellamy's text ends in a wish-fulfilment fantasy; Morris's in the grim reality of late nineteenth-century England. Feminist writers use the love story in a way similar to Morris, using the traveller's romance to illustrate alternative possibilities for inter-personal relationships, but returning the traveller to a present in which those possibilities are suppressed. So Connie Ramos returns to her nightmare existence in twentieth-century America, with only a memory of the love she experienced in the utopian society.

Feminist utopian texts are part of the second flowering of the genre. Fredric Jameson noted the resurgence of interest in the genre in the 1960s when it became a means of speculation about the nature of the state by political activists from a variety of political backgrounds – from environmentalists, peace activists and civil rights campaigners as well as feminists. Feminist utopian fiction constitutes an intervention in the dominant ideological formation, and the subject positions it constructs, in the same way as does feminist science fiction and fantasy. It constructs for readers a feminist reading position from which the institutional practices of patriarchy become visible, thereby reducing their ability to position the reader so easily, to naturalize her or him so compliantly into patriarchal subject positions.

Feminist detective fiction is more problematic. The detective fiction narrative is one of revelation *and* concealment, discovery (whodunit) in its representational practice, mystification in its ideological practice. Conventionally in detective fiction a crime is committed and a detective finds out who committed the crime. The detective does not situate the crime in a particular social formation, as a construct of that formation, nor does s/he situate the criminal as a subject of that formation. The criminal is simply a villain and that villainy is given the most conservative ideological character. So, female villains are usually transgressively active women whose self-determination is the quality most indicative of evil. Male villains also transgress the social order in some way, but often their crime is that they come too close to deconstructing that order, their avarice or viciousness too clearly indicative of the ideological basis of that order. The conventional detective narrative handles crime and criminals by a process of individuation: the crime is an aberrant act unrelated and inimical to the social order (not a product of it) and the criminal is an aberrant individual (not a subject or product of the social order). So how can feminists use this genre which seems superficially to be about detection and revelation, but which is (ideologically) about concealment and mystification, as part of feminist practice?

Some writers attempt to use it as a genre of detection, despite its contradictory ideological premise. In order to do so, however, these writers must challenge the genre at its very basis. This often results in such a radical reworking that conventional readers might be expected to respond negatively. So Valerie Miner's *Murder in the English Department* operates effectively as a text about the institutional practice of sexism in tertiary education, but is arguably less successful as a thriller. This is because Miner radically reworks so many conventions of the genre: for example, both the detective and the victim are situated in terms of gender, class and race (rather than being situated romantically outside society, outside ideology, in the case of the detective or rendered faceless or irrelevant in the case of the victim); the crime is explained as a construct of patriarchal ideology (rather than as an aberration from it); and the criminal is situated as a male patriarchal subject (rather than as an aberrant individual). Other texts compromise more with genre convention, as for example Amanda Cross's Kate Fansler mysteries, but the danger is that these texts are co-opted by the ideology they set out to expose – exactly what seems to happen in Cross's *Death in a Tenured Position*, which also concerns the institutional practice of sexism in tertiary education. The Cross novel works well as detective fiction, but reinforces the sexism it seems concerned to deconstruct; the Miner novel deconstructs sexist practices at universities, but fails (comparatively) as detective fiction.

Another option is represented by Barbara Wilson's *Murder in the Collective* which co-operates with some conventions, modifies others. Wilson contextualizes her detective, victim and crime in much the same way as Miner, but not so her criminal; he is characterized as aberrant, rather than as a particular subject positioning – alien to his society, rather than a product of it. Though the Wilson novel uses other strategies to avoid the co-option of the text by the dominant ideological formation, it does succumb in this important aspect to its mystificatory practice. The sexism which is discovered in the narrative is the fault of an aberrant individual, not a construct of patriarchal ideology. The sexist individual of the narrative is shown to be a thorough villain by his treachery towards political radicals and his co-operation with covert CIA activities overseas while his sexism and racism are not established as a construct of a patriarchal, colonialist society (even though those aspects of the society are described in other ways in the text). The pay-off is that Wilson's novel operates more effectively as detective fiction.

Another recent change to the detective fiction genre, often related to the feminist movement is the characterization of the professional female detective. This change necessitates other modifications of the narrative; for example, the treatment of sexual relationships has to be different if the female detective is to avoid being positioned as either a transgressively, active woman (which would align her with the criminal) or as a passive, powerless woman (which would prevent her doing her job). So, even if the writer is not constructing a feminist reading position in the text, certain changes necessitated by this new kind of character do operate to deconstruct the function of particular conventions, for example the exploitative macho detective who acts out the fear of women of the patriarchal masculine subject.

Detective fiction is a relatively new field for feminist writers, even though there have been many celebrated female writers of the genre. Like feminist writing in the genres of science fiction, fantasy and utopian fiction, feminist detective fiction is liable to co-option by conservative (patriarchal, bourgeois) discourses coded into the conventions of the genre. The detective fiction narrative seems particularly prone to this co-option, functioning as it does (and did, historically) to reproduce a bourgeois individualist narrative of social order and aberration. Readers are positioned by this narrative as bourgeois individualist subjects, and that discursive positioning, with its mystification of class, race and gender relations, is almost invariably aligned with a patriarchal discourse, so that readers are also positioned as patriarchal subjects. And when the writer uses the narrative to articulate another kind of discourse, a feminist discourse which reveals patriarchal practices, the result is unsatisfactory: the text is not satisfying detective fiction. The reason for this is that the detective fiction narrative, as it developed in the nineteenth century, is not a narrative of detection at all, but one of concealment.

The same kind of contradiction is evident in feminist attempts to revise the genre of romance. Romantic fiction was seen to be premised on the naturalization of a particular kind of female/male interaction, constructing a particular kind of male (masculine) and female (feminine) subject; that is, a strong, assertive male and a weak, passive female in a relationship of unequal power which verges on sado-masochism. It was also noted, however, that romantic fiction fetishises gender relations as a displacement of their fundamental (discursive) preoccupation with money and status, i.e. with class. These texts are not just about sexuality and romance; they are about the ways sexuality and romance are constructed in our society – which is in terms of class (and race). Romances describe how masculinity and femininity are constructed in a bourgeois, patriarchal society, and they situate readers to accept, to naturalize, this definition of gender roles as the price of material success: so it becomes 'natural' that a powerful, attractive, successful, wealthy, older man will fall in love with a powerless, but beautiful, naïve, poor, younger woman – whether or not it is 'realistically' probable they would ever meet – or, if they meet, have anything in common which allows them to discover their 'love'. In other words, these romantic narratives mystify (in fact, deny) the role of class (and race) in personal interactions. They are the patriarchal (white supremacist) bourgeois individualist myth *par excellence*: the myth that any goose-girl can marry a king (if she is sufficiently beautiful – which defines the subject position of women in this discursive formation) and that any boy can be president (if he is sufficiently hard-working – which defines the subject position of men).

Subverting this genre seems an almost impossible task, given the discourses it encodes and its fetishisation of an unequal gender relationship. The feminist texts in which romance is used tend to be far more complex than the conventional Mills & Boon/Harlequin novella, situating the romance text within another narrative which deconstructs its representation of gender relations without necessarily addressing issues of class or race. Margaret Atwood in *Lady Oracle* tells the story of a romance novelist and includes part of one of her novelist's Regency romances in the text, the resultant dialogue between the realist narrative of the novelist's life and the romance narrative of her work constructing the feminist reading position of the text whereby readers are positioned to see the role of such romance in the construction of the feminine and masculine subjects of patriarchy. Fay Weldon's *Life and Loves of a She-Devil* also deals with the life of a romance novelist, but here through the eyes of a woman marginalized by the patriarchal discourse/society which romance novels reproduce (that is, for which they operate as discursive practice) – a woman who does not fit the patriarchal definition of femininity, a woman who becomes an active, not compliant or passive subject, a she-devil. In these texts the conventional romance narrative is situated within a metatext which reveals its patriarchal practice. The same occurs when romance is situated within estranged genres such as science fiction, fantasy and utopian fiction; other genres and other narratives contextualize the romantic narrative to reveal its ideological function. A feminist romance which describes a happy, equal sexual relationship seems as far away as the discursive formation for which this would be the 'natural' kind of interpersonal relationship.

That discursive formation would have to be very different from the bourgeois construct which produces the mystified texts of class relationships currently fetishised as romance.

In summary, then, this study of feminist revisions of generic fiction points to a series of issues which must be addressed when evaluating such fiction:

1 Genre fiction is encoded with ideological discourses which articulate the socio-historical formation in which the particular text is written.

2 These discourses are coded into the conventions of the genre.

3 A historical study of the development of the genre enables the critic to identify the discourses coded into particular conventions, and into the (socio-historically determined) modifications of conventions.

4 Feminist writers are using generic fiction both to describe or reveal (sometimes in the representational or story level of the text, sometimes in the dialogue which constitutes the feminist reading position of the text) the naturalization of patriarchal subject positions and causal sequences or narratives, and to explore the use of fiction as ideological practice.

5 The major strategy employed by feminist writers is the construction within the text of a feminist reading position; that is, a position at which the contradictions within the text are explained if the reader sees them from the perspective of a feminist discourse.

6 Construction of this reading position may involve changing to some extent the conventions of the genre, reworking them to express a changed socio-historical (discursive) formation; and it may involve voicing a patriarchal discourse which is then contextualized or placed in dialogue with other discourses.

7 In constructing this reading position, however, feminist writers have to be constantly aware that conservative (patriarchal) discourses are coded into generic conventions and that these discourses may subvert the feminist discourse and reading position they are constructing in the text.

8 In some woman-centred texts writers (who may or may not be feminist) concentrate their attention on the representational or story level of the text; that is, they tell stories about the oppression of women in which women are the major characters, but they pay little attention to other semiotic practices of their texts. The result is that these texts can still position readers in terms of a patriarchal

discourse, even if oppositional voices are sometimes heard.

9 Other feminist writers work comprehensively with the semiotic practices of the text to construct a reading position at which the discourses operating in the text, coded into narrative(s) and generic conventions, are aligned by a feminist discourse to be mutually explicable.

10 Feminist writers working at this comprehensive level have also to be aware that texts are often constructed from not only more than one narrative, but also more than one genre: horror within science fiction as in *Alien* and *The Word for World is Forest*, romance within utopian fiction as in *Looking Backward* and *Woman on the Edge of Time*, fantasy within detective fiction as in the earliest stories of Edgar Allan Poe. In this case the writer must be aware of the dialogic nature of the text, and take account of the encoded discourses of all these textual conventions, as well as the semiotic significance of the particular generic mix in constructing a feminist reading position. I have not dealt with the mixing of genres at any length in this study since it demands a full-length analysis in its own right (it is basically a complication of the dialogic model of semiotic practice used in my analysis of separate genres). As Derrida argues, one can never not mix genres; texts almost inevitably carry traces of other genres, in the very process defining themselves as primarily texts not of that trace genre(s) (Derrida, 1980 (A)). But the traces must be taken into account, since they too encode discourses of various kinds.

As this summary shows, the process of analysing the feminist revision of genre fiction is a complex one, and feminist generic texts are not simply texts which tell stories in which women are given roles usually taken by men. Analysing feminist generic fiction means understanding the semiotic practice of a particular genre, which in turn means understanding the history of the genre and so the discourses that are encoded in the conventions of the genre. This model of textual analysis is grounded in the semiotic theory of Bakhtin:[1] a particular text is constructed in terms of one dominant genre (though traces of other genres will also be found); those genres are themselves constructed as a dialogue of literary conventions, which developed at a particular time and place, in a particular social formation; these conventions encode discourses constitutive of this social formation; changes to the conventions (and so to their encoded discourses) are the indicative of changes to the social formation (as is evident in the historical study of a particular genre), since the social formation is itself a construct or negotiation of many discourses (about gender, race, class, etc.).

As Gunther Kress notes, discourses (for example, sexist and feminist discourses) are essentially sets of statements which define, describe and delimit the possibilities of action and of thought, of representation and self-representation, of a particular institution or site of power: in other words, discourses are the textual realizations of ideology (Kress, 1985 (A), pp. 6–7). Sexist discourse, for example, defines, describes and delimits the possibilities of action and of thought, of representation and self-representation, for subjects of patriarchy, an institutionalization of gender relations whereby masculinity is located as the site of power, femininity as powerlessness. Every text renegotiates a set of discourses that will almost inevitably involve some of the dominant discourses of a particular social formation; after all, the text has to be intelligible to readers whose subjectivity is constituted in terms of those discourses. This renegotiation may simply be a restatement of the contemporary dominant or hegemonic ideological formation: that is, the negotiation of discourses which constitutes the text may reproduce in whole or in part the negotiation of discourses which constitutes the contemporary dominant ideological formation. In that case the text would be a patriarchal, bourgeois, white supremacist text – and probably a best-seller. On the other hand, a text may be a renegotiation which includes oppositional discourses such as feminism. In this case the text would probably not be a best-seller. It will make readers uneasy or uncomfortable because it is oppositional (at least in part) not only to the dominant ideological formation, but also to those subjects who are compliant with it, and that means most of the market. These oppositional texts mark changes in the dominant ideological formation, a new negotiation of meaning, new meanings being constructed. And subjects, too, negotiate these texts and may be changed by them – are given access to new meanings.

Analysis of feminist genre fiction means analysing the dialogue of voices or discourses which constructs the text and locating the position at which this dialogue is not resolved or negated, but at which it makes sense. If this position is recognizably an articulation of a feminist discourse, then the text may be described as a feminist text. Sometimes this position is not so clear; the text may articulate oppositional voices but operate basically from a different kind of premise (for example bourgeois individualist – as in most romance and detective fiction). The critic then needs to evaluate more carefully how this text can be seen to function as a feminist text; whether it might be seen to have been co-opted by a discourse inimical to feminism.

One undeniable point is that feminist generic fiction is interesting and fun. It is also highly innovative and participates in the (re)construction of the genres of which it is a part, and with which it is in dialogue. Feminist writers have a particular political aim for this dialogue, which is the construction of a feminist subject – the female subject that de Lauretis describes as being both inside and outside patriarchal discourse, both the idealist patriarchal construct, Woman and the experiential subject, women. This feminist subject detects the boundaries of patriarchy, the statements and practices which define that discourse, in the same way that generic texts detect the boundaries of their own (principal) genre – by going outside those boundaries, introducing contradictions which are resolved by a particular alignment of discourses within the text, the reading position. So the feminist subject resolves the contradictions which arise from her positioning as a feminine subject of patriarchy and her experience of that positioning (which so often contradicts the patriarchal myth) in terms of a particular alignment of discourses, which is feminist.

> 'What women do is survive. We live by ones and twos in the chinks of your world-machine.'
>
> 'Sounds like a guerilla operation.' I'm not really joking, here in the 'gator den. In fact, I'm wondering if I spent too much thought on mahogany logs.
>
> 'Guerillas have something to hope for.' Suddenly she switches on a jolly smile. 'Think of us as opossums, Don. Did you know there are opossums living all over? Even in New York City.'
>
> I smile back with my neck prickling. I thought I was the paranoid one.
>
> 'Men and women aren't different species, Ruth. Women do everything men do.'
>
> 'Do they?' Our eyes meet, but she seems to be seeing ghosts between us in the rain. She mutters something that could be 'My Lai' and looks away. 'All the endless wars . . .' Her voice is a whisper. 'All the huge authoritarian organizations for doing unreal things. Men have to struggle against each other; we're just part of the battlefields. It'll never change unless you change the whole world. I dream sometimes of – of going away –' She checks and abruptly changes voice. 'Forgive me, Don, it's so stupid saying all this.'
>
> 'Men hate wars too, Ruth,' I say as gently as I can.
>
> 'I know.' She shrugs and climbs to her feet. 'But that's your problem, isn't it?'
>
> End of communication. Mrs. Ruth Parsons isn't even living in the same world with me. (Tiptree, 1975 (B), p. 154)

Notes

Chapter 1 Introduction

1 Louis James, *Fiction for the Working Man, 1830–1850: A study of the literature produced for the working classes in early Victorian urban England* (Harmondsworth: Penguin, 1973); Margaret Dalziel. *Popular Fiction 100 Years Ago* (London, 1957).

2 Linda Dowling, The decadent and the New Woman in the 1890s, *Nineteenth-Century Fiction*, 33 (1979), 434–53.

3 For example, this century women have only had a *major* presence in science fiction since the 1960s, although there have always been women writers of SF.

4 Craig Owens, The discourse of others: feminists and postmodernism. In Hal Foster (ed.), *Postmodern Culture* (London and Sydney: Pluto Press, 1985). Owens's article is poised dangerously on the brink of co-option, exploring the sexism endemic to modernist and postmodernist theory, but still validating feminism in terms of its relationship to postmodernism.

5 *An Anthology of Chartist Literature* (Moscow, 1956).

6 Lyman Tower Sargent, Themes in utopian fiction in English before Wells, *Science-Fiction Studies*, Vol. 3 (1976) 275–82.

7 See my The Strategy of Utopia: A Study of Conflict and Ideology in William Morris's *News from Nowhere*. In T. Threadgold, E.A. Grosz, G. Kress and M.A.K. Halliday (eds), *Semiotics/Ideology/Language* (Sydney: Pathfinder Press, 1986), 75–91.

8 See, for example, the discussion of *Frankenstein* in Ellen Moers, *Literary Women* (New York: Anchor Press/Doubleday, 1977).

9 See, for example, the discussion of Wells's work in Robert Scholes and Eric S. Rabkin, *Science Fiction: History, Science, Vision* (London: OUP, 1977).

10 See particularly *News from Nowhere*, chapter XVI, in which discussion of the subject matter of a series of tapestries constitutes an interrogation of textual practice as political intervention.

11 *News from Nowhere* argues for the freedom of women from patriarchal gender ideology, and yet employs that ideology in the construction of female characters; see my 'The Strategy of Utopia' in *Semiotics/Language/Ideology*.

12 See Rachel Blau DuPlessis, *Writing beyond the Ending: Narrative Strategies of*

Twentieth-Century Women Writers (Bloomington: Indiana University Press, 1985), p. 44 on the desire mechanism encoded in much Gothic fiction.

13 See Teresa de Lauretis, *Alice Doesn't: Feminism, Semiotics, Cinema* (London: Macmillan 1984), p. 114 on the use of contradiction by contemporary feminist filmmakers.

14 See, for example, M.A.K. Halliday and Ruqaiya Hasan. *Language, context and text: Aspects of language in a social-semiotic perspective* (Geelong, Victoria: Deakin University Press, 1985) [Oxford: OUP, 1989]; J.R. Martin, *Factual writing: exploring and challenging social reality* (Geelong, Victoria: Deakin University Press, 1985) [Oxford: OUP, 1989].

15 See Derrida, The law of genre, *Glyph*, 7 (1980), 202–32.

16 See V. Blain, P. Clements and I. Grundy (eds), *The Feminist Companion to Literature in English* (London: Batsford, [1989]).

17 This formulation of subject position derives originally from Althusser's essay, Ideology and Ideological State Apparatuses. In Ben Brewster (tr.), *Lenin and Philosophy and other essays* (New York: Monthly Review Press, 1970). It has been developed by critics such as Catherine Belsey in *Critical Practice* (London and New York: Methuen, 1980) and Constructing the subject: deconstructing the text, in J. Newton and D. Rosenfelt (eds), *Feminist Criticism and Social Change* (New York and London: Methuen), 45–64.

Chapter 2   Feminist Science Fiction

1 Silverberg's argument for his designation of Tiptree as an 'ineluctably masculine' writer is worth considering in detail, with particular attention to the language Silverberg uses to characterize 'masculine' writing.

2 Marge Piercy in Dear Frontiers: Letters from Women fantasy and science fiction writers, *Frontiers*, II, 3 (1977), 64.

3 V. Garbarini, Everyone needs a hand to hold on to, *Musician*, October 1987, 96.

Chapter 3   Feminist Fantasy

1 'Dear Frontiers': Letters from women fantasy and science fiction writers, *Frontiers*, Volume II (1977), 62.

2 'Dear Frontiers', 63–4.

3 See Tanith Lee, *Sabella or The Blood Stone* (New York: Daw, 1980); Jody Scott, *I, Vampire* (London: Women's Press, 1986); Suzy McKee Charnas, *The Vampire Tapestry* (London: Granda, 1980).

4 See Anne Cranny-Francis, Sexual Politics and Political Repression in Bram Stoker's *Dracula*. In C. Bloom, B. Docherty, J. Gibb and K. Shand (eds), *Nineteenth Century Suspense: from Poe to Conan Doyle* (London: Macmillan, 1988), 64–79.

5 'Dear Frontiers', 65.

Chapter 4   Feminist Utopian Fiction

1 Edward Bellamy, *Looking Backward (2000–1887) or, Life in the Year 2000A.D.* repr. (London: William Reeves, [n.d.]).
2 See Fredric Jameson, Of islands and trenches: naturalization and the production of utopian unconscious, *Diacritics: a review of contemporary criticism*, summer 1977, 2–21; Louis Marin, Theses on ideology and utopia, *Minnesota Review*, 6 (1976), 71–5; E.P. Thompson, Postcript: 1976. In *William Morris: Romantic to Revolutionary*, rev. edn) (London: Merlin Press, 1977).

Chapter 5   Feminist Detective Fiction

1 See, for example, Holmes's musings on the role of the detective in 'The Hound of the Baskervilles', Sir Arthur Conan Doyle, *The Penguin Complete Sherlock Holmes* (Harmondsworth: Penguin, 1981), 687.
2 I conducted a preliminary analysis of 'By Shadowed Paths' in my Ph.D. thesis, 'William Morris's *News from Nowhere*: the propaganda of desire', University of East Anglia, 1983.
3 On *Cagney and Lacey* see Julie D'Acci, 'Woman', Television and the Case of *Cagney and Lacey*, paper presented to the 1986 International Television Studies Conference, London, July 1986.
4 On Sjöwahl and Wahlöö see Stephen Knight, Radical Thrillers. In *Leftwright* (Sydney: Intervention Publication, 1986), 49–59.

Chapter 6   Feminist Romance

1 Other non-fictional genres which might reward similar analysis include travel writing, biography and autobiography.
2 I am indebted to Dorothy Jones for suggesting *Wuthering Heights and Jane Eyre* as the pattern of contemporary romantic fiction.
3 See Terry Eagleton, *Myths of Power: A Marxist Study of the Brontes* (London: Macmillan, 1975).
4 See, for example, the essays in Jack Zipes, *Don't Bet on the Prince*.

Chapter 7   Gender and Genre

1 As elaborated in Bakhtin's writing, particularly *The Dialogic Imagination: Four Essays*, ed. M. Holquist, tr. C. Emerson and M. Holquist (Austin: University of Texas Press, 1981), 84–258; *Problems of Dostoyevsky's Poetics*, ed. and tr. C. Emerson (Manchester: Manchester University Press, 1984); *Rabelais and his World*, tr. H. Iswolsky (Cambridge, Mass.: Harvard Universi-

ty Press, 1968); *Speech Genres and Other Late Essays*, ed. C. Emerson and M. Holquist, tr. V. McGee (Austin: University of Texas Press, 1986); and *Marxism and the Philosophy of Language*, tr. L. Matejka and I.R. Titunik (N.Y.: Seminar Press, 1973), which was published under the name V.N. Volosinov, but which is widely attributed to Bakhtin.

References and Bibliography

The references and bibliography is divided into six sections, A–F, in the same order as the discussion of the different genres in the text.

A   General Critism

Allott, Miriam, (ed.) 1974: *The Brontes: The Criticial Heritage*. London: RKP.

Althusser, Louis 1971: *Lenin and Philosophy and Other Essays*. Ben Brewster (tr.) New York Monthly Review Press.

Althusser, Louis 1977: *For Marx*. Ben Brewster (tr.). London: New Left Books.

Bakhtin, M.M. 1981: *The Dialogic Imagination: Four Essays*. C. Emerson and M. Holquist (trs). M. Holquist (ed.). Austin: University of Texas Press.

Bakhtin, M.M. 1984: *Problems of Dostoyevsky's Poetics*. C. Emerson (tr. and ed.). Manchester: Manchester University Press.

Bakhtin, M.M. 1968: *Rabelais and his World*. H. Iswolsky (tr.). Cambridge, Mass.: MIT Press.

Bakhtin, M.M. 1986: *Speech Genres and Other Late Essays*. Vern McGee (tr.). C. Emerson and M. Holquist (eds). Austin: University of Texas Press.

Bakhtin, M.M. *See also* Volosinov, V.N.

Bal, Mieke 1985: *Narratology: Introduction to the Theory of Narrative*. Christine van Boheemen (tr.). Toronto: University of Toronto Press.

Barthes, Roland 1977: *Image/Music/Text*. Stephen Heath (tr.). London: Fontana.

Belsey, C. 1980: *Critical Practice*. London: Methuen.

Benjamin, Walter 1973: *Illuminations*. Harry Zohn (tr.). Hannah Arendt (ed.). Glasgow: Fontana.

Bersani, Leo 1978: *A Future for Astyanax: Character and Desire in Literature*. London: The Library Association.

Blain, V., Clements, P. and Grundy I. (eds) 1989: *The Feminist Companion to Literature in English*. London: Batsford.

Brooks, Peter 1984: *Reading for the Plot: Design and Intention in Narrative*. New York: Alfred A. Knopf.

Carter, Angela 1979: *The Sadeian Woman: An Exercise in Cultural History*. London: Virago.

Chambers, Ross 1984: *Story and Situation: Narrative Seduction and the Power of Fiction*. Manchester: Manchester University Press.

De Lauretis, Teresa 1987: *Technologies of Gender: Essays on Theory, Film and Fiction*. Bloomington and Indianapolis: Indiana University Press.

De Lauretis, Teresa 1984: *Alice Doesn't: Feminism, Semiotics, Cinema*. London: Macmillan.

Derrida, Jacques 1980: La loi du genre/The Law of Genre. *Glyph*, 7, 176–232.

Doane, Mary Ann, Patricia Mellencamp and Linda Williams (eds) 1984: *Re-Vision: Essays in Feminist Film Criticism*. Los Angeles: American Film Institute.

DuPlessis, Rachel Blau 1985: *Writing beyond the Ending: Narrative Strategies of Twentieth-Century Women Writers*. Bloomington: Indiana University Press.

Ecker, Gisela (ed.) 1985: *Feminist Aesthetics*. Harriet Anderson (tr.). London: Women's Press.

Figes, Eva 1978: *Patriarchal Attitudes: Women in Society*. London: Virago.

Foucalt, Michel 1981: *The History of Sexuality Volume 1: An Introduction*. Robert Hurley (tr.). Harmondsworth: Penguin.

Foucault, Michel 1977: *Language, Counter-Memory, Practice: Selected Essays and Interviews*. Donald F. Bouchard and Sherry Simon (trs). Donald F. Bouchard (ed.). Oxford: Basil Blackwell.

Fowler, Alastair 1982: *Kinds of Literature: An Introduction to the Theory of Genres and Modes*. Oxford: Clarendon Press.

Freadman, Anne 1985: Taking things literally (sins of my old age). *Southern Review*, 18 (July), 161–88.

Gallop, Jane 1982: *Feminism and Psychoanalysis: The Daughter's Seduction*. London: Macmillan.

Greene, Gayle and Coppelia Kahn (eds) 1985: *Making A Difference: Feminist Literary Criticism*. London and New York: Methuen.

Halliday, M.A.K. 1978: *Language as social semiotic: The social interpretation of language and meaning*. London: Edward Arnold.

Halliday, M.A.K. and Hasan, Ruqaiya 1985: *Language, context, and text: Aspects of language in a social-semiotic perspective*. Geelong, Victoria: Deakin University Press, 1985; Oxford: OUP, 1989.

Heath, Stephen 1981: *Questions of Cinema*. London: Macmillan.

Hodge, Robert and Kress, Gunther 1988: *Social Semiotics*. Cambridge: Polity Press.

Huyssen, Andreas 1986: *After the Great Divide: Modernism, Mass Culture, Postmodernism*. Bloomington and Indianapolis: Indiana University Press.

Irigaray, Luce 1985: *This Sex Which Is Not One*. Catherine Porter and Carolyn Burke (trs). Ithaca, NY.: Cornell University Press.

Jameson, Fredric 1981: *The Political Unconscious: Narrative as a Socially Symbolic Act*. London: Methuen.

Jameson, Fredric 1985: Postmodernism and Consumer Society. In Hal Foster (ed.) *Postmodern Culture*. London and Sydney: Pluto Press, 111–25.

Kaplan, Cora 1986: *Sea Changes: Essays on Culture and Feminism*. London: Verso.

Kress, Gunther 1985: *Linguistic processes in sociocultural practice*. Geelong, Victoria: Deakin University Press, 1985; Oxford: OUP, 1989.

Kress, Gunther and Hodge Robert 1979: *Language as Ideology*. London: RKP.

Kuhn, Annette 1985: *The power of the image: Essays on representation and sexuality*. London: RKP.

Lovell, Terry 1987: *Consuming Fiction*. London: Verso.

Lovell, Terry 1980: *Pictures of Reality: Aesthetics, Politics, Pleasure*. London: British Film Institute.

Lyotard, Jean-François 1984: *The Postmodern Condition: A report on Knowledge*. Geoff Bennington and Brian Massumi (trs). Manchester: Manchester University Press.

Marks, Elaine and de Courtivron, Isabelle (eds) 1981: *New French Feminisms: An Anthology*. Brighton: Harvester.

Martin, J.R. 1985: *Factual writing: exploring and challenging social reality*. Geelong, Victoria: Deakin University Press 1985; Oxford: OUP, 1989.

Masterman, Len 1983: Media education: theoretical issues and practical possibilities. *Metro*, 60, 5–10.

Mathews, Sue 1984: *35mm Dreams*. Ringwood, Victoria: Penguin.

Modleski, Tania 1986: Feminism and the Power of Interpretation: Some Critical Readings. In Teresa de Lauretis (ed.) *Feminist Studies/Critical Studies*. Bloomington: Indiana University Press, 121–38.

Moers, Ellen 1977: *Literary Women*. New York: Anchor Press/Doubleday.

Morson, Gary Saul 1981: *The Boundaries of Genre: Dostoyevsky's* Diary of a Writer *and the Traditions of Literary Utopia*. Austin: University of Texas Press.

Neale, Steve 1980: *Genre*. London: British Film Institute.

Newton, Judith and Rosenfeld Deborah (eds) 1985: *Feminist Criticism and Social Change: Sex, Class and Race in Literature and Culture*. New York and London: Methuen.

Nichols, Bill 1976: *Movies and Methods: An Anthology*. Berkeley: University of California Press.

Owens, Craig 1985: The Discourse of Others: Feminists and Postmodernism. In Hal Foster (ed.) *Postmodern Culture*. London and Sydney: Pluto Press, 57–82.

Pawling, Christopher (ed.) 1984: *Popular Fiction and Social Change*. London: Macmillan.

Poynton, Cate 1985: *Language and gender: making the difference*. Geelong, Victoria: Deakin University Press, 1985; Oxford: OUP, 1989.

Prince, Gerard 1982: *Narratology: The Form and Functioning of Narrative*. Berlin: Mouton.

Rabinowitz, Peter 1987: *Before Reading: Narrative Conventions and the Politics of Interpretation*. Ithaca, NY and London: Cornell University Press.

Rimmon-Kenan, Shlomith 1983: *Narrative Fiction: Contemporary Poetics*. London and New York: Methuen.

Rosenberg, Betty 1982: *Genreflecting: A Guide to Reading Interests in Genre Fiction*. Littleton, Colorado: Libraries Unlimited Inc.

Rosmarin, Adena 1985: *The Power of Genre*. Minneapolis: University of Minnesota Press.

Russ, Joanna 1984: *How to Suppress Women's Writing*. London: Women's Press.

Showalter, Elaine (ed.) 1986: *The New Feminist Criticism: Essays on Women, Literature, and Theory*. London: Virago.

Steedman, Carolyn 1986: *Landscape for a Good Woman: A Story of Two Lives*. London: Virago.

Threadgold, Terry, Grosz, E.A., Kress, Gunther, and Halliday, M.A.K. 1986: *Semiotics/Ideology/Language*. Sydney: Pathfinder Press.

Todorov, Tzevetan 1984: *Mikhail Bakhtin: The Dialogical Principle*. Wlad Godzich (tr.). Manchester: Manchester University Press.

White, Hayden 1987: *The Content of Form: Narrative Discourse and Historical Representation*. Baltimore: Johns Hopkins University Press.

Williams, Raymond 1980: *Problems in Materialism and Culture: Selected Essays*. London: Verso.

B   *Science Fiction*

FICTION CITED

Charnas, Suzy McKee 1978: *Walk to the End of the World*. New York: Berkley.

Elgin, Suzette Haden 1984: *Native Tongue*. New York: Daw.

Ellison, Harlan (ed.) 1972: *Again, Dangerous Visions*. New York: New American Library.

Green, Jen and LeFanu Sarah (eds) 1985: *Despatches from the Frontiers of the Female Mind*. London: Women's Press.

LeGuin, Ursula K. 1981: *The Left Hand of Darkness*. London: Futura.

LeGuin, Ursula K. 1980: *The Word for World Is Forest*. London: Granada.

Lem, Stanislaw 1971: *Solaris*. Joanna Kilmartin and Steve Cox (trs). New York: Berkley.

McCaffrey, Anne 1978: *Dragonsinger*. London: Corgi.

Sargent, Pamela (ed.) 1978: *Women of Wonder: Science-fiction Stories by Women about Women*. Harmondsworth: Penguin.

Shelley, Mary W. 1968: *Frankenstein*. In Peter Fairclough (ed.) *Three Gothic Novels*. Harmondsworth: Penguin.

Tiptree, Jr., James 1981: *Out of the Everywhere, and Other Extraordinary Visions*. New York: Ballantine.

Tiptree, Jr., James 1975: *Warm Worlds and Otherwise*. Robert Silverberg (ed.). New York: Ballantine.

Tiptree, Jr., James 1976: 'Houston, Houston, Do You Read?'. In Susan Anderson and Vonda McIntyre (eds) *Aurora: Beyond Equality*. New York: Fawcett.

CRITICAL BACKGROUND

'Dear Frontiers': Letters from women fantasy and science fiction writers. *Frontiers*, Vol. II, No. 3 (1977).

Angenot, Marc 1979: The absent paradigm: an introduction to the semiotics of science fiction. *Science-Fiction Studies*. 6, 9–18.

Angenot, Marc and Darko Suvin 1979: Not only but also: reflections on cognition and ideology in science fiction and SF criticism. *Science-Fiction Studies*, 6, 168–78.

Cook, Diane 1985: 'Yes, Virginia, there's always been Women's Science Fiction ... Feminist, Even'. In *Contrary Modes*. Proceedings of the World Science Fiction Conference 1985. Melbourne: Ebony.

Delany, Samuel 1978: *The Jewel-Hinged Jaw: Notes on the Language of Science Fiction*. New York: Berkley Windhover.

LeGuin, Ursula K. 1979: *The Language of the Night: Essays on Fantasy and Science Fiction*. Susan Wood (ed.). New York: Perigee.

Parrinder, Patrick (ed.) 1979: *Science Fiction: A Critical Guide*. London and New York: Longman.

Parrinder, Patrick 1980: *Science Fiction: Its Criticism and Teaching*. London and New York: Methuen.

Rose, Mark (ed.) 1976: *Science Fiction: A Collection of Critical Essays*. Engelwood Cliffs, NJ: Prentice-Hall.

Sargent, Pamela 1978: Introduction: Women in Science Fiction. In Pamela Sergent (ed.) *Women of Wonder: Science-fiction Stories by Women about Women*. Harmondsworth: Penguin.

Staicar, Tom (ed.) 1982: *The Feminine Eye: Science Fiction and the Women Who Write It*. New York: Frederick Ungar.

Suvin, Darko 1979: *Metamorphoses of Science Fiction: On the Poetics and History of a Literary Genre*. New Haven and London: Yale University Press.

Tulloch, John and Alvarado, Manuel 1983: *Doctor Who: the Unfolding Text*. London: Macmillan.

C   Fantasy

FICTION CITED

Bradley, Marion Zimmer 1978: *The Shattered Chain*. London: Arrow.

Carter, Angela 1979: *The Bloody Chamber and other stories*. London: Gollancz.

Charnas, Suzy McKee 1980: *The Vampire Tapestry*. London: Granada.

Lee, Tanith 1983: *Red as Blood, Or Tales from the Sisters Grimmer*. New York: Daw.

Lee, Tanith 1980: *Sabella or The Blood Stone*. New York: Daw.

Lynn, Elizabeth 1981: *The Northern Girl*. New York: Berkley.

Scott, Jody 1986: *I, Vampire*. London: Women's Press.

Voirst, Judith 1976: ... And Then The Prince Knelt Down and Tried to Put the Glass Slipper on Cinderella's Foot. In Jack Zipes (ed.), *Don't Bet on the Prince: Contemporary Feminist Fairy Tales in North America and England*. Aldershot: Gower.

CRITICAL BACKGROUND

Bentley, C.F. 1972: The monster in the bedroom: sexual symbolism in Bram Stoker's *Dracula*. *Literature & Psychology*, 22, 27–34.

Bettelheim, Bruno 1978: *The Uses of Enchantment: The Meaning and Importance of Fairy Tales*. Harmondsworth: Penguin.

Boyer, R.H. and Zahorski, K.J. (eds) 1984: *Fantasists on Fantasy: A Collection of Critical Reflections*. New York: Avon.

Burgin, Victor, James, Donald and Kaplan, Cora (eds) 1986: *Formations of Fantasy*. London and New York: Methuen.

Day, William Patrick 1985: *In the Circles of Fear and Desire: A Study of Gothic Fantasy*. Chicago and London: University of Chicago Press.

Demetrakopoulos, Stephanie 1977: Feminism, sex role exchanges, and other subliminal fantasies in Bram Stoker's *Dracula*. *Frontiers*, II, no. 3, 104–13.

Dowling, Linda 1979: The decadent and the New Woman in the 1980s. *Nineteenth-Century Fiction*, 33, 434–53.

Jackson, Rosemary 1981: *Fantasy: the Literature of Subversion*. London and New York: Methuen.

LeGuin, Ursula K. 1979: *The Language of the Night: Essays on Fantasy and Science Fiction*. Susan Wood (ed.). New York: Perigee.

Punter, David 1980: *The Literature of Terror: A History of Gothic Fictions from 1765 to the present day*. London: Longman.

Roth, Phyllis A. 1982: *Bram Stoker*. Boston: Twayne.

Roth, Phyllis A. 1977: Suddenly sexual women in Bram Stoker's *Dracula*. *Literature & Psychology*, 26, 113–21.

Senf, Carol A. 1982: 'Dracula': Stoker's response to the New Woman. *Victorian Studies*, 26, 1, 33–49.

Todorov, Tzevetan 1975: *The Fantastic: A Structural Approach to a Literary Genre*. Richard Howard (tr.). Ithaca, NY: Cornell University Press.

Zipes, Jack 1979: *Breaking the Magic Spell: Radical Theories of Folk and Fairy Tales*. London: Heinemann.

Zipes, Jack 1986: *Don't Bet on the Prince: Contemporary Feminist Fairy Tales in North America and England*. Aldershot: Gower.

Zipes, Jack 1983: *The Trials and Tribulations of Little Red Riding Hood: Versions of the Tale in Sociocultural Context*. London: Heinemann.

D   *Utopian Fiction*

FICTION CITED

Atwood, Margaret 1985: *The Handmaid's Tale*. London: Women's Press.

Bellamy, Edward. *Looking Backward (2000–1987) or, Life in the year 2000A.D.* repr. London: William Reeves [n.d.]

Charnas, Suzy McKee 1978: *Walk to the End of the World*. New York: Berkley.

Delany, Samuel 1977: *Triton*. London: Corgi.

Gilman, Charlotte Perkins 1979: *Herland*. London: Women's Press.

LeGuin, Ursula 1975: *The Dispossessed*. St Albans: Granada.

MacNie, Louis (Ismar Thiusen) 1889: *The Diothas, Or, A Far Look Ahead*. 2nd edn. Repr. 1971. New York: Arno Press and the New York Times.

More, St Thomas 1964: *Utopia*. Edward Surtz (ed.). New Haven and London: Yale University Press.

Morris, William 1970: *News from Nowhere, or, an epoch of rest, being some chapters from a utopian romance*. James Redmond (ed.). London: RKP.

Piercy, Marge 1979: *Woman on the Edge of Time*. London: Women's Press.

Russ, Joanna 1985: *The Female Man*. London: Women's Press.

Tiptree Jr., James 1981: Angel Fix. In *Out of the Everywhere and Other Extraordinary Visions*. New York: Ballantine.

CRITICAL BACKGROUND

Abrash, Merrit 1977: Missing the point in More's *Utopia*, *Extrapolation*, 18, 27–38.

Anderson, Perry 1980: *Arguments Within English Marxism*. London: Verso.

Barr, Marlene, S. (ed.) 1981: *Future Females: A Critical Anthology*. Bowling Green, Ohio: Bowling Green State University Popular Press.

Barthes, Roland 1976: *Sade/Fourier/Loyola*. Richard Miller (tr.). New York Hill and Wang.

Bellamy, Edward 1977: How I came to write *Looking Backward*. *Science-Fiction Studies*, 4, 194–5.

Bierman, Judah 1975: Ambiguity in Utopia; *The Dispossessed Science-Fiction Studies*, 2, 249–55.

Block, Ernst 1970: *A Philosophy of the Future*. John Cumming (tr.). New York: Herder and Herder.

Brantlinger, Patrick 1975–6: 'News from Nowhere': Morris's socialist anti-novel. *Victorian Studies*, 19, 35–49.

Clarke, I.F. (ed.) 1978: *Tale of the Future: From the Beginning to the Present Day*. 3rd edn. London: The Library Association.

Elliott, Robert C. 1970: *The Shape of Utopia: Studies in a Literary Genre*. Chicago: University of Chicago Press.

Engels, Frederick 1954: *Socialism: Utopian and Scientific*. Moscow: Progress Publications.

Fekete, John 1979: *The Dispossessed and Triton:* act and system in utopian science fiction. *Science-Fiction Studies*, 6, 129–43.

Fitting, Peter 1979: The modern Anglo-American SF novel: utopian longing and capitalist cooptation. *Science-Fiction Studies*, 6, 59–75.

Gerber, Richard 1955: *Utopian Fantasy: A Study of English Utopian Fiction since the end of the Nineteenth Century*. London: RKP.

Goode, John 1971: William Morris and the Dream of Revolution. In John Lucas (ed.) *Literature and Politics in the Nineteenth Century*. London: Methuen, 221–80.

Jameson, Fredric 1976: Introduction/prospectus: to reconsider the relationship of Marxism to utopian thought. *Minnesota Review*, n.s. 6, 53–8.

Jameson, Fredric 1971: *Marxism and Form: Twentieth-Century Dialectical Theories of Literature*. Princeton: Princeton University Press.

Jameson, Fredric 1977: Of islands and trenches: naturalization and the production of utopian discourse. *Diacritics: a review of contemporary criticism*, June, 2–21.

Jameson, Fredric 1975: World reduction in LeGuin: the emergence of utopian narrative. *Science-Fiction Studies*, 2, 221–30.

Kessler, Carole (ed.) 1984: *Daring to Dream: Utopian Stories by United States Women 1836–1919*. Boston: Pandora.

Klaus, H. Gustav (ed.) 1982: *The Socialist Novel in Britain: Towards the Recovery of a Tradition*. Brighton: Harvester.

Manuel, Frank E. (ed.) 1973: *Utopias and Utopian Thought*. London: Souvenir.

Marcuse, Herbert 1978: *The Aesthetic Dimension*. London: Macmillan.

Marcuse, Herbert 1972: *Eros and Civilization: A Philosophical Inquiry into Freud*. London: Abacus.

Marin, Louis 1976: Theses on ideology and utopia. Fredric Jameson (tr.). *Minnesota Review*, n.s. 6, 71–5.

Meier, Paul 1978: *William Morris: the Marxist Dreamer*. Frank Gubb (tr.). 2 vols. Hassocks, Sussex: Harvester.

Morris, William 1889: 'Looking Backward'. *Commonweal*, 22 June 1889, p. 194 col. 1–p. 195 col. 1.

Morton, A.L. 1969: The English Utopia. London: Lawrence & Wishart.

Moylan, Tom 1986: *Demand the Impossible: Science fiction and the utopian imagination*. New York and London: Methuen.

Negley, Glenn and Max Patrick J. 1952: *The Quest for Utopia: An Anthology of Imaginary Societies*. New York: Harry Schuman.

Pearson, Carol 1977: Women's fantasies and feminist utopias. *Frontiers*, II, 3, 50–61.

Pfaezler, Jean 1976: American utopian fiction 1888–1896: the political origins of form. *Minnesota Review*, n.s. 6, 114–17.

Sargent, Lyman Tower 1977: Ambiguous legacy: the role and position of women in the English Utopia. *Extrapolation*, 19, 39–49.

Sargent, Lyman Tower 1976: Themes in utopian fiction in English before Wells. *Science-Fiction Studies*, 3, 3, 275–82.

Somay, Bülent 1984: Towards an open-ended utopia. *Science-Fiction Studies*, 11, 25–38.

Thompson, E.P. 1977: Postcript: 1976. *William Morris: Romantic to Revolutionary*. London: Merlin.

Walsh, Chad 1962: *From Utopia to Nightmare*. London: Geoffrey Blas.

Williams, Raymond 1978: Utopia and science fiction. *Science-Fiction Studies*, 5, 203–14.

E   *Detective Fiction*

FICTION CITED

Cross, Amanda 1981: *Death in a Tenured Position*. New York: Ballantine.

Day, Marele 1988: *The Life and Crimes of Harry Lavender*. Sydney: Allen & Unwin.

Doyle, Sir Arthur Conan 1981: *The Penguin Complete Sherlock Holmes*. Harmondsworth: Penguin.

Hume, Fergus 1894: The Lone Inn. *Labour Leader*, 7 July–6 October 1894.

Jiles, Paulette 1986: *Sitting in the Club Car Drinking Rum and Karma-Kola: A Manual of Etiquette for Ladies Crossing Canada by Train*. Winlaw, BC: Polestar.

Marles, Albert T. (Yorick the Younger) 1894: By Shadowed Paths. *Labour Leader*, 13 April 1984–30 November 1984.

McDermid, Val 1987: *Report for Murder*. London: Women's Press.
Miner, Valerie 1982: *Murder in the English Department*. London: Women's Press.
Muller, Marcia 1985: The Broken Men. In Martin Greenberg and Bill Prozini (eds) *Academy Mystery Novellas Volume 1: Women Sleuths*. Chicago: Academy Chicago Publications.
Poe, Edgar Allan 1967: *Selected Writings: Poems, Tales, Essays and Reviews*. D. Galloway (ed.). Harmondsworth: Penguin.
Slovo, Gillian 1987: *Death Comes Staccato*. London: Women's Press.
Slovo, Gillian 1984: *Morbid Symptoms*. London: Women's Press.
Wilson, Barbara 1984: *Murder in the Collective*. London: Women's Press.
Wilson, Barbara 1987: *Sisters of the Road*. London: Women's Press.
Wings, Mary 1986: *She Came Too Late*. London: Women's Press.

CRITICAL BACKGROUND

Bloom, Clive, Docherty Brian, Gibb, Jane and Shand, Keith (eds) 1988: *Nineteenth-Century Suspense: From Poe to Conan Doyle*. London: Macmillan.
Cawelti, John G. 1976: *Adventure, Mystery, and Romance: Formula Stories as Art and Popular Culture*. Chicago and London: University of Chicago Press.
Cranny-Francis, Anne 1988: Gender and genre: feminist rewritings of detective fiction. *Women's Studies International Forum*, 11, 1, 69–84.
Greenberg, Martin H. and Pronzini, Bill (eds) 1985: *Academy Mystery Novellas: Volume 1: Women Sleuths*. Chicago: Academy Chicago Publications.
Knight, Stephen 1981: The case of the great detective. *Meanjin*, 40, 2, 175–85.
Knight, Stephen 1980: *Form and Ideology in Crime Fiction*. London: Macmillan.
Knight, Stephen 1986: Radical Thrillers. In *Leftwright*. Sydney: Intervention Publications.
Palmer, J. 1979: *Thrillers: Genesis and Structure of a Popular Genre*. London: Edward Arnold.
Slung, Michele B. (ed.) 1977: *Crime on her Mind: Fifteen Stories of Female Sleuths From the Victorian Era to the Forties*. Harmondsworth: Penguin.
Stasio, Marilyn 1985: Lady Gumshoes: boiled less hard. *New York Times Book Review*, April 28, 1985, pp. 1, 38.
Victorian Detective Fiction: A Catalogue of the Collection Made By Dorothy Glover and Graham Greene Bibliographically Arranged by Eric Osbourne and Introduced by John Carter, with a Preface by Graham Greene. London: Bodley Head, 1966.

F   Romantic Fiction

FICTION CITED

Atwood, Margaret 1982: *Lady Oracle*. London: Virago.
Brontë, Charlotte 1966: *Jane Eyre*. Harmondsworth: Penguin.
Brontë, Emily 1966: *Wuthering Heights*. London: Heron.
Fielding, Henry 1965: *Joseph Andrews* and *Shamela*. M.C. Battestin (ed.). London: Methuen.
James, Sarah 1984: *Public Affair*. Toronto: Harlequin.

Loring, Jenny 1984: *The Right Woman*. Toronto: Harlequin.

Martin, Michelle 1986: *Pembroke Park*. Tallahassee, Fla. Naiad.

Richardson, Samuel 1962: *Pamela*. Vol 1. London: Dent.

Rule, Jane 1986: *Desert of the Heart*. London: Pandora.

Weldon, Fay 1983: *The Life and Loves of a She-Devil*. London: Hodder & Stoughton.

CRITICAL BACKGROUND

Ang, Ien 1985: *Watching* Dallas: *Soap opera and the melodramatic imagination*. Della Couling (tr.). London and New York: Methuen.

Beer, Patricia 1974: *Reader, I Married Him*. London: Macmillan.

Curti, Linda 1986: Gender and genre. International Television Studies Conference, London.

D'Acci, Julie 1986: 'Woman', Television and the case of *Cagney and Lacey*. International Television Studies Conference, London.

Figes, Eva 1982: *Sex and Subterfuge: Women Writers to 1850*. London: Macmillan.

Gilbert, Sandra M. and Gubar, Susan 1979: *The Madwoman in the Attic: The Woman Writer and the Nineteenth-Century Literary Imagination*. New Haven: Yale University Press.

Modleski, Tania 1982: *Loving with a Vengeance: Mass-Produced Fantasies for Women*. New York and London: Methuen.

Radway, Janice A. (ed.) 1986: *The Progress of Romance: the Politics of Popular Fiction*. London: RKP.

Radway, Janice A. 1984: *Reading the Romance: Women, Patriarchy, and Popular Culture*. Chapel Hill, NC and London: University of North Carolina Press.

Russ, Joanna 1973: Somebody's trying to kill me and I think it's my husband: the modern Gothic. *Journal of Popular Culture*, 6, 4, 666–91.

Thurston, Carol 1987: *The Romance Revolution: Erotic Novels for Women and the Quest for a New Sexual Identity*. Urbana, Ill. and Chicago: University of Illinois Press.

Index